Redefining Global Economic Thinking for the Welfare of Society

Md Mashiur Rahman
Bank Asia Ltd., Bangladesh

Richa Goel
Amity University, Noida, India

Anthony P. Gomes
TeamPeople, USA

Md Almas Uzzaman
Independent Researcher, Australia

A volume in the Advances in Finance, Accounting, and Economics (AFAE) Book Series

IGI Global
PUBLISHER of TIMELY KNOWLEDGE

Published in the United States of America by
IGI Global
Business Science Reference (an imprint of IGI Global)
701 E. Chocolate Avenue
Hershey PA, USA 17033
Tel: 717-533-8845
Fax: 717-533-8661
E-mail: cust@igi-global.com
Web site: http://www.igi-global.com

Library of Congress Cataloging-in-Publication Data

Names: Rahman, Md. Mashiur, editor.
Title: Redefining global economic thinking for the welfare of society / Md. Mashiur Rahman [and three others], editor.
Description: Hershey, PA : Business Science Reference, [2021] | Includes bibliographical references. | Summary: "This book digs into the current climate of global wealth by examining some prevailing economic theories to uncover deficiencies of existing economic thinking and suggests guidelines for redefining the global economic atmosphere to create a world economy with more parity to the benefit of all of social"-- Provided by publisher.
Identifiers: LCCN 2021018330 (print) | LCCN 2021018331 (ebook) | ISBN 9781799882589 (hardcover) | ISBN 9781799882596 (paperback) | ISBN 9781799882602 (ebook)
Subjects: LCSH: Welfare economics. | Economics--Moral and ethical aspects. | Economics--Sociological aspects.
Classification: LCC HB846 .R44 2021 (print) | LCC HB846 (ebook) | DDC 330.15/56--dc23
LC record available at https://lccn.loc.gov/2021018330
LC ebook record available at https://lccn.loc.gov/2021018331

This book is published in the IGI Global book series Advances in Finance, Accounting, and Economics (AFAE) (ISSN: 2327-5677; eISSN: 2327-5685)

British Cataloguing in Publication Data
A Cataloguing in Publication record for this book is available from the British Library.

Advances in Finance, Accounting, and Economics (AFAE) Book Series

ISSN:2327-5677
EISSN:2327-5685

Editor-in-Chief: Ahmed Driouchi, Al Akhawayn University, Morocco

MISSION

In our changing economic and business environment, it is important to consider the financial changes occurring internationally as well as within individual organizations and business environments. Understanding these changes as well as the factors that influence them is crucial in preparing for our financial future and ensuring economic sustainability and growth.

The **Advances in Finance, Accounting, and Economics (AFAE)** book series aims to publish comprehensive and informative titles in all areas of economics and economic theory, finance, and accounting to assist in advancing the available knowledge and providing for further research development in these dynamic fields.

COVERAGE

- Corporate Finance
- Economics of Risks, Uncertainty, Ambiguity, and Insurance
- Accounting information systems
- Microfinance
- Banking
- Theoretical Issues in Economics, Finance, and Accounting
- Bankruptcy
- Risk Analysis and Management
- Taxes
- Applied Accounting

IGI Global is currently accepting manuscripts for publication within this series. To submit a proposal for a volume in this series, please contact our Acquisition Editors at Acquisitions@igi-global.com or visit: http://www.igi-global.com/publish/.

The Advances in Finance, Accounting, and Economics (AFAE) Book Series (ISSN 2327-5677) is published by IGI Global, 701 E. Chocolate Avenue, Hershey, PA 17033-1240, USA, www.igi-global.com. This series is composed of titles available for purchase individually; each title is edited to be contextually exclusive from any other title within the series. For pricing and ordering information please visit http://www.igi-global.com/book-series/advances-finance-accounting-economics/73685. Postmaster: Send all address changes to above address.

Titles in this Series

For a list of additional titles in this series, please visit:
http://www.igi-global.com/book-series/advances-finance-accounting-economics/73685

FinTech Development for Financial Inclusiveness
Muhammad Anshari (Universiti Brunei Darussalam, Brunei) Mohamad Nabil Almunawar (Universiti Brunei Darussalam, Brunei) and Masairol Masri (Universiti Brunei Darussalam, Brunei)
Business Science Reference • © 2022 • 269pp • H/C (ISBN: 9781799884477) • US $225.00

Evaluating Trade and Economic Relations Between India and Southeast Asia
Anita Medhekar (Central Queensland University, Australia) and Harpreet Kaur (Central Queensland University, Australia)
Business Science Reference • © 2022 • 347pp • H/C (ISBN: 9781799857747) • US $195.00

Handbook of Research on Global Aspects of Sustainable Finance in Times of Crises
Ibrahim Yasar Gok (Süleyman Demirel University, Turkey & Freie Universität Berlin, Germany)
Business Science Reference • © 2022 • 442pp • H/C (ISBN: 9781799885016) • US $285.00

Handbook of Research on Developing Circular, Digital, and Green Economies in Asia
Patricia Ordóñez de Pablos (The University of Oviedo, Spain)
Business Science Reference • © 2022 • 521pp • H/C (ISBN: 9781799886785) • US $225.00

Handbook of Research on Climate Change and the Sustainable Financial Sector
Odunayo Magret Olarewaju (Durban University of Technology, South Africa) and Idris Olayiwola Ganiyu (University of KwaZulu-Natal, South Africa)
Business Science Reference • © 2021 • 573pp • H/C (ISBN: 9781799879671) • US $295.00

CSR and Management Accounting Challenges in a Time of Global Crises
Ionica Oncioiu (Titu Maiorescu University, Romania)
Business Science Reference • © 2021 • 278pp • H/C (ISBN: 9781799880691) • US $215.00

Impact of Global Issues on International Trade

For an entire list of titles in this series, please visit:
http://www.igi-global.com/book-series/advances-finance-accounting-economics/73685

IGI Global
PUBLISHER of TIMELY KNOWLEDGE

701 East Chocolate Avenue, Hershey, PA 17033, USA
Tel: 717-533-8845 x100 • Fax: 717-533-8661
E-Mail: cust@igi-global.com • www.igi-global.com

Table of Contents

Detailed Table of Contents

The 17 Sustainable Development Goals officially come into force upon the signing of 193 countries arranged by the United Nations, and the time duration for achieving the goals is 2030. In view of the goals, this study redefines the process of 6 SDGs: (1) no poverty; (2) zero hunger; (3) quality education; (4) gender equality; (5) peace, justice, and strong institutions; and (6) partnership for the goals. The signing countries are not legally bound to achieve the goals. It comes into force as gentlemen commitment. For the purpose of study, secondary data, bulletin, papers, articles, holy books, and in-depth interviews with some experts based on open-ended questionnaires have been taken. Upon analyzing the study, the authors found that to achieve the SDG competition for good works understanding that work is worship, sharing prosperity in terms of monetary and non-monetary aspects like knowledge with poor and marginal people, truthfulness in education with opportunity for all, building mindset for treating all genders as human, transparency and justice from court as well as social leaders, trust among all stakeholders in enterprise, corporation, society, and state are essentially required. The study has also shown that happiness comes to mind when a person can pay for others. These will also be supportive for achieving all other SDGs.

This study discusses the inadequacy of GDP alone as a measure of welfare in the global economic age and examines alternative welfare indicators and measurement methods. This study, which discusses the human development index (HDI), the inequality adjusted human development index (I-HDI), the gender inequality index (GII), the multidimensional poverty index (MPI), the social progress index (SPI), the happy planet index (HPI), the better life index (BLI), the Legatum prosperity index(LPI), the human capital index (HCI), and the ecological footprint (EF) methods, shares the country rankings of these methods and reveals the differences in the results depending on the method. It also draws attention to the differences between the economic size and welfare level by sharing the rankings of the world's 10 largest economies in alternative methods. In addition, the study examines the obstacles to the inability to establish a complete, precise, and generally accepted method of measuring welfare.

This chapter examines the legal and financial control issues regarding compliance with labor legislation. On the one hand, the legal analysis shows that legislation is one of the main factors influencing the financial control practice for compliance with labour legislation. On the other hand, the problems and specifics of the control procedures applied by the General Labor Inspectorate Executive Agency in Bulgaria are presented. The overall inspection process is presented sequentially, analyzing the individual stages that the control procedures go through. The problems and the specifics of carrying out an independent inspection activity by the agency are presented, and the peculiarities of carrying out joint control activities with executive bodies or their administrative structures by the specialized administration are examined. Different types of factors that influence the implementation of control procedures by the General Labor Inspectorate Executive Agency in Bulgaria are considered.

Globally, prominent sharing-based services include Uber, Lyft, and Airbnb, which have become behemoths in terms of their valuation, revenue, and number of users. Uber is reported to have over 100 million users globally. Bangladesh has also witnessed a rise in sharing-based services of both global and local origins. Sharing services have severely disrupted traditional business models and the economy they collectively encompass is referred to as the "sharing economy." Based on a systematic literature review of top management journals and other scholarly works, the authors present the most overarching conceptualization of sharing-based services. Taking this knowledge forward, this chapter not only conceptualizes and compares sharing-based services in Bangladesh but also identifies "collaborative consumption" as the most dominant type of sharing-based services among them. This chapter also presents scholarly works on the customers' motivators and barriers, which creates grounds for future research efforts in Bangladesh concerning collaborative consumption services.

Linear economic models have led us to a point where our planet can no longer sustain itself and heal its natural resources. Thus, circular economy has provided us the opportunity to hope for increasing resource value, extending its life as a means to put waste back into the consumption chain. In emerging economies, circular economy-based business models are not as pertinent. However, in the past decade, the Sustainable Development Goals (SDGs) have provided a guideline for businesses, legislators, and academics. It has been witnessed that a few notable initiatives in the field of the circular economy have taken place in emerging economies which has led to achieving different SDGs to a certain extent. This chapter discusses the potential circular economy-based business models held in the attainment of different sustainable development goals.

Today, despite the increase in global wealth, the income gap between the rich and the poor gradually widens. This gap is significant in both developed and developing nations. Thus, increasing income inequality adversely affects several socio-economic indicators. Previous studies demonstrated that one of the socio-economic indicators that were negatively affected by income inequality is population health. The income inequality experienced by the individuals or throughout life adversely affects several populations' health outputs, especially life expectancy at birth. The present study aimed to test the correlation between income inequality and population health output indicators with canonical correlation method and based on the most current data available for several nations. To determine the correlation between the two datasets, the 2017 data for 29 European countries and Turkey were analyzed. Canonical correlation analysis revealed a significant correlation between the income inequality and population health indicator datasets.

Capital is one of the first and foremost requisites of economic development for every country in this world. However, not every country is given abundant capital. Foreign direct investment (FDI) occurs as a good cure to solve capital-related issues. In this study, the net FDI inflow and economic growth correlation was researched in Turkey for the period of 2010:1-2018:3 by employing quarterly data as well as applying the Augmented Dickey Fuller Test (ADF); Phillips-Perron (PP); Kwiatkowski, Phillips, Schmidt, Shin (KPSS); Elliott, Rothenberg, and Stock (ERS) Point Optimal; Ng-Perron Unit Root Tests; and Toda-Yamamoto Causality Tests. According to the findings of the study, there is a unidirectional causality running from net FDI to economic growth in Turkey.

The notion of spirituality is a divisive area when it moves to its applicability in organizations. In today's scenario with so much of chaos and volatility in organization especially after the pandemic, one cannot ignore the significance of spiritual practices. With changing time, the significance of spirituality becomes more pertinent for employee wellbeing. With numerous studies being conducted in this field, however the research gap provides enough space for authors to work on understanding and deciding the substantial factors affecting spirituality among academicians. This study employs a positivist research approach, comprising of a quantitative basis of enquiry, and assembled data via survey questionnaires. A total of 358 questionnaires were allocated, and finally, 240 usable cases were selected for study. The factor structure was proved by using SEM. This study raises awareness on the significance of spirituality in the university wellbeing which will ultimately contribute to improving academic delivery and bringing more satisfaction. Further factor loading helps in assessment.

The richest one percent of the entire population of the world now owns more than half of the global wealth which shows global wealth is unequally distributed. Moreover, this is assumed that sustainable growth is impossible based on impossibility theorem. Considering the above, the study has been conducted and critically overviewed the wealth distribution of an ancient period based on Islamic rules and practice. Upon study, it has been found that people are very much self-centered and unaware of the broader perspective like searching happiness instead of immediate wealth maximization. The finding has also shown that right of inheritances, relatives, neighbors, society, and state should be defined clearly and need distribution of wealth based on definition. If we become more self-centered, we will find ourselves helpless. Here, wealth means knowledge and physical assets.

Foreword

Redefining Global Economic Thinking for the Welfare of Society is a comprehensive reference source that examines the prevailing economic theories and thinking, determines the deficiency of some of the existing economic thinking, and sets up guidelines and transformation of existing economic thinking. The richest one percent of the entire population of the world now owns more than half of the global wealth. Global wealth is unequally distributed, gross domestic product (GDP) and consumption are in a declining trend, and poverty is in an increasing trend. Each participant's gain or loss of utility is exactly balanced by the losses or gains of the utility of the other participants, which certainly drives an unhealthy and unhappy globe. As such, global economic thinking must be redefined in order to encourage inclusive development and better problem solving. Covering topics that include economic development, circular economy, and population health, serve as an excellent resource for economists, sociologists, government officials, policymakers, practitioners, faculties of universities and colleges, students, researchers, and academics.

This book offers an insight into the important components of global economic thinking and find out ways of redefining thoughts and processes by offering a thorough and strong introduction. It explores areas of Circular Economy, Digital Age, Economic Development& Growth, Economic Empowerment& Wellbeing, Economy Conceptualization& Policy making, Gender Gap, Global Economy, Happiness Concept, Humanizing Work, Income Inequality, Labor Force Participation and many more key applications.

I assume that academics, students, corporates, masses in all fields can improve and expand their knowledge with the learning of the basic trends and activities in this book. This book offers a valuable guide to the intellectual and practical work and calls for need to rethink and examines the consequences for future management of innovation. I am pleased to write this foreword as the Editors of this Book has given full hearted effort for a great solution and innovation. All chapters in this book have been selected based on peer review where reviewers were very much expert in the sector.

Mohammad Humayun Kabir
Bank Alfalah Limited, Bangladesh

Preface

Redefining Global Economic Thinking for the Welfare of Society is a comprehensive reference source that examines the prevailing economic theories and thinking, determines the deficiency of some of the existing economic thinking, and sets up guidelines and transformation of existing economic thinking. Covering topics that include economic development, circular economy, and population health, this serves as an excellent resource for economists, sociologists, government officials, policymakers, practitioners, faculties of universities and colleges, students, researchers, and academicians. The book is covered by following chapters where have also chapters' synopsis:

CHAPTER 1: ADOPTION OF SUSTAINABLE DEVELOPMENT GOALS THROUGH REDEFINING THE PROCESS AND ACHIEVING HAPPINESS

In this study redefines the process of 6 SDGs out of 17 SDGs, i.e. no poverty, zero hunger, quality education, gender equality, peace, justice & strong institutions and partnership for the goals. Although, the signing countries are not legally bound to achieve the goals and it comes into force as gentlemen commitment. For the purpose of study, secondary data, bulletin, papers, articles, holy books and in-depth interviews with some experts based on open-ended questionnaires have been taken. Upon analyzing the study we have found that for achieving the SDGs competition for good works with understanding that work is worship, sharing prosperity in terms of monetary and non-monetary like knowledge with poor and marginal people, truthfulness in education with opportunity for all, building mind set for treating all genders are human, transparency and justice from court as well as social leaders, trust among all stakeholders in enterprise, corporation, society and state are essentially required. The study has also shown that happiness comes to mind when a person can expense for others.

CHAPTER 2: NEW INDICATORS AND MEASUREMENT METHODS FOR WELFARE IN THE GLOBAL ECONOMY ERA

This study discusses the inadequacy of GDP alone as a measure of welfare in the global economic age and examines alternative welfare indicators and measurement methods. This study, which discusses the Human Development Index (HDI), the Inequality Adjusted Human Development Index (I-HDI), the Gender Inequality Index (GII), the Multidimensional Poverty Index (MPI), the Social Progress Index (SPI), the Happy Planet Index (HPI), the Better Life Index (BLI), the Legatum Prosperity Index(LPI), the Human Capital Index (HCI) and the Ecological Footprint (EF) methods, shares the country rankings of these methods and reveals the differences in the results depending on the method. It also draws attention to the differences between the economic size and welfare level by sharing the rankings of the world's ten largest economies in alternative methods. In addition, the study examines the obstacles to the inability to establish a complete, precise, and generally accepted method of measuring welfare.

CHAPTER 3: NEW FEATURES IN THE BULGARIAN LEGAL FRAMEWORK AND FINANCIAL CONTROL PRACTICE FOR COMPLIANCE WITH LAB

This paper examines the legal and financial control issues regarding compliance with labor legislation. On the one hand, the legal analysis shows that legislation is one of the main factors influencing the financial control practice for compliance with labour legislation. On the other hand, the problems and specifics of the control procedures applied by the General Labor Inspectorate Executive Agency in Bulgaria are presented. The overall inspection process is presented sequentially, analyzing the individual stages that the control procedures go through. The problems and the specifics of carrying out an independent inspection activity by the Agency are presented, and the peculiarities of carrying out joint control activities with executive bodies or their administrative structures by the specialized administration are examined. Different types of factors that influence the implementation of control procedures by the General Labor Inspectorate Executive Agency in Bulgaria are considered.

CHAPTER 4: SHARING ECONOMY-CONCEPTUALIZATION, MOTIVATORS AND BARRIERS, AND AVENUES FOR RESEARCH IN BANGLADESH

Globally, prominent sharing-based services include Uber, Lyft, and Airbnb, which have become behemoths in terms of their valuation, revenue, and number of users. Uber is reported to have over 100 million users globally. Bangladesh has also witnessed a rise in sharing-based services of both global and local origins. Sharing services have severely disrupted traditional business models and the economy they collectively encompass is referred to as the "Sharing Economy." Based on a systematic literature review of top management journals and other scholarly works, we present the most overarching conceptualization of sharing-based services. Taking this knowledge forward, this paper not only conceptualizes and compares sharing-based services in Bangladesh but also identifies ''collaborative consumption'' as the most dominant type of sharing-based services among them. This paper also presents scholarly works on the customers' motivators and barriers, which creates grounds for future research efforts in Bangladesh concerning collaborative consumption services.

CHAPTER 5: SUSTAINABLE DEVELOPMENT THROUGH THE CIRCULAR ECONOMY – EXPERIENCE FROM EMERGING ECONOMIES

Linear economic models have led us to a point where our planet can no longer sustain itself and heal its natural resources. Thus, circular economy has provided us the opportunity to hope for increasing resource value, extending its life as a means to put waste back into the consumption chain. In emerging economies, circular economy-based business models are not as pertinent. However, in the past decade, Sustainable Development Goals (SDGs) have provided a guideline for businesses, legislators, and academics. It has been witnessed that a few notable initiatives in the field of the circular economy have taken place in emerging economies which has led to achieving different SDGs to a certain extent. This chapter discusses the potential circular economy-based business models held in the attainment of different sustainable development goals.

CHAPTER 6: THE CORRELATION BETWEEN INCOME INEQUALITY AND POPULATION HEALTH – AN EMPIRICAL STUDY

Today, despite the increase in global wealth, the income gap between the rich and the poor gradually widens. This gap is significant in both developed and developing nations. Thus, increasing income inequality adversely affects several socio-economic indicators. Previous studies demonstrated that one of the socio-economic indicators that were negatively affected by income inequality is population health. The income inequality experienced by the individuals or throughout life adversely affects several population health outputs, especially life expectancy at birth. The present study aimed to test the correlation between income inequality and population health output indicators with canonical correlation method and based on the most current data available for several nations. To determine the correlation between the two datasets, the 2017 data for 29 European countries and Turkey were analyzed. Canonical correlation analysis revealed a significant correlation between the income inequality and population health indicators datasets.

CHAPTER 7: THE EFFECT OF NET FDI INFLOW ON ECONOMIC GROWTH IN TURKEY – AN APPLICATION WITH TODA-YAMAMOTO APPROACH

Capital is one of the first and foremost requisite of economic development for every country in this world. However, not every country is given abundant capital. At that rate foreign direct investment (FDI) occurs as a good cure to solve capital related issues. In this study, the net FDI inflow and economic growth correlation was researched in Turkey for the period of the period of 2010:1-2018:3 by employing quarterly data as well as applying the Augmented Dickey Fuller Test (ADF), Phillips-Perron (PP), Kwiatkowski, Phillips, Schmidt, Shin (KPSS), Elliott, Rothenberg and Stock (ERS) Point Optimal, Ng-Perron unit root tests and Toda-Yamamoto causality tests. According to the findings of the study, there is a unidirectional causality running from net FDI to economic growth in Turkey.

CHAPTER 8: IMPACT OF THE PANDEMIC ON THE INDIAN ECONOMY AND WELLBEING

The goal of the study is to look at the impact of COVID 19 on major industries including automobiles, wellness, education, tourism, and many others, as well as migrant workers' status. COVID-19, a sudden epidemic, has had a devastating impact on the Indian economy. The migrant population was also affected by this situation. They were concerned about labor shortages, monthly rationing, and social insurance shortages. In this investigation, secondary data was gathered. The study focuses on the influence of COVID 19 on important industries such as automotive, wellness, education, tourism, and so on, as well as the position of migrant workers. Secondary data was acquired for this inquiry. Blogs, magazines, newspapers, news from foreign agencies, written academic papers, government materials, and websites are examples of secondary sources. Educational institutions, customers, legislators, the government, and the community will all profit from this research.

CHAPTER 9: FACETS OF GENDER GAP IN LABOR FORCE PARTICIPATION AND ECONOMIC EMPOWERMENT DISRUPTION – A STUDY OF COMPETING NEEDS OF FAMILY AND WORK

According to Centre for Monitoring Indian Economy (CMIE) data, the average employment for January 2019-March 2020 was 403 million, which declined to 282 million in April 2020 and recovered steadily thereafter to reach 393million by August 2020. In India, female labour force participation is abysmally poor and has declined over the years, despite a rise in education. The causes for this are complex and, aside from objective factors, include a whole variety of social and cultural aspects. One of the factors causing this is the social mentality of women becoming homemakers. Furthermore, the scarcity of schooling and work-oriented courses, the lack of mobility and sexism in the workplace have been deterrents to women's access to the public workspace. Therefore, initiatives that aim to fix this void need to be holistic. Legislation alone is not enough, and to close this gap, all stakeholders should join hands. The article attempts to analyse facets of gender gap in labour force participation and economic empowerment disruption through Pandemic.

CHAPTER 10: A BIBLIOGRAPHIC ANALYSIS OF E-WASTE RECYCLING RESEARCH

The tremendous increase in the amount of e-waste and its impact on the environment and human health is a concern for the whole world nowadays. The low rate of recycling of e-waste as compared to the rate at which e-waste is increasing is a matter of concern and needs immediate action. Negative environmental consequences of e-waste have prompted the interest of both academia and industry alike. The objective of the study is to study the yearly growth pattern for the last twenty years, recognize relevant scholars, and explore collaborations among various institutes, authors, and countries over time. The study also intends to identify any shift in the field of e-waste recycling. So to better understand the development of this field in the past twenty years its require to study the yearly growth pattern of publication. To identify the relevant collaborations among authors, institutes, and countries that contributed to this field. In line with this, this study is conducted to examine the research landscape of e-waste recycling by using comprehensive bibliometric analysis.

CHAPTER 11: ON HUMANIZING WORK IN THE DIGITAL AGE

The present study addresses the problem of humanization of labor in the digital age. With technological advancement worldwide, notwithstanding economic and political differences among individual states, digitalization has invariably put its mark on human relationships. And it is about to transform both individual and social relations also in the labor law. The purpose of the present study is to examine the acts and documents at European level and offer an up-to-date analysis on applicable aspects of introducing AI in the labor process, its role in facilitating employees work alongside potential threats and negatives. Based on said analysis, the authors offer their views on the challenges to be faced and outline ongoing trends in the doctrine, the European community and legislation, to put in place a regulatory framework towards humanization of work in the digital age.

CHAPTER 12: INTEGRATING SPIRITUALITY AT THE WORKPLACE FOR WELL BEING – A STUDY ON ACADEMIA IN HIGHER EDUCATION

The notion of spirituality is a divisive area when it moves to its applicability in organizations. In today's scenario with so much of chaos and volatility in organization especially after the Pandemic one cannot ignore the significance of spiritual practices. With changing time, the significance of spirituality becomes more pertinent for employee wellbeing. With numerous studies being conducted in this field, however the research gap provides enough space for authors to work on understanding and deciding the substantial factors affecting spirituality among academicians. This study employs a positivist research approach, comprising of a quantitative basis of enquiry, and assembled data via survey questionnaires. A total of 358 questionnaires were allocated and finally 240 usable cases were selected for study. The factor structure was proved by using SEM This study raises awareness on the significance of spirituality in the university wellbeing which will ultimately; contribute to improving academic delivery and bringing more satisfaction. Further factor loading helps in assessment.

CHAPTER 13: DISTRIBUTION OF WEALTH FOR SUSTAINABLE HAPPINESS

The richest one percent of the entire population of the world now owns more than half of the global wealth which shows global wealth is unequally distributed. Moreover, this is assumed that sustainable growth is impossible based on impossibility theorem. Considering the above, the study has been conducted and critically overviewed the wealth distribution an ancient period based on Islamic rules and practice. Upon study, it has been found that now a day's peoples are very much self-centered and unconscious about broader perspective like searching happiness instead of immediate wealth maximization. The finding has also shown that right of inheritances, relatives, neighbors, society and state should be defined clearly and need to distribution of wealth based on definition. If we become more self-centered, we will find ourselves as helpless. Here, wealth means knowledge and physical assets.

All the chapters have been selected based on peer review process, and we are hopeful this book will be helpful for you.

Acknowledgment

We want to praise our Almighty God first and foremost. We learned how true is this talent of writing in the process of putting this book together. You have given us the ability to believe and follow our ambitions in our passion. Without trust in you, we could never have done this. Our most sincere gratitude to our family, who have provided us with support during the difficult process of creating this book.

All the people involved in this project and in particular the writers and reviewers that participated in the review process would be grateful to the editors. This book would not have been a reality without their assistance. First, each of the authors wishes to thank them for their efforts. Our heartfelt appreciation goes to the authors of this chapter who have given this book their time and expertise. Second, the editors recognize the evaluators' important contributions in improving the quality, consistency, and substance of chapters. Most of the authors were also reviewers and we respect their enormous work.

We owe a tremendous debt of appreciation to our experts who have commented on several chapters in length and constructively and have urged us to clarify concepts, to examine certain features of insight, to explain reasons for specific recommendations.

We also like to thank many people who have helped us learn and practice both the art and science of networking throughout the years.

Md Mashiur Rahman

Richa Goel

Anthony P. Gomes

Md Almas Uzzaman

Chapter 1
Adoption of Sustainable Development Goals Through Redefining the Process and Achieving Happiness

Md Mashiur Rahman
Bank Asia Ltd., Bangladesh

Richa Goel
Amity University, Noida, India

ABSTRACT

The 17 Sustainable Development Goals officially come into force upon the signing of 193 countries arranged by the United Nations, and the time duration for achieving the goals is 2030. In view of the goals, this study redefines the process of 6 SDGs: (1) no poverty; (2) zero hunger; (3) quality education; (4) gender equality; (5) peace, justice, and strong institutions; and (6) partnership for the goals. The signing countries are not legally bound to achieve the goals. It comes into force as gentlemen commitment. For the purpose of study, secondary data, bulletin, papers, articles, holy books, and in-depth interviews with some experts based on open-ended questionnaires have been taken. Upon analyzing the study, the authors found that to achieve the SDG competition for good works understanding that work is worship, sharing prosperity in terms of monetary and non-monetary aspects like knowledge with poor and marginal people, truthfulness in education with opportunity for all, building mindset for treating all genders as human, transparency and justice from court as well as social leaders, trust among all stakeholders in enterprise, corporation, society, and state are essentially required. The study has also shown that happiness comes to mind when a person can pay for others. These will also be supportive for achieving all other SDGs.

DOI: 10.4018/978-1-7998-8258-9.ch001

INTRODUCTION AND LITERATURE REVIEW

Sustainable development goals consist with 17 number of items which is announced and directed by United Nations. Target to achieve all the goals are 2030. The goals are required to adopt irrespective of culture, nationality, religion, language and income inequality. Several authors have explained in different ways for adoption of the goals. In this chapter we shall redefine the process of 6 SDGs like, (i) no poverty, (ii) zero hunger, (iii) quality education, (iv) gender equality, (v) peace, justice & strong institutions and (vi) partnership for happiness.

Sabrine Dhahri (June 2020) & others: They found FDI and foreign aids have positive impact on food security and poverty reductions as well as food security. In this connection they conclude that zero hunger and no poverty depends on development of agricultural sector, inflow of foreign direct investment and composition of foreign aids provided to the host countries.

Ellen Boeren (15 March 2019) This article explains the existing focus of education policies around the globe with benchmarks, indicators and targets. Agency and structure theory form an important opening point of this article, to be separated and viewed from micro-, meso- and macro-level perspectives. This study explores the idea that reaching the SDG 4 aims is a responsibility shared among people, education and training institutions, and regulating governments

Lorraine Eden (2021) & Others: Evidence-based policymaking (EBP) contends that when informed by evidence is executed policy decisions comes to successful. They recommend that governments adopt an Evidence-based policymaking approach employing public–private partnerships to address gender equality. They also recommend that multinational enterprises executives use our new Sustainable Development Goals (SDG) Materiality Matrix, designed on Evidence-based policymaking principles, to build gender equality into their global corporate social responsibility strategies.

Isabel B. Franco (14 November 2019) It examines the role of women and livelihood options in encouragement sustainable peace. Study was conducted in rural peoples in the vicinity of Risaralda, Colombia. The results show that the heterogeneous alignment of communities, particularly women and their personalities, which explains distinct perceptions towards project development. Secondly, results entail a practical measurement which suggests that in the process of calculation, development and management of resources, differences related to communal identity, religion and context-based aspects must be accepted and taken into account to adoptive sustainable peace and overall local sustainability.

M. Larionova (2020) This article assessed the COVID-19 pandemic impact on economic growth and sustainable development goals and offer recommendations partnerships for the SDGs. It looks at the international institutions' edges to support developing countries in response to the pandemic and related economic shocks. The study concludes by outlining priorities for reinforcement international assistance on sustainable development goals which include incorporation of components of digitalization into the sustainable development goals as concrete targets and indicators and a comprehensive G20-led debt relief initiative for the released amounts allocation to poverty and inequality eradication, health and education - related to sustainable development goals.

JUSTIFICATION OF THE STUDY

There the 193 countries signed for achieving sustainable development goal in 2015 where target to achieving the goals is 2030 but in 2021 we find that we are far away from the achievement. We find from column of the New York Times written by Maria Abi Habib on 30 April 2020 here she mentioned that poverty is increasing specially in last two years even in the USA and Europe including South Asia and Africa.

On the other hand, a UNICEF report shows that estimated 617 million kids and youths around the globe are unable to reach minimum levels in reading and mathematics, even though two thirds of them are in school.

These are the justification for redefining process of SDGs and achieving happiness.

METHODOLOGY

Primary data have been observed and taken answers through open ended questions to the experts like, senior teacher, banker, economist, socialist, and political leaders. Secondary data is used in this study work, such as articles, newspaper, magazines, statements, journals, blogs and etc. The usage of a systematic literature review procedure has been employed to carry out the existing investigation. The literature review strategy is a well-established technique for secondary data base reviews. They provide as a firm foundation for future research. However, conducting a literature review and using the results for strategy purposes is always challenging.

FINDING OF THE STUDY

(i) No Poverty and Zero Hunger

Eliminating poverty is not a job of charity, it's an action of justice and the key to exposing a gigantic human potential; mentioned in Global Goals for Sustainable Development (n.d.).

When people get required food to survive we called it the people have no hunger and when we can run life without begging we may call it no poverty. Considering the fact, scientific and sustainable wealth distribution in terms of material and non-material are required among successor, neighbors and poor. However, economists are yet to provide a universal sustainable assets distribution process but we find a solution in Holy Quran which is a book of all mankind.

We also need to know the justification of no poverty and zero hunger. If people are under mal nutrition it means lack of efficiency, skilled and attitude. Those people have been maintaining minimum state and corporate rules and regulations which create inefficiency, less security and peace of all because rules and religion is not applicable for the people those cannot fill-up their hungry. For mitigating the above problems, sustainability as well as happiness no poverty and zero hunger are essentially important.

Moreover, peoples' attitude drives to economic activities like food for hungry people but types of food varied based on their attitude lice rice, burger, pizza etc. As the study of research conclude that **attitude means economics** and **good attitude means welfare economics** where sustainability and happiness means good attitude like doing something for betterment of others. Elizebeth Dunn, researcher said that people get more happiness by spending money on others.

Considering the fact, human comes to good human when he/she make payment of right of successors, sharing prosperity it may be at least 2.50% of un-utilized assets based on Holy Quran to the poor relatives, neighbors and hungry people. This is also good to pay more than 2.50% for the human welfare. Sharing of good knowledge is also very important. Good knowledge mean that knowledge doesn't make harms to the other and/or misguide others. This is all about good attitude which is called welfare economics.

(ii) Quality Education

There are many assumptions regarding education like education is the light, backbone and happiness. But we find from observations on society a good number of people are not happy and not wealthy although they have formal institutional education. On the other hand, some people have no formal education but enlighten. **Truly**

enlightenment depend on attitude that shows in research study and mentioned in above. Those have good attitude they are practicing welfare economics and get happiness.

This is found from the interview and observations that quality of education can only be possible when truthfulness is established in the education but unfortunately there have huge poor quality of literature but people are widely following. Finding of the study show that in some locality one human observed other human as God and seeks help the such a false God which drives to in the line of bad attitude and bad economy ultimately tension and un-happiness.

So quality education means truthful education for all irrespective of language, culture, religion and nationality.

(iii) Gender Equality

Gender equality report (1019) published by University of Minnesota (Audette, 2019) shows in summary that if for happiness we should work toward gender equality irrespective of any gender. happier, we should work towards gender equality

Data from past few years persist gender in-equality makes several problems like freedom of thinking and working. Gender in-equality makes problem for all gender like women, men and common gender.

Sometime meaning of gender equality creates confusion, where finding of the study show that **gender equality means justice** in the family, society and corporation which to be ensured through rules and regulations as well as practicing culture and fair justice through court. This will ensure sustainability and happiness.

(iv) Peace, Justice & Strong Institutions

The 16th no. goals of SDGs is peace, justice and strong institutions which is makes the society sustainable. As reported by the European Commission (n.d.), absence of these corruption comes to force. We also talked with several politicians, justice, social workers and corporate executives and the study founds under open ended questions and summery secondary study which is as follows for sustainability:

- Legal system should be based on strong humanitarian philosophy as stated in holy books, human should have strong personality like no begging, no bribery personality.
- Transparency to be ensured in corporation and social culture.
- Strong bonding to be formed among family members.
- Fundamental rights irrespective of religion, nationality and culture to be followed.

- Strong commitment culture to be formed among the peoples for peace and progress.

(v) Partnership

German depression foundations show that 5.30 million people between the ages of 18 and 79 are diagnosed with depression in German each year – women are affected up to three times as much as men. The report also shows that every fourth person in Germany has a family member or friend who suffers from depression consequently 84% withdraw from social life, 45% break up with their partner and 72% feel disconnected from others.

Culture of partnership in family, friends and countries are in downward trend as opined the experts as because truthfulness and attitude of work is worship as well as competition of good works are demolished. The study find from several biography of good human that they were succeed based on single philosophy that is called trust. Trust to family members, friends, colleagues, society, state governance and even trust to the animals. As such we observed biography of successful and happy human like Bill Clinton, Obama, Dalailama and Muhammod – the messenger of God. The study found that Muhammad was trusted human for every religions and cultural people specially in finance as no people can told he did not return the deposit of others and laterally he succeeds is sustainable happiness. He was also a happy and sustainable business man.

CONCLUSIONS AND RECOMMENDATIONS

In this chapter, study find that sustainability is required for happiness and here we explained the five number of goals out of seventeen goals. The finding agreed with the title of goals and redefined the adoption process. This is very important for human, corporation, state governance as well as making good attitude which will drive the society in the welfare economy. The study also find that attitude means economics and good attitude means welfare economics where truly enlightenment depend on attitude. Moreover, gender equality means justice and sustainability as well as happiness depends on the philosophy of Trust i.e. trusted to all stakeholders like family, society, corporation and state governance.

Upon analyzing the study we have recommended that for achieving the SDGs (i) competition for good works with understanding that work is worship, (ii) sharing prosperity in terms of monetary and non-monetary like knowledge with poor and marginal people, (iii) truthfulness in education with opportunity for all, (iv) building mind set for treating all genders are human, (v) transparency in culture and justice from court as well as social leaders, (vi) trust among all stakeholders in enterprise, corporation, society and state are essentially required. The study has also shown that happiness comes to mind when a person can expense for others. These will also be supportive for achieving all other SDGs which is required for happiness of all people and making the society as sustainable.

REFERENCES

Larionova. (2020). Saving the SDGs? Strengthening Partnership for Achieving SDGs in the Post-Covid-19 Digital World. Academic Press.

Montañez. (2017). The Persistent Problem of Gender Inequality. *Scientific American*.

Good Deeds Day. (2021). *What You Can Do to End Poverty and Hunger*. https://www.good-deeds-day.org/sdg-1/

European Commission. (n.d.). Retrieved from https://ec.europa.eu/international-partnerships/sdg/peace-justice-and-strong-institutions_en

Global Goals for Sustainable Development. (n.d.). *No Poverty*. Retrieved from https://www.globalgoals.org/1-no-poverty

Abi-Habib. (2020). Millions Had Risen Out of Poverty. *New York Times*.

Audette. (2019). *Gender report policy*. https://genderpolicyreport.umn.edu/gender-equality-supports-happiness/

Vergin, J. (2019). *Psychology: A happy partner is the elixir of longer life*. DW News. Retrieved from https://www.dw.com/en/psychology-a-happy-partner-is-the-elixir-of-longer-life/a-48762543

Chapter 2
New Indicators and Measurement Methods for Welfare in the Global Economy Era

Mikail Kar
Bursa Uludag University, Turkey

ABSTRACT

This study discusses the inadequacy of GDP alone as a measure of welfare in the global economic age and examines alternative welfare indicators and measurement methods. This study, which discusses the human development index (HDI), the inequality adjusted human development index (I-HDI), the gender inequality index (GII), the multidimensional poverty index (MPI), the social progress index (SPI), the happy planet index (HPI), the better life index (BLI), the Legatum prosperity index(LPI), the human capital index (HCI), and the ecological footprint (EF) methods, shares the country rankings of these methods and reveals the differences in the results depending on the method. It also draws attention to the differences between the economic size and welfare level by sharing the rankings of the world's 10 largest economies in alternative methods. In addition, the study examines the obstacles to the inability to establish a complete, precise, and generally accepted method of measuring welfare.

DOI: 10.4018/978-1-7998-8258-9.ch002

INTRODUCTION

Humanity has always been in an effort to become better in addition to maintaining its current situation in every period it has won the struggle to survive. This struggle of humanity to achieve the better has been discussed in every period as one of the important fields for economics, which focuses on meeting the demands and needs of individuals with scarce resources. At this point, starting with Adam Smith, economists have thought about how to use scarce resources in order to improve the situation of the individual and society. In this context, different approaches and schools, using concepts such as quality of life, well-being, subjective wellbeing, happiness, life satisfaction, have scrutinized the subject of welfare. Welfare has become one of the most important goals with industrialization, modernization, and the spread of capitalism, and has become one of the focal points for all economies, regardless of developed or developing countries. Especially in recent years, with the effect of globalization, determining the welfare level of individuals and societies, evaluating their change, and making international comparisons have become one of the hot topics of the theoretical and empirical literature.

One of the most fundamental goals of individuals and societies is to reach a good level of welfare and to maintain and increase this standard. Evaluating the effort and struggle given for this purpose is only possible by measuring welfare. At this point, GDP has been used as a welfare indicator and measurement method in measuring and comparing welfare for many years. It can be said that GDP has been generally accepted as an important indicator of welfare, especially since the 1960s. In other words, the level of welfare, whether it has changed, and how it is compared to other societies is expressed by GDP (GDP per capita). Even for many years, economic growth and wealth increase have been used as synonyms. However, especially towards the end of the 20th century, international organizations, universities, academics, and non-governmental organizations started to speak loudly that the GDP was not sufficient in measuring welfare and that new indicators and measurement methods should be found and used. It has been argued that economically developed countries may not be welfare countries, and individuals with high-income levels may not be prosperous, and it has been stated that besides economic performance, many other social indicators should be considered in the evaluation of welfare. At this point, different indicators and methods have emerged in the literature that takes into account factors such as environment, social structure, life satisfaction, security, housing quality, education, health, and personal freedom for the determination and evaluation of welfare.

The purpose of this book chapter is to discuss the inadequacy of GDP alone as a measure of welfare in the global economic era and to examine alternative welfare indicators and measurement methods. The study shares the country rankings of the alternative methods it deals with, revealing the differences in the results depending on the method. It also draws attention to the differences that arise between economic size and welfare by sharing the rankings of the world's ten largest economies in alternative methods. In addition, the study examines the obstacles to the inability to establish a complete, precise, and generally accepted method of measuring welfare. While contributing to the discussions in the literature by considering the alternative methods and their most up-to-date data together, the study becomes an important resource by examining the obstacles to establishing a complete, precise, and generally accepted welfare measurement method. In line with the purpose stated above, the study is structured in six sections. After this introduction, the subject of welfare is discussed in the second section. In the third section, the use and insufficiency of GDP in measuring welfare are discussed, the need for new indicators and measurement methods is emphasized. In the fourth section, alternative welfare assessment and measurement methods in the literature are shared and country evaluations are made with the most up-to-date data at the end of each method. In the fifth section, obstacles to introducing a generally accepted and used method of measuring welfare are discussed. In the sixth section, which is the last section, a general summary and evaluation are made and some suggestions are shared.

WELFARE

It is clear to what extent economics, which focuses on how to meet unlimited human needs with scarce resources, is intertwined with welfare, which is defined as meeting the preferences of individuals. One of the main objectives of economics is how to establish welfare, how to preserve and develop the current level. Indeed, whether different economic approaches and schools use the same name or not, the main theme of their policies is which economic policies will increase welfare more. Since the indicators and level of welfare will change according to the definition of welfare, it is important to make a definition that sets out the limits of welfare. However, the unity of the goals of economic approaches was unfortunately not captured in the definitions and therefore an agreed definition of welfare could not be put forward. There are different views in defining the concept of welfare. In this context, different approaches and branches of science examined welfare by making references to concepts such as quality of life, well-being, subjective well-being, happiness, and life satisfaction. Welfare, which is expressed as meeting the preferences of individuals in its simplest form, can be evaluated as well-being, reaching happiness or satisfaction. Welfare, as a measure of a person's well-being, expresses a set of conditions that make up the quality of life. Welfare is the level of satisfaction and happiness. With the economic approach, welfare word, when used alone, means that the individual is better than the previous situation in terms of income and benefit level. According to another definition, welfare is how well an individual's life is compared to another individual (Costanza et al., 2009; Hausman & McPherson, 2009; Somers & Block, 2005; Bryson, 1992)

Welfare can also be analyzed in the literature in three categories: individual welfare, social welfare, and the relationship between individual welfare and social welfare. While individual welfare refers to the satisfaction of a single individual, social welfare describes the state of the entire community consisting of individuals, that is, the society. Individual welfare also expressed as subjective welfare includes all variables such as health, nutrition, education, employment, etc. related to the welfare of the individual. If the changes in these variables have a positive effect on the life of the individual, it can be said that the individual's welfare increases, but if they cause dissatisfaction, it can be said to decrease welfare. Social welfare refers to the general welfare state of the society. There are approaches that social welfare is achieved by collecting individual welfare within certain rules and assumptions. In general, it can be said that individual welfare is very important in achieving social welfare and that social welfare is an increasing function of the welfare of individuals. Although the increase in the welfare of each individual increases social welfare, the opposite is not true. In other words, increased social welfare does not mean that the welfare of every individual will increase (Veenhoven, 2009; Veenhoven, 2002; Sen, 1999; Islam & Clarke, 2001; Somers & Block, 2005).

With the criticism that economists are only concerned with a certain part of welfare, welfare is also discussed by dividing it into economic welfare and social welfare. Pigou explained the concept of economic welfare in his book "The Economics of Welfare". He defined economic welfare as only one part of total welfare, as welfare that can be measured in monetary terms. He stated that although there is no clear boundary between economic and non-economic welfare, monetary measurement is sufficient to draw a line. According to Pigou, economic welfare is only a part of total welfare, while total welfare can change while economic welfare remains the same. It has been argued with some studies that welfare has versatility, but the only part that economists focus on is economic welfare, and therefore the evaluations made at this point are incomplete (Bryson, 1992; Islam & Clarke, 2001).

Considering the welfare studies in the literature, it is revealed that welfare depends on various economic, social, and political variables. Variables such as economic growth, inflation, employment, public expenditure, income distribution, and savings are the prominent economic variables that affect the level of welfare in a society. Among the prominent social variables affecting welfare are variables such as poverty, social capital, population growth, education, health, and entrepreneurship. In addition to economic and social variables, political variables that affect the welfare level of a society can be considered as the democratic structure of the countries, political administration, and individual freedoms (Costanza et al., 2009).

USE OF GDP IN MEASURING WELFARE AND NEED FOR NEW METHODS

Based on the importance of welfare in economics, determining the welfare level of individuals and societies, making comparisons, and evaluating the welfare effects of the policies are becoming one of important topics of the literature. At this point, the most widely used indicator for the welfare level is GDP (GDP per capita). Especially after 1960, most of the economic analyzes focused on GDP, which refers to the total income generated within the borders of a country. GDP, which is the measure of the success of countries and the focal point of international comparisons, guides the policies implemented. The main idea underlying the use of GDP in welfare measurement, which is concrete and easy to understand, is the approach that if the income in the country increases, the additional income will somehow reach the poor (McCulla & Smith, 2007; Brinkman & Brinkman, 2011; Holcombe, 2009; Somers & Block, 2005),

It is not easy to measure people's wishes and desires and to determine their satisfaction and benefits. Therefore, because income is measurable, it is also used as an important indicator of welfare. According to Pigou (1962), although the GDP growth is not the sum of all economic activities since the increase in welfare can only be achieved by the economic growth of the countries, it is the closest tool among the tools to be used in measuring welfare. That is why he sees economic growth as the reason for the increase in welfare in a country. Economic growth and development enable the production process to be more effective, enabling the production of more goods and services that the society can consume. The increase in income obtained by economic growth increases the choice of consumers by expanding the mix of goods and services they can consume. At this point, many theoretical and empirical studies in the literature have examined the same directional relationship between income and welfare (Holcombe, 2009; McCulla & Smith, 2007; England, 1998; Brinkman & Brinkman, 2011; Islam & Clarke, 2001; Grasso & Canova, 2008)

For many years, countries have made the determination of the welfare level and international comparisons over the concept of GDP per capita obtained by dividing the GDP by the population of that country. Countries with a certain level of per capita income are considered rich and prosperous, and countries below a certain level are considered poor and undeveloped countries. There is no economic theory under this use of the GDP for welfare. In fact, let alone the use of GDP as an indicator of welfare, GDP calculations are controversial even in terms of revealing the total income generated within the borders of a country. At this point, although there are many criticisms against the GDP, there are four that stand out. First, the GDP is inadequate to measure the informal economy. Second, it cannot observe changes in the quality of goods and services. Third, it does not evaluate the consumption of natural resources and the creation of environmental damage during production, since it only considers output. Fourth, although it is called GDP per capita, it does not give any information about how the economic size created is shared among individuals. An important example of the criticism brought to the GDP is the effects of natural disasters. It includes in the calculation the expenditures made to avoid this destruction without looking at the destruction caused by a natural disaster. It implies that the disaster experienced will in fact cause economic growth and increase welfare (Costanza et al., 2009; Cobb et al., 1995; Lawn, 2003; Lawn, 2005; England, 1998; Veenhoven, 2009; Veenhoven, 2002; Sen, 1999; Islam & Clarke, 2001).

In the report of Commision on the Measurement of Economic Performance and Social Progress 2009, also known as the Stiglitz Commission, it was stated that the GDP is not a criterion that shows the welfare level and market conditions very well (Stiglitz, Sen & Fitoussi, 2009). Growth in an economy does not necessarily conclude that welfare has increased, and people's living standards are improving. In countries with high growth rates, there may be situations that indicate that social peace is not high, such as political instability, inequality in income distribution, environmental problems, and high crime rates. GDP is insufficient to reveal these situations. The GDP interprets every expenditure as a contributor to welfare and overestimates welfare, without distinguishing between welfare enhancement and welfare reduction activity. The GDP does not accurately represent a country's wealth as it ignores how money is shared. GDP ignores factors such as clean air, health, life expectancy, gender equality, opportunity, and education, which are many important indicators of measuring the welfare of a country. So much so that an extensive theoretical and empirical literature has emerged in which the use of GDP alone as a measure of welfare is criticized and alternative indicators are proposed (Delhey & Kroll, 2012; Costanza et al., 2009; Cobb et al., 1995; Goossens et al., 2007; Lawn, 2005; Veenhoven, 2009).

As people's expectations, priorities, production structure, and social life changed, the need for new welfare indicators and measurement methods that would fully reflect this change and suitable for new conditions emerged. The Commission on the Measurement of Economic Performance and Social Progress argued that other criteria are required to measure the quality of life and welfare. This commission stated that the quality of life and welfare in a country should be measured by eight criteria: health, education, personal activities including business life, materials required for the standard of living, policy, and management, social relations and communications, environment, and trust. Since the level of per capita income does not show all aspects related to human welfare, it has led to the emergence of new indexes that include different dimensions of welfare such as environment, social structure, life satisfaction, security, accommodation quality, education, health, and personal freedom, with a large number of indicators. As a result, although GDP continues to be used as the traditional measure of economic welfare, a number of alternative indicators and measurement methods have been developed based on the above-mentioned need. The most important of these are Human Development Index (HDI), Inequality Adjusted Human Development Index (I-HDI), Gender Inequality Index (GII), Multidimensional Poverty Index (MPI), Social Progress Index (SPI), The Happy Planet Index (HPI), Better Life Index (BLI), Legatum Prosperity Index (LPI), Human Capital Index (HCI) and Ecological Footprint (EF). These methods, which have been introduced as an alternative to GDP to be used in welfare measurements, are examined in the next section (Costanza et al., 2009; Goossens et al., 2007; England, 1998; Veenhoven, 2009; Veenhoven, 2002; Delhey & Kroll, 2012; Holcombe, 2009).

NEW METHODS OF MEASURING WELFARE

Human Development Index (HDI)

The most widely accepted and used index that is put forward as an alternative to the GDP in measuring welfare is the Human Development Index (HDI). This index was developed by Pakistani economist Mahbub ul Haq in 1990, based on the views of Amartya Kumar Sen. The HDI has been used by the United Nations Development Program (UNDP) in annual development reports, first in 1990. According to the UNDP's Human Development Report (HDR) in 1990, welfare is the process of increasing people's choices, such as living a long and healthy life, being educated, and having a good standard of living. The HDI was created to emphasize that people and the conditions they face should be the ultimate criterion in assessing a country's welfare, not economic growth alone. The HDI also provides the opportunity to question policy choices and reveals how two countries with the same per capita income have different human development outcomes (UNDP, 2010; UNDP, 2021a; UNDP, 2021b; Costanza et al., 2009; Hicks, 1997).

The HDI is a method that evaluates welfare with a single composite index by combining three indicators related to the human standard of living, education standard, and health standard. The human standard of living is achieved by purchasing power parity (PPP), which is calculated by taking into account the cost of living in the country. The education standard is calculated by the duration that individuals aged 25 and over can receive education during their lifetime and the expected school attendance time for children at school starting age. The health standard is determined by the average life expectancy after birth. The index value is determined between 0.00 and 1.00, the value of 0.00 denoting the minimum welfare level and the value of 1.00 denoting the maximum welfare level. In other words, as the HDI values of the countries approach towards 1, their welfare levels increase, and the further away from 1, their welfare levels decrease. In addition, a quadruple classification is made for countries according to the index value obtained. Index values between 0-0.550 are considered as low welfare level, between 0.551-0.699 as medium welfare level, between 0.700-0.799 as high welfare level, and between 0.800-1 as very high welfare level (UNDP, 2010; UNDP, 2021a; UNDP, 2021b).

The HDI is among the most used indicators as an alternative to GDP with its simplicity, transparency, and comparability feature. The HDI has not remained as it was first put forward, and over the years, updates have been dynamically made in accordance with new conditions and criticisms. Important innovations were made especially in 1991, 1994, 1995, 1999, and 2010. At this point, the Inequality Adjusted Human Development Index (I-HDI), the Gender Inequality Index (GII), and the Multidimensional Poverty Index (MPI) have been put forward in order to reveal more dimensions of welfare within the scope of the HDR published in 2010 (Hicks, 1997; UNDP, 2010).

Inequality Adjusted Human Development Index (I-HDI): Like all average-based measurement methods, the HDI does not make visible the inequalities in the country-level distribution of welfare. The increase in inequality in any country increases the loss of that country in welfare. The The Inequality Adjusted Human Development Index (I-HDI) was created as a result of the HDI revealing only the health, education, and income level of countries and not including inequality within the country and between different regions. So the I-HDI not only takes into account a country's average gains in health, education, and income but also evaluates how the gains are distributed across the population. After the average value of each dimension of the HDI is taken, the equality level is subtracted from this value and the I-HDI is found.

Gender Inequality Index (GII): The World Health Organization (WHO) defines gender equality as non-discrimination based on gender in terms of decision-making, selection, use of opportunities, allocation, and use of resources. The Gender Inequality Index (GII) shows the potential welfare losses caused by the differences between the gains of women and men in power and economic fields. The GII combines the Gender Related Development Index (GDI) and the Gender Empowerment Measure (GEM) methods introduced in 1995 and tries to overcome the limitations and constraints of these two indices. This index is a composite measure that reflects the inequality between men and women in terms of gains with the help of three dimensions and five indicators. The GII ranges from 0 to 1, having a high GII value means that gains are low and gender inequality is high.

Multidimensional Poverty Index (MPI): The Multidimensional Poverty Index (MPI) was created with the aim of defining the deprivation at the household level with the dimensions of living standards, health, and education, revealing the deprivation of poor households and determining the average number of poor people. In fact, it is a further developed version of the Human Poverty Index (HPI) introduced in 1997. This index reveals the more detailed contents of the bigger picture, which cannot be understood only by looking at the HDI in general. In the MPI, education and health dimensions are addressed on the basis of two sub-indicators and the standard of living dimension on six sub-indicators.

According to the latest published data of the HDI, the top ten countries with the highest level of human development are listed as Norway, Ireland, Switzerland, Hong Kong, Iceland, Germany, Sweden, Australia, Netherlands, and Denmark. The last ten countries at the point of human development are Eritrea, Mozambique, Burkina Faso, Sierra Leone, Mali, Burundi, South Sudan, Chad, Central African Republic, and Niger. According to the results, there are 66 countries in the very high human development country category, 53 in the high human development country category, 37 in the medium human development country category, and 33 in the low human development country category (UNDP, 2021b)

When we pay attention to the ranking of the countries that make up the ten largest economies of the world, United States is 17th, China is 85th, Japan is 19th, Germany is 6th, India is 131st, United Kingdom is 13th, France is 26th, Italy is 29th, Brazil is 84th, and Canada is ranked 16th. It is noteworthy that none of them except Germany are in the top ten, China and Brazil are in the high human development category and India is in the medium human development classification (UNDP, 2021b).

According to the Inequality Adjusted Human Development Index (I-HDI), the top ten countries are ranked as Norway, Iceland, Switzerland, Finland, Ireland, Denmark, Sweden, Netherlands, Slovenia, and Germany. The last ten countries are Comoros, Haiti, Burundi, Guinea-Bissau, Sierra Leone, Mali, Niger, South Sudan, Chad, and Central African Republic (UNDP, 2021b).

When we pay attention to the I-HDI ranking of the countries that make up the ten largest economies of the world, United States is 28th, China is 83rd, Japan is 18th, Germany is 10th, India is 132th, United Kingdom is 16th, France is 24th, Italy is 35th, Brazil is 104th, and Canada is ranked 17th. According to these rankings, when compared to HDI rankings, United States and Brazil stand out as the countries with the greatest difference (UNDP, 2021b).

According to the Gender Inequality Index, the top ten countries with the least gender inequality are Switzerland, Denmark, Sweden, Netherlands, Belgium, Norway, Finland, France, Iceland, and Slovenia. The ten countries with the highest gender inequality are Yemen, Papua New Guinea, Chad, Central African Republic, Mali, Afghanistan, Liberia, Sierra Leone, Niger, and Haiti (UNDP, 2021b).

Considering the GII rank of the countries that make up the world's ten largest economies, United States is 46th, China is 39th, Japan is 24th, Germany is 20th, India is 123rd, United Kingdom is 31st, France is 8th, Italy is 14th, Brazil is 95th, and Canada is ranked 19th. One of the most striking points in these results is that United States, Japan, Germany, United Kingdom, Brazil, and Canada rank worse than the HDI rankings, and China, India, France, and Italy rank better than the HDI rankings (UNDP, 2021b).

Social Progress Index (SPI)

One of the most important index calculations put forward in response to income-oriented welfare calculations is the Social Progress Index (SPI). The SPI was first introduced in 2014 by The Social Progress Imperative, a Washington DC based nonprofit organization. The SPI is designed to clearly and directly measure the welfare based on its four core principles consisting of actionable, relevant to all communities, exclusive of social and environmental factors, and focus on outcomes not inputs. This index includes three dimensions: basic human needs, welfare facility, and opportunity. The basic human needs dimension includes the level of meeting the most basic needs of the people of the country, the welfare facility dimension includes the level of establishment of building blocks that will enhance and sustain the welfare of individuals and communities, and the opportunity dimension examines the level of opportunity given to each individual to enable them to reach their full potential. In this index, calculations are made by giving equal weights to all dimensions (SPI, 2021).

While the SPI provides information on the basic development struggle of countries, it shows through its dimensions and components in which areas countries are successful and in which areas they are underperforming. SPI addresses all aspects of social progress, from basic needs such as housing and nutrition to long-term goals such as rights and freedoms. One of the most important features of this index is that for the first time, a community's social and environmental progress is evaluated independently of economic development by removing economic values from the index. This index focuses on the results that are important to people's lives. It is not based on how much is spent on a service, but on what level of results are obtained from there. The index has made differences in its calculations according to the developments over time. However, according to the last method put forward, it allowed comparisons by calculating the annual values for the period until 2014. The SPI calculations are made for 163 countries covering 99% of the world population. In addition, partial results are shared in 22 countries for which all data cannot be obtained (SPI, 2021).

According to the latest shared 2020 data, the top ten countries among 163 countries evaluated in the Social Progress Index calculations are Norway, Denmark, Finland, New Zealand, Sweden, Switzerland, Canada, Australia, Iceland, and Netherlands. The last ten countries in the SPI ranking are South Sudan, Chad, Central African Republic, Eritrea, Somalia, Burundi, Niger, Democratic Republic of Congo, Afghanistan, and Guinea. According to basic human needs the top three countries are Iceland, Japan, and Singapore, and the last three are Central African Republic, Chad, and South Sudan. According to the foundations of wellbeing the top three countries are Norway, Iceland, and New Zealand, and the last three are South Sudan, Chad, and Eritrea. According to Opportunity, the first three countries are Denmark, Finland, and Norway, and the last three countries are South Sudan, Eritrea, and Chad (SPI, 2021).

When considering the SPI rankings of the countries that make up the ten largest economies of the world, United States is 80th, China is 100th, Japan is 13th, Germany is 11th, India is 117th, United Kingdom is 20th, France is 18th, Italy is 23rd, Brazil is 61st, and Canada is ranked 7th. According to these results, while only Canada is in the top ten, it can be said that the rankings of United States, China, India, and Brazil are quite bad (SPI, 2021).

Happy Planet Index (HPI)

The Happy Planet Index (HPI), developed by the New Economics Foundation (NEF) and first introduced in 2006, compares differences in happiness between countries. The HPI actually measures sustainable welfare for all. While making this measurement, it tries to reveal how successful nations are in achieving long, happy and sustainable lives. Four different basic variables such as life expectancy, wellbeing, inequality of outcomes, ecological footprint are used in the calculation of the HPI. Life expectancy data are obtained from United Nations Human Development Reports, wellbeing data are obtained from self-reports by "Gallup World Poll", and ecological footprint is obtained from Global Footprint Network. Inequality of outcomes data are calculated from the available data. 140 countries took part in the last study. The HPI also makes evaluations by dividing the countries into 6 different regions as Americas, Asia Pacific, Europe, Middle East and North Africa, Post-communist and Sub Saharan Africa (HPI, 2021; Jeffrey et al., 2016).

According to the latest the Happy Planet Index data, the happiest ten countries are Costa Rica, Mexico, Colombia, Vanuatu, Vietnam, Panama, Nicaragua, Bangladesh, Thailand, and Ecuador. These countries are the countries of the Americas and Asia Pacific regions and there are no European countries in the top ten. The last ten countries in the ranking are Burundi, Swaziland, Sierra Leone, Turkmenistan, Cote d'Ivoire, Mongolia, Benin, Togo, Luxembourg, and Chad. These countries are generally the countries of the Sub Saharan Africa region. The top 3 countries of the Americas region are Costa Rica, Mexico, and Colombia, and the last 3 countries are Bolivia, United States of America, and Trinidad. The first 3 countries of the Asia Pacific region are Vanuatu, Vietnam, and Bangladesh, and the last 3 countries are Australia, Hong Kong, and Mongolia. The top 3 countries of the Europe region are Norway, Spain, and Netherlands, and the last three countries are Belgium, Greece, and Luxembourg. The top 3 countries of the Middle East and North Africa region are Palestine, Algeria, and Morocco, and the last 3 countries are Oman, Afghanistan, and Syria. The first 3 countries of the post-communist region are Albania, Tajikistan, and Kyrgyzstan, and the last 3 countries are Estonia, Latvia, and Turkmenistan. In the Sub Saharan Africa region, the first 3 countries are Mauritius, Ethiopia, and Zambia and the last 3 countries Benin, Togo, and Chad (HPI, 2021; Jeffrey et al., 2016).

Considering the HPI rankings of the countries that make up the world's ten largest economies, United States is 108th, China is 72nd, Japan is 58th, Germany is 49th, India is 50th, United Kingdom is 34th, France is 44th, Italy is 60th, Brazil is 23rd, and Canada is ranked 85th. According to these results, it is striking that while none of these ten countries are in the top ten, United States is in the worst situation and Brazil is in the best position (HPI, 2021; Jeffrey et al., 2016).

Better Life Index (BLI)

With its efforts to measure welfare more broadly, the Organization for Economic Cooperation and Development (OECD) developed an alternative method with the Better Life Index (BLI), which it put into practice in 2011. With this index, a wide variety of social indicators are taken into account in addition to the income indicators of the countries such as GDP. There are 11 basic components and 24 different sub-areas that make up these components in the BLI. While the basic components are "housing, income, jobs, community, education, environment, civic engagement, health, life satisfaction, safety, and work-life balance" 24 subtitles consist of "dwellings without basic facilities, housing expenditure, rooms per person, household net adjusted disposable income, household net wealth, labour market insecurity, employment rate, long-term unemployment rate, personal earnings, quality of support network, educational attainment, student skills, years in education, air pollution, water quality, stakeholder engagement for developing regulations, voter turnout, life expectancy, self-reported health, life satisfaction, feeling safe walking alone at night, homicide rate, employees working very long hours, time devoted to leisure, and personal care". With this index, OECD reveals the differences between current material living conditions and living standards, and also discusses their sustainability over time. According to the latest shared the BLI data, calculations were made for 40 countries with the addition of Brazil, Russia, and South Africa, which are not members of the

OEDC. In the BLI, OECD allows researchers to make their own rankings according to the importance they attribute to the titles with the interactive structure it creates. The researcher can make the evaluation by highlighting the variable he wants to evaluate or by giving different weights to different variables specific to the country. One of the main purposes of this index is to leave the discussion of what is important to the researcher. The system also reveals the differences between the genders by sharing the results according to the distinction between men and women (BLI, 2021; Kasparian & Rolland, 2012; Kerenyi, 2011).

In the BLI ranking made by weighing all variables equally, the top ten countries are ranked as Norway, Australia, Iceland, Canada, Denmark, Switzerland, Netherlands, Sweden, Finland, and United States. The last ten countries are Hungary, Latvia, Russia, Chile, Brazil, Greece, Turkey, Colombia, Mexico, and South Africa (BLI, 2021).

When we pay attention to the BLI rankings of the countries that make up the ten largest economies of the world, United States is 10th, Japan is 25th, Germany is 15th, United Kingdom is 14th, France is 18th, Italy is 24th, Brazil is 35th, and Canada is ranked 4th. China and India are not included in the calculated countries. According to these results, it can be said that Canada is in a good condition, while other large economies do not appear to be parallel to their size in terms of a better life (BLI, 2021).

Legatum Prosperity Index (LPI)

The Legatum Prosperity Index (LPI), published by the Legatum Institute and first reported in 2007, covers 167 countries. While setting the index, Legatum Institute set the goal of generating and allocating capital and ideas to people that will create a more prosperous life. Within the framework of the LPI, it was thought that welfare was not just about GDP growth per capita, and an index was created to measure the welfare in human life and the progress of this welfare. Here, it is aimed to measure the satisfaction of individuals with their lives and it is thought that the welfare levels of countries and thus societies will be revealed more clearly. In this index calculation, 66 different policy elements belonging to 12 different welfare areas and 294 different indicators are used accordingly. Some of these elements can be expressed as health, safety, social capital, education, environment, economic quality, business environment, personal freedom, infrastructure, and management. While calculating this index, secondary data obtained from global databases are used. The LPI index has been shared every year since 2007. At this point, more than 96% of the world's population is covered. The LPI methodology is reviewed every year and changes are made in the placement of indicators, the structure of the elements, and the data sources used, thus increasing its strength and up-to-dateness (LPI, 2021; Khan & Ahmad, 2019).

According to the latest the LPI data published in 2020, the top ten countries are Denmark, Norway, Switzerland, Sweden, Finland, Netherlands, New Zealand, Germany, Luxembourg, and Austria. Of these countries, only New Zealand is from the Asia-Pacific region, while all other countries are countries of the Western Europe region. The last ten countries are South Sudan, Central African Republic, Yemen, Chad, Somalia, Afghanistan, Democratic Republic of Congo, Eritrea, Sudan, and Syria. Among these countries, Afghanistan is a Asia-Pacific region country, Yemen and Syria are Middle East and North Africa region country and all others are classified as Sub-Saharan Africa region countries. The ranking obtained in the calculations for the regions is North America, Western Europe, Eastern Europe, Latin America and the Caribbean, Asia-Pacific, Middle East and North Africa, and Sub-Saharan Africa in descending order (LPI, 2021).

When the LPI rankings of the countries that make up the world's ten largest economies are considered, United States is 18th, China is 54th, Japan is 19th, Germany is 8th, India is 101st, United Kingdom is 13th, France is 22nd, Italy is 31st, Brazil is 70th, and Canada is ranked 14th. According to these results, while only Germany is in the top ten, the situation of China, India, and Brazil is very bad (LPI, 2021).

Human Capital Index (HCI)

Human capital can be defined as positive values such as knowledge, skills, experience, and dynamism possessed by the labor force participating in production and emphasizing the quality of human. In other words, human capital refers to the sum of the knowledge of individuals in the society, their ability to learn, and transfer this knowledge and their abilities. The living conditions of the individual directly affect the human capital. Human capital is very important in terms of welfare as it is in a position to affect both as a result of welfare and as a determinant of future welfare. The Human Capital Index (HCI) is a measurement method that tries to determine the skill potential that a newborn can acquire until the age of 18, in the light of the prevailing health and education conditions in the country where he lives. In this index, which was created with the data of the World Bank, a value between 0 and 1 was calculated for 174 countries around the world and the countries were ranked according to their human capital potential. The HCI value, which is calculated annually, is calculated separately for men and women to show the differences between the sexes (HCI, 2021; Kraay, 2018; Pasquini & Rosati, 2020).

According to the latest the HCI general values published in September 2020, the top ten countries are listed as Singapore, Hong Kong, Japan, Korea, Rep., Canada, Finland, Macao, Sweden, Ireland, and Netherlands. The top ten countries, when the ranking is made for men only, is Singapore, Canada, Korea, Ireland, Sweden, Hong Kong, United Kingdom, Macao, Netherlands, and Finland, while for women only, Singapore, Hong Kong, Finland, Macao, Korea, Estonia, Canada, Sweden, Netherlands, and Ireland. All of these countries are in the class of high income countries. The ten countries with the worst conditions in the overall results are listed as Central African Republic, Chad, South Sudan, Niger, Mali, Liberia, Nigeria, Mozambique, Angola, and Sierra Leone. Of these countries, only Nigeria and Angola are lower middle income countries, while all others are from low income countries (HCI, 2021).

When considering the HCI rankings of the countries that make up the ten largest economies of the world, United States is 35th, China is 45th, Japan is 3rd, Germany is 25th, India is 116th, United Kingdom is 11th, France is 18th, Italy is 30th, Brazil is 91st, and Canada is ranked 5th. When these results are considered, it can be observed that Japan and Canada are very good in human capital and India and Brazil are in very bad conditions. The rankings of United States, China, and Germany are also at bad levels (HCI, 2021).

Ecological Footprint (EF)

One of the most important criticisms of the welfare measurements made with the GDP is that it only focuses on economic outputs and ignores the resources consumed and the losses caused in production and consumption. When discussing welfare, it should be discussed how much nature is consumed and whether it is possible to recover it. The state of nature and natural resources is indispensable for the sustainability of an increase in welfare that can be achieved. At this point, the Ecological Footprint (EF) calculates the natural limits of the world and to what extent people in the race for production and consumption exceed these limits. The EF can be defined as the value of biologically fertile land and water space required to produce resources consumed by an individual, community or activity and to dispose of the waste it generates, with current technology and resource management. In other words, the EF reveals the area required for the reproduction of the consumed natural resource. In this way, the EF demonstrates the sustainability of the process by providing the opportunity to evaluate between the speed of people in consuming earth resources and the renewal capacity of the existing ecosystem. The EF was included in the literature in the 1990s as a result of the work of William Rees and Mathis Wackernagel. There are many factors within the EF of a community such as air to breathe, clean water, food for healthy nutrition, wood products consumed, cooling and heating activities, waste generated at the end of all kinds of consumption, resources consumed for the preparation of living spaces. It is attempted to determine how much human activities demand the regeneration capacity of the biosphere by calculations in many sub-headings such as carbon capture footprint, grassland footprint, fishing field footprint, agricultural land footprint, built-up area footprint. For any area, if EF is more than biocapacity, this is an ecological deficit; If EF is less than biocapacity, it is considered as an ecological surplus. While the first situation does not allow sustainability, the second is a precondition for sustainability. The growth of EF means that resources tend to disappear (EF, 2021; Costanza et al., 2009; Venetoulis & Talberth, 2006).

According to the data of 2020, top ten countries with biocapacity reserve percentage that biocapacity exceeds ecological footprint (ecological surplus) and their percentage values are listed as Suriname (2,930%), Guyana (2,090%), Gabon (888%), Congo (738%), Central African Republic (540%), Bolivia (402%), Congo, Democratic Republic of (234%), Paraguay (218%), and Eritrea (212%). Top ten countries with biocapacity deficit percentage that ecological footprint exceeds biocapacity (ecological deficit) and their percentage values are listed as Singapore (10,300%), Bermuda (5,610%), Réunion (2,580%), Israel (2,450%), Barbados (2,130%), Cayman Islands (1,880%), Bahrain (1,690%), United Arab Emirates (1,570%), Kuwait (1,570%), and Cyprus (1,540%). According to the results where the data of 188 countries are shared, 49 countries have ecological surplus and 139 countries have ecological deficits (EF, 2021).

Considering the EF rankings of the countries that make up the ten largest economies in the world, United States, China, Japan, Germany, India, United Kingdom, France, and Italy are in the group of countries with ecological deficits, while only Brazil and Canada are in the group of ecological surplus countries. In the ecological deficit group, which includes 139 countries, United States is 66th with 133%, China is 39th with 302%, Japan is 24th with 684%, Germany is 51st with 204%, India is 57th with 177%, United Kingdom is 67th with 287%, France is 96th with 82%, and Italy is 31st with 404%. In the ecological surplus group, which includes 49 countries, Brazil is 11th with 206% and Canada is 27th with 85%. As can be seen, the situation of countries in terms of EF seems very bad. Large countries take urgent measures at this point as an indispensable condition for sustainability (EF, 2021).

OBSTACLES TO MEASURING WELFARE

As discussed in the relevant titles of the study, GDP is widely used although it is considered insufficient in measuring welfare. Alternative methods, on the other hand, are criticized from various aspects, are found insufficient, not widely accepted and not preferred in international evaluations. There are important reasons why a generally accepted welfare measurement method cannot be put forward. These obstacles are generally discussed in the literature under three main headings: data-related obstacles, methodology-related obstacles, and institutional obstacles (Costanza et al., 2009; Lawn, 2003; Lawn, 2005; England, 1998; Brinkman & Brinkman, 2011).

Data-related obstacles: The data constraint problem, which is the most important problem faced by researchers in many empirical analyzes of economics, is also one of the most important problems in measuring welfare. The first step in measuring welfare is determining the indicators that will indicate the welfare level. Indicators may vary from person to person, as well as large differences between societies. At this point, it is quite difficult to determine generally accepted indicators. After determining the indicators, the data of these indicators should be obtained in a reliable, usable and periodic manner. Usability is related to the timeliness, scale and scope of the data collected. It is very difficult to obtain the data of the welfare indicators determined comprehensively from each society in accordance with the scales determined in an updated and comprehensive way. Its reliability is basically whether a change in the indicator is an accurate signal of change in welfare expected to measure. At this point, the fact that the indicators have different priorities according to individuals and especially societies causes questioning the reliability of the data obtained regarding this indicator. The fact that the data to be included in the calculation are the data of the same period is very important for the correct result. However, obtaining data for many indicators frequently and in the same period requires a highly developed infrastructure and a large financial resource. This does not seem possible for almost all societies in the world, although there are various differences (Costanza et al., 2009).

At this point, GDP has been calculated for many years. The studies in this process have at this point led to the formation of international acceptances and the development of an important infrastructure and expertise in the calculation of GDP. Over time, a much smoother process was achieved at the point of collecting, processing, analyzing and reporting GDP data. GDP data can be collected quickly, reliably and comparatively. In this respect, the alternative methods put forward have not prevented the use of GDP in measuring welfare.

Methodology-related obstacles: The subject of methodology is very important for the method to be generally accepted and to be used in international comparisons and evaluations. The methodology includes the issues of which items are selected, how these items are measured, and how different items are combined in the creation of an alternative method. The items chosen should reflect the choices, values and goals of the person or community. As individuals and societies change, so do choices, values, and goals, and consequently indicators and methods must change to reflect this transformation. At this point, it is very difficult to determine indicators and methods that can be generally accepted and vary according to variable situations. In other words, it does not seem possible to achieve a standardization that covers all societies. In addition, most of the information used for alternative methods is based on surveys on individuals' perceptions of welfare. This is often considered very subjective data and causes criticism of alternative methods (Costanza et al., 2009; Lawn, 2003; Lawn, 2005; Neumayer, 1999; Neumayer, 2000)

At this point, a standard system, which is now internationally accepted and used by almost all countries, has been established for the GDP. The results obtained are used in all comparisons and evaluations in the international arena, and guide decisions and policies. Although GDP is criticized with some missing measures, standardization that cannot be achieved in alternative methods is provided in GDP measurements.

Institutional obstacles: One of the obstacles to the acceptance and spread of alternative methods in measuring welfare is institutional obstacles. Institutional obstacles can be expressed as resistance to change. As other obstacles are more technical, they seem relatively easy to overcome over time. However, since overcoming institutional obstacles requires a change in mentality, it can be considered as more difficult obstacles to solve. Managing authorities think that economic growth is the solution to most of the problems and they develop and implement policies in this direction. Basically, GDP, which has a continuous growth trend, becomes an indispensable data for these managing authorities. In addition, political authorities do not support these alternative methods because they fear that the results of alternative methods show that their policies are not as successful as they mentioned. Political authorities convince the society that the increase in the GDP will increase the welfare of the society as a result of their belief in economic growth. The fact that both governments and society believe that GDP is the most important indicator prevents the adoption of a new alternative method and its spread (Costanza et al., 2009).

At this point, there is a willingness to maintain the status quo and a lack of innovation in the tradition of state institutions in general. This situation, combined with the concern that the results of alternative methods may indicate some failures, prevents the political authorities from using alternative methods to the GDP to measure welfare. Although statements are made in support of GDP criticism and innovations from time to time, no will is put in place to change the GDP and the current situation is preserved.

FUTURE RESEARCH DIRECTIONS

The issue of welfare has been the favorite subject of the literature so far, and will be discussed extensively in the coming periods. As humanity continues its rapid development, efforts and struggle will always continue for the better. At this point, welfare measurements, evaluations and comparisons will continue to increase in importance. In this respect, studies on welfare should always be developed and updated.

This study can be improved by focusing on the differences between the results of the alternative methods presented and the reasons for these differences. This kind of work contributes to efforts to find a new indicator and method. In addition, the sources of the difference between income and welfare can be determined and propositions can be made by examining the economic approaches of the countries that rank first in alternative methods.

CONCLUSION

In this book chapter, the insufficiency of GDP alone as a measure of welfare in the global economic era is discussed and alternative welfare indicators and measurement methods are examined. Determining the welfare level, evaluating its change, and making international comparisons are one of the most important fields of the theoretical and empirical economics literature. At this point, GDP has been used as a welfare indicator in measuring and comparing welfare for many years. In other words, the level of welfare, whether the welfare has changed or not, and how it is compared to other societies are expressed in terms of GDP per capita. However, especially towards the end of the 20th century, it was stated by international organizations, universities, academics, and non-governmental organizations that the GDP was not sufficient in measuring welfare and that new indicators and measurement methods should be found and used. At this point, different indicators and indices that take into account many factors in economic, social, and political fields have emerged in the literature in order to determine and evaluate welfare and to be used in international comparisons.

The welfare of people is influenced by economic variables such as economic growth, inflation, employment, public spending, income distribution, and savings, social variables such as poverty, social capital, population growth, education, health, and entrepreneurship, and political variables such as democratic structure, political governance, and individual freedoms. In other words, in welfare analysis, it is necessary to observe the interactions of people with the life and environment they live in, rather than just the total output and income. At this point, many alternative indicators, ways, and methods have been put forward to measure welfare over time. While some of these alternatives aimed to measure only certain dimensions of welfare, some others wanted to reveal the welfare level of the society in general. Some of them were accepted and used, some remained specific to some countries and regions, and some were not well known. In this study, the prominent methods introduced as an alternative to GDP in welfare measurements were examined. These methods are the Human Development Index (HDI), the Inequality Adjusted Human Development Index (I-HDI), the Gender Inequality Index (GII), the Multidimensional

Poverty Index (MPI), the Social Progress Index (SPI), the The Happy Planet Index (HPI), the Better Life Index (BLI), the Legatum Prosperity Index (LPI), the Human Capital Index (HCI) and the Ecological Footprint (EF).

The study also revealed the differences in the results depending on the method by sharing the country rankings of these alternative methods. It was observed that the rankings of both the best countries and the worst countries changed depending on the focus and priorities of the method. In addition, by sharing the rankings of the world's ten largest economies in alternative methods, the differences between the economic size and welfare indicators were highlighted. The rankings of these countries, which direct the world economy and are generally considered to be prosperous, in alternative methods, are quite striking. In these comparisons, it is evaluated that countries that are not known in world politics and who do not have a say in economic meetings are at the top and are in a much better situation than big countries.

In this study, it is also discussed that it is not possible for now due to the data, methodological and institutional obstacles to establishing a generally accepted, complete, and clear method of measuring welfare. In other words, it is not possible to say that the world has a welfare indicator and measurement method that can be used in all evaluations other than GDP, or that it will be in the near future. The alternative methods introduced do not serve as a substitute for the GDP for now, but perhaps as a complement to it. However, with the strengthening of the infrastructure and institutional transformation in time, it is possible to introduce new alternatives and to update and strengthen the existing ones. At this point, efforts of a country, a university, or an institute will not be enough for a solution. An international will is required for a strong result. For now, the approaches are to share superficial criticisms of the insufficiency of the current situation but not to put a strong will in terms of innovation and solution.

REFERENCES

BLI. (2021, March 15). *Better life index.* http://www.oecdbetterlifeindex.org/#/11111111111

Brinkman, R. L., & Brinkman, J. E. (2011). GDP as a measure of progress and human development: A process of conceptual evolution. *Journal of Economic Issues, 45*(2), 447–456. doi:10.2753/JEI0021-3624450222

Bryson, L. (1992). *Welfare and the state: Who benefits?* Macmillan/British Sociological Association. doi:10.1007/978-1-349-22282-7

Cobb, C., Halstead, T., & Rowe, J. (1995). If the GDP is up, why is America down? *Atlantic Monthly, 276*, 59–78.

Costanza, R., Hart, M., Posner, S., & Talberth, J. (2009). *Beyond GDP: The need for new measures of progress. The Pardee Papers, No. 4*. Boston University.

Delhey, J., & Kroll, C. (2012). "Happiness Test" for the new measures of national well- being: how much better than gdp are they? *Wissenschaftszentrum Berlin für Sozialforsclung (WZB) Discussion Paper,* (201), 1-33.

EF. (2021, March 15). *Ecological footprint*. https://www.footprintnetwork.org/our-work/ecological-footprint/

England, R. W. (1998). Measurement of social well-being: Alternatives to gross domestic product. *Ecological Economics, 25*(1), 89–103. doi:10.1016/S0921-8009(97)00098-0

Goossens, Y., Schepelmann, P., & Kuhndtand, M. (2007). *Alternative progress indicators to Gross Domestic Product (GDP) as a means towards sustainable development*. European Parliament, Policy Department A: Economic and Scientific Policy.

Grasso, M., & Canova, L. (2008). An assessment of the quality of life in the european union based on the social ındicators approach. *Social Indicators Research: An International and Interdisciplinary Journal for Quality-of-Life Measurement, Springer, 87*(1), 1–25. doi:10.100711205-007-9158-7

Hausman, D., & McPherson, M. (2009). Preference satisfaction and welfare economics. *Economics and Philosophy, 25*(1), 1–25. doi:10.1017/S0266267108002253

HCI. (2021, March 15). *Human capital index*. https://datacatalog.worldbank.org/dataset/human-capital-index

Hicks, D. A. (1997). The inequality-adjusted human development ındex: A constructive proposal. *World Development, 25*(2), 1283–1298. doi:10.1016/S0305-750X(97)00034-X

Holcombe, R. (2009). A reformulation of the foundations of welfare economics. The Review of Austrian Economics, *Springer. Society for the Development of Austrian Economics, 22*(3), 209–224. doi:10.100711138-009-0089-1

HPI. (2021, March 15). *Happy planet index*. https://happyplanetindex.org/

Islam, S. M., & Clarke, M. (2001). The relationship between economic development and social welfare: A new adjusted gdp measure of welfare. *Social Indicators Research, 57*(2), 201–228. doi:10.1023/A:1014481414637

Jeffrey, K., Wheatley, H., & Abdallah, S. (2016). *The happy planet index: 2016. A global index of sustainable well-being*. New Economics Foundation.

Kasparian, J., & Rolland, A. (2012). OECD's better life index: Can any country be well ranked? *Journal of Applied Statistics, 39*(10), 2223–2230. doi:10.1080/02664763.2012.706265

Kerenyi, A. (2011). The better life ındex of the organisation for economic co-operationand development. *Public Finance Quarterly, 56*(4), 518–538.

Khan, A., & Ahmad, H. (2019). Prosperity and instability: an evaluation of legatum prosperity index. *Papers and Proceedings*, 407-431.

Kraay, A. C. (2018). Methodology for a world bank human capital index. *Political Economy - Development: International Development Efforts & Strategies.*

Lawn, P. A. (2003). A theoretical foundation to support the index of sustainable economic welfare (ISEW), genuine progress indicator (GPI), and other related indexes. *Ecological Economics, 44*(1), 105–119. doi:10.1016/S0921-8009(02)00258-6

Lawn, P. A. (2005). An assessment of the valuation methods used to calculate the index of sustainable economic welfare (ISEW), genuine progress indicator (GPI), and sustainable net benefit index (SNB). *Environment, Development and Sustainability, 7*(2), 185–208. doi:10.100710668-005-7312-4

LPI. (2021, March 15). *Legatum prosperity index*. https://www.prosperity.com/rankings

McCulla, S. H., & Smith, S. (2007). *Measuring the economy: A primer on gdp and the national ıncome and product accounts*. Bureau of Economic Analysis: US Department of Commerce.

Pasquini, A., & Rosati, F. (2020). *A human capital index for the Italian provinces*. Discussion Paper Series. IZA Institute of Labor Economics.

Pigou, A. C. (1962). *The economics of welfare*. Macmillian.

Sen, A. (1999). *Development as freedom*. Alfred A. Knopf.

Somers, M. R., & Block, F. (2005). From Poverty to perversity: Ideas, markets, and ınstitutions over 200 years of welfare debate. *American Sociological Review, 70*(2), 260–287. doi:10.1177/000312240507000204

SPI. (2021, March 15). *Social progress imperative*. https://www.socialprogress.org/

Stiglitz, J., Sen, A., & Fitoussi, J. P. (2009). *The measurement of economic performance and social progress revisited: Reflections and Overview*. Commission on the Measurement of Economic Performance and Social Progress.

UNDP. (2010). Human Development Report 2010. United Nations Development Programme (UNDP).

UNDP. (2021a, March 15). *United Nations Development Programme*. http://hdr.undp.org/en/content/human-development-index-hdi

UNDP. (2021b, March 15). *United Nations Development Programme*. http://hdr.undp.org/en/data

UNDR. (1990). Human development report: overview. United Nations Development Programme.

Veenhoven, R. (2002). Why social policy needs subjective indicators. *Social Indicators Research, 11*(1/3), 33–45. doi:10.1023/A:1015723614574

Veenhoven, R. (2009). Well-being in nations and well-being of nations Is there a conflict between individual and society. *Social Indicators Research, 91*(1), 5–21. doi:10.100711205-008-9323-7

Venetoulis, J., & Talberth, J. (2006). Refining the ecological footprint. *Environment, Development and Sustainability, 10*(4), 441–469. doi:10.100710668-006-9074-z

ADDITIONAL READING

Andrews, F., & Withey, S. (1976). *Social indicators of wellbeing: American perceptions of quality of life*. Plenum Press. doi:10.1007/978-1-4684-2253-5

Braun, A. (2009). *Gross national happiness in Bhutan: A living example of an alternative approach to progress*. Wharton School of the University of Pennsylvania.

Coyle, D. (2014). *GDP: A brief but affectionate history*. Princeton University Press.

Dolan, P., Peasgood, T., & White, M. (2008). Do we really know what makes us happy? A review of the economic literature on the factors associated with subjective wellbeing. *Journal of Economic Psychology, 29*(1), 94–122. doi:10.1016/j.joep.2007.09.001

Johnson, D., Fisher, J., Smeeding, T., & Thompson, J. (2018). Inequality in 3D: income, consumption, and wealth. *Working Paper*, Washington Center for Equitable Growth.

Jones, C. I., & Klenow, P. J. (2016). Beyond GDP? Welfare across countries and time. *The American Economic Review*, *106*(9), 2426–2457. doi:10.1257/aer.20110236

Jorgenson, D. W. (2018). Production and welfare: Progress in economic measurement. *Journal of Economic Literature*, *56*(3), 867–919. doi:10.1257/jel.20171358

Jorgenson, D. W., & Schreyer, P. (2017). Measuring individual economic well-being and social welfare within the framework of the system of national accounts. *Review of Income and Wealth*, *63*(2), 460–477. doi:10.1111/roiw.12326

Oulton, N. (2012). How to measure living standards and productivity? *Review of Income and Wealth*, *58*(3), 424–456. doi:10.1111/j.1475-4991.2012.00498.x

Pilling, D. (2018). *The growth delusion the wealth and well-being of nations*. Bloomsbury Publishing.

Van, W. K. (1997). *Social welfare: a world view*. Nelson–Hall Publishers.

Wagener, H. (2004). Good governance, welfare, and transformation. *The European Journal of Comparative Economics*, *1*(1), 127–143.

Wilensky, H. L., & Lebeaux, C. N. (1965). *Industrial society and social welfare*. Free Press.

KEY TERMS AND DEFINITIONS

Better Life Index (BLI): This index, developed by the OECD, takes into account a wide variety of social indicators in addition to income indicators in the welfare measurement.

Ecological Footprint (EF): The value of biologically fertile land and water space required to produce resources consumed by an individual, community, or activity and to dispose of the waste it generates, with current technology and resource management.

Gender Inequality Index (GII): This index shows the potential welfare losses caused by the differences between the gains of women and men in power and economic fields.

Happy Planet Index (HPI): This index, developed by the New Economics Foundation (NEF), compares differences in happiness between countries.

Human Capital Index (HCI): It is a measurement method that tries to determine the skill potential that a newborn can acquire until the age of 18, in the light of the prevailing health and education conditions in the country where he lives.

Human Development Index (HDI): This index is a method that evaluates welfare with a single composite index by combining three indicators related to the human standard of living, education standard, and health standard.

Inequality Adjusted Human Development Index (I-HDI): This index not only takes into account a country's average gains in health, education, and income but also evaluates how the gains are distributed across the population.

Legatum Prosperity Index (LPI): This index is an index that aims to measure the welfare in human life and the progress of this prosperity with the aim of generating and allocating capital and ideas that will create a more prosperous life.

Multidimensional Poverty Index (MPI): This index is created with the aim of defining the deprivation at the household level with the dimensions of living standards, health, and education, revealing the deprivation of poor households and determining the average number of poor people.

Social Progress Index (SPI): This index evaluates the social and environmental welfare of a community independent of economic development by subtracting economic values from the index.

Welfare: Welfare, which is expressed as meeting the preferences of individuals in its simplest form, can be evaluated as well-being, reaching happiness or satisfaction.

Chapter 3
Redefining Global Economic Thinking for the Welfare of Society:
New Features in the Bulgarian Legal Framework and Financial Control Practice for Compliance With LAB

Plamena Nedyalkova
University of Economics, Varna, Bulgaria

Darina Dimitrova
University of Economics, Varna, Bulgaria

Hristosko Bogdanov
University of Economics, Varna, Bulgaria

ABSTRACT

This chapter examines the legal and financial control issues regarding compliance with labor legislation. On the one hand, the legal analysis shows that legislation is one of the main factors influencing the financial control practice for compliance with labour legislation. On the other hand, the problems and specifics of the control procedures applied by the General Labor Inspectorate Executive Agency in Bulgaria are presented. The overall inspection process is presented sequentially, analyzing the individual stages that the control procedures go through. The problems and the specifics of carrying out an independent inspection activity by the agency are presented, and the peculiarities of carrying out joint control activities with executive bodies or their administrative structures by the specialized administration are examined. Different types of factors that influence the implementation of control procedures by the General Labor Inspectorate Executive Agency in Bulgaria are considered.

DOI: 10.4018/978-1-7998-8258-9.ch003

INTRODUCTION

Labour right, in terms of rights deriving from employment, is a fundamental human right. The obligation of the countries to take appropriate measures to protect this right is regulated in a number of international acts: the International Covenant on Economic, Social and Cultural Rights; EU Treaty; Treaty on the Functioning of the EU; EU Charter of Fundamental Rights. The International Covenant on Economic, Social and Cultural Rights, adopted by the UN, has been ratified and enforced in Bulgaria in 1976. От 2007 г. Bulgaria is an EU member state, and in this sense, the principles of precedence over the national law of the Member States and direct effect of the norms of European law are applicable to the law of the Union (primary and derivative).

According to the provisions of the EU Treaty and the Treaty on the Functioning of the EU, the Union does not have exclusive competence in the field of labour and social policy. As regards labour law, the EU complements Member States' initiatives by setting minimum standards on working conditions, informing and consulting workers. EU membership and the subsequent reforms of Member States' legislation, as well as the accompanying processes of globalization, lead to many challenges and raise a number of fears of job losses and social injustice. Therefore, each state has a responsibility to respect the rights of its citizens and workers at a national level, as well as within international institutions. And in the beginning, it should be clarified that **the subject of the research is the control for compliance with labour legislation, under which the employers are the main subject**, and the responsibility of the state is not considered.

Given that the EU has 27 Member States and more than 240 million workers, respect for labour rights is of direct benefit to a large number of citizens and has a positive impact on one of the most important and tangible areas of their daily lives. Respect for the basic labour rights of employees goes hand in hand with the united market. The free movement of goods, services, funds and workers must be accompanied by appropriate rules to ensure that the Member States and the companies compete on the basis of the quality of their products and not by lowering the labour law standards. (1). Therefore, monitoring compliance with labour law in both its legal and economic aspects is of great importance given the impact of globalization on the labour market. (Blagoycheva, H. 2016) (Andreeva, A., Yolova, G., 2017) (Blagoycheva, H., Andreeva, A., Yolova, G., 2018).

In view of the above, **the relevance of the topic** is determined by the importance of the issues concerning the legal framework and financial control practice for the observance of labour rights in accordance with the commitments arising from Bulgaria's membership in the EU. At present, the chosen topic is relevant given the changed social reality of working in the digital environment, when employers have expanded their employer's power, despite the lack of such regulations at the legal level. The pandemic situation and the measures taken to preserve public health have changed the rules of labour law, giving other priorities. This implies increased administrative control by the state to respect the labour rights of employees, so as not to obtain arbitrariness on the part of the employers.

The scientific purpose of this work is to explore, from a legal and economic point of view, some new features in legislation, control procedures and financial control practices for the observance of labour legislation. To achieve this goal, the authors set the following **research tasks**:

1. To analyze the new features in the legal framework of the control for the observance of labour legislation in the context of the membership of Bulgaria in the EU
2. To analyze the control procedures performed by the General Labour Inspectorate Executive Agency and to give some guidelines for improving the performed inspections;
3. To investigate the factors that influence the control practice regarding the observance of labour legislation;
4. To draw conclusions and summaries on the applicability of legal regulations and financial control problems regarding compliance with labour legislation.

According to the approved subject and object of research, the inductive approach is applied (from the general to the particular), and for the study of the individual factors that influence the control practice, factor analysis is applied with the help of the software program SPSS. The present study is adapted from the theoretical model of Jae-On Kim and Charles W. Mueller (Jae-On Kim § Mueller, 1978).

1. TRANSPOSITION OF EUROPEAN NORMS IN THE FIELD OF CONTROL FOR COMPLIANCE WITH LABOUR LEGISLATION IN BULGARIA

The legal regulations set the framework in which public relations are developed in each area, including the ones in the field of state control for the observance of labour legislation. The protection of labour right requires an active influence on the part of the state through appropriate legislation, given the fact that employees are the weaker party in the employment relationship, due to the subordinate position in which they are to the employer and the established order of work. (Dimitrova, D., 2020).

The specificity of the legal regulations concerning the control for the observance of the labour legislation is determined by the sources of the labour law, being the main branch of our national legal system. In Bulgaria, the sources of labour law are characterized by diversity both in terms of their legal force (given the subordination of legal acts) and in terms of the entities entitled to issue acts - sources of this legal branch (Andreeva, A., Yolova, G., 2020, p. 19).

Among the national sources in the field of labour law, the main spot is occupied by the laws, which regulate in detail the labour legal relations, the basic labour rights of the employees, as well as the control by the state over the observance of the labour legislation. Among the legal acts, the purpose of which is directly aimed at regulating the state control over the observance of the rights coming as a result of the employment, the following must be indicated: the Labour Code, the Health and Safety at Work Act, the Labour Inspection Act, the Act on Labour Migration and Labour Mobility, the Employment Promotion Act.

From the mentioned normative acts the Labour Code (promulgated in Official Gazette issue 26/April 1, 1986, last amended in OG issue 109/December 22, 2020) can be determined as the most significant source of labour law in Bulgaria, due to its codified nature and the substantive rules relating to a wide range of issues. Since its adoption in 1986, it has undergone dozens of amendments, including the ones with regard to the regulations concerning compliance control and administrative liability for breaches of labour law.

According to the current legal framework, the overall control over the observance of labour legislation is carried out by the General Labour Inspectorate Executive Agency under the Minister of Labour and Social Policy (Article 399, paragraph 1 of the Labour Code). If, as a result of the exercised control, violations of the labour legislation are established, the Labour Code provides in Art. 412a an imposition of administrative penalties.

In addition to exercising control over compliance with labour legislation and imposing penalties for its violation within the national state, the General Labour Inspectorate Executive Agency also has functions to carry out administrative cooperation through the Internal Market Information System with the competent authorities of the EU member states (Article 417, paragraph 1 of the Labour Code). Thus, in 2016, pursuant to Chapters 3 and 6 of Directive 2014/67 / EU in the Labour Code, a new Chapter 20 - "Administrative cooperation through the Internal Market Information System and cross-border enforcement of imposed financial administrative sanctions and fines, including fees and accruals" - was created. (Official Gazette, issue 105/2016).

According to Art. 417, para. 2 and 3 of the Labour Code, as the main body exercising control over the observance of labour legislation, the General Labour Inspectorate Executive Agency is competent to receive and send requests through the Internal Market Information System:

- Requests for collection of public receivables under Art. 162, para. 7 of the Tax and Social Insurance Procedure Code (promulgated in OG issue 105/ December 29, 2005, last amended and supplemented in OG issue 105/ December 11, 2020) (2);
- Requests for collection of receivables under imposed property sanctions or fines, for violations of labour legislation regarding the posting and sending of workers or employees within the framework of the provision of services, the implementation of which cannot be performed on the territory of Bulgaria.

The types of administrative cooperation are regulated, including the sending and receiving of documents through the Internal Market Information System, with the competent authorities of other countries and the terms in which it is carried out (Article 418 of the Labour Code). The implementation of the enforced acts sent with a request for collection of receivables through the Internal Market Information System is also regulated, by which the competent authorities of another EU member state impose financial administrative sanctions or fines on Bulgarian employers for violations of labour legislation regarding the posting or sending of workers or employees (Art. 419, para. 1 of the Labour Code).

The General Labour Inspectorate Executive Agency is also competent to send a request for collection of amounts of imposed administrative penalties. The penal decrees that have entered into force, by which fines or property sanctions have been imposed on an employer under Art. 121a, para. 1, item 2 and para. 2, item 2 of the Labour Code (3) for violations of the labour legislation regarding the posting or sending of workers or employees within the provision of services, the implementation of which cannot be performed on the territory of Bulgaria, shall be sent together with the collected amounts to the competent body of the state for registration of the employer or of the company, which provides temporary work, with a request for collection through the Information system of the internal market (art. 422, para 1 of the Labour Code).

The reasons for the adoption of the considered changes in the Bulgarian labour legislation derive from the obligation of the member states to apply the EU law (4). The amendments to the Labour Code (OG, issue 105/2016) introduced the requirements of two European directives (Directive 96/71 / EC and Directive 2014/67 / EU), providing for mandatory rules for minimum protection, which must be observed by employers in the host country, as well as rules for administrative cooperation and control between the competent authorities of the member states.

Directive 96/71 / EC introduces mandatory minimum protection rules that need to be observed in the host country by employers who send workers on business trips for temporary employment in the territory of the member state, where service is provided related to the following: the maximum length of the employment and the minimum length of the rest, the minimum paid days off, the minimum rates of pay, including overtime rates, the conditions for offering workers for employment, in particular by companies providing temporary work, health, safety and hygiene at work, protective measures with regard to the conditions of employment of pregnant women or women in labour, children and young people, equal treatment for men and women and other nondiscrimination provisions.

Accordingly, Directive 2014/67 / EU introduces a package of measures to ensure better protection of the sent workers in the framework of the service provision, to ensure also fight against so-called "social dumping" and a more transparent and predictable legal framework for service providers. It aims to improve the process of implementation and enforcement of Directive 96/71 / EC by introducing rules for administrative cooperation and control between the competent authorities of the member states, the administrative requirements for service providers and the control measures at a national level.

The full functioning of the EU presupposes the right of the Union not only to be established but also to be applied and respected throughout the EU. Accordingly, member states are required to adapt their national law to the requirements of European law. Given the fact that the acts mentioned above are directives, their application in the domestic legal order is done by transposition into the national law, for in general, they are not directly applicable and have no direct effect.

In the years after Bulgaria's membership in the EU, in addition to the already mentioned directives, the provisions of a number of other directives relevant to the state control over the observance of the rights of the employees have been transposed into our national labour legislation (5). Directives are the Union's main legislative way of creating the united internal market and implementing its policies as a whole, which is why their correct and timely implementation in the member states must be ensured. The process of transposing the EU law is complex and no measure can be effectively implemented in the same way as the relevant European institution or body has adopted it without any national administrative measure. (Popova, Zh., 2011, p. 396) (Dimitrova, D., 2019).

At the time of developing this study, a legislative procedure for amending the Labour Code (6) is underway, which is already a fact (Official Gazette issue 109/22 December 2020), and a large part of the changes concern the control and sanctioning activities relating the observance of the labour law. The imposition of administrative sanctions by the control bodies in case of violation of the labour legislation provides protection to the employees and ensures fair competition between the companies, which supports the functioning of the labour market. The latest amendments to the Labour Code have the main goal of improving the adequacy of the labour legislation in terms of labour market trends, the level of the industrial relations, the socio-economic conditions in the country and the international acts and standards.

In this sense, it is necessary to develop the legislation in the field of labour law in accordance with the EU law, the standards of the International Labour Organization and the national socio-economic peculiarities.

Due to the changes in the labour market related to the processes of globalization and digitalization (Andreeva, A., Yolova, G., 2019) (Andreeva, A., 2020) (Andreeva, A., & Yolova, G., 2020), the number of employment relationships that have a cross-border element is increasing. Labour mobility and job change is an increasingly common trend in the labour market, especially among young people seeking realization and suitable employment. The adoption of the proposed bill into our national legislation introduces the requirements of Directive (EU) 2018/957 of the European Parliament and of the Council of 28 June 2018 amending Directive 96/71 / EC on the sending of workers in the framework of the provision of services (OJ L 173/16, 9 July 2018).

The above shows that Bulgaria's membership in the EU has a significant impact on the development of national law in the field of control over compliance with labour legislation. EU labour law covers two main areas:

- **working conditions** concerning full-time work, part-time work, fixed-term work and sending workers on a business trip; and
- **informing and consulting workers** on collective redundancies, transfers of companies, etc. (7)

As already mentioned, the EU does not have exclusive competence in the field of labour law, but only complements the initiatives of individual member states by setting minimum standards regarding the working conditions and informing and consulting the employees. Nevertheless, the EU labour law benefits not only the employees but also the employers and the society as a whole, because it provides a clear framework of rights and obligations in the workplace, protects the health of the workforce and promotes sustainable economic growth.

As a result of the analysis of the new features in the legal framework, and in particular, the transposition of the European norms in the field of the control for the observance of the labour legislation in Bulgaria, the following conclusions and summaries can be made regarding the applicable legislation concerning the considered issues:

First, the provision of the workforce in today's globalization requires the creation of regulatory guarantees for the observance of the rights resulting from employment. The provision of employment is related to the economic and organizational dependence of the employee on the employer. In view of this, the legislation must determine the limits within which the counter-rights and obligations under the employment relationship may be exercised in the conditions of a dependent position of the employee by the employer.

Second, the protection of the right to work requires the active influence of the state through the relevant legislation. The regulation of the right to work, including its recognition as a fundamental right in a number of international acts, shows its function and its importance both for the society and for the individual.

Third, the modern social conditions of globalization and digitalisation set new challenges to the legal framework requiring administrative protection of the fundamental labour rights (for example, health and safety at work, right to remuneration, right to have a vacation or a leave, etc.). In this sense, the administrative control and administrative punitive liability provided for in the labour legislation are of great practical importance.

Fourth, some of the considered changes in the Labour Code aim at more effective implementation of the control activity and better prevention in connection with the envisaged administrative sanctions in case of violation of the labour legislation. This, on the one hand, shows the role and importance of administrative-legal protection in ensuring the necessary level of protection of the labour right. On the other hand, the national legislation, which transposes the European norms in the field of control for the observance of the labour rights of the employees, is one of the main factors influencing the control procedures and the financial control practice for the observance of the labour legislation.

2. CONTROL PROCEDURES PERFORMED BY THE BODIES OF THE GENERAL LABOUR INSPECTORATE EXECUTIVE AGENCY. SOME GUIDELINES FOR IMPROVING THESE INSPECTIONS

The objective related to the effective and efficient functioning of the control system carried out by the General Labour Inspectorate Executive Agency to ensure appropriate working conditions is part of the strategic objectives of the Agency and the meaning of its existence. In this way, the social character of the control activity of the General Labour Inspectorate Executive Agency stands out. Through the control exercised by the agency, the socio-economic goals in the government's policy are achieved, because organizationally, the agency is a structure under the Minister of Labour and Social Policy. The purpose of the General Labour Inspectorate Executive Agency is exercising comprehensive control over compliance with labour legislation in all sectors and activities of the state.

Depending on the tasks set before Agency for the respective year, the specific control activity is carried out and planned. During the different periods, the General

Labour Inspectorate Executive Agency has had different priorities. Depending on these priorities, different goals have been set in these particular years, related to the scope of control to ensure compliance with labour legislation and legal requirements to ensure healthy and safe working conditions. The main form used by the agency to exercise control is doing inspections in the companies (8).

The control procedures applied by the General Labour Inspectorate Executive Agency have the character of preventive, ongoing and follow-up control. Of considerable interest are the inspections carried out on enterprises, which have the character of ex-post control. The elements of the inspection technology performed by labour inspectors may consist of the following procedures and guidelines:

2.1. Selection of the Object for the Inspection

Here, an object can be understood as an entire company as well as its individual parts. The selection of the object for inspection is related to the annual inspection plan of the General Labour Inspectorate Executive Agency, the specific priorities for the year and the objectives through which these priorities should be achieved.

In carrying out its control activities, the Agency cooperates with other state control bodies. In this regard, as a result of the control activity of another state body, it may determine the object of the inspection carried out by the inspectors of the General Labour Inspectorate Executive Agency. In many cases, these are signals of the lack of employment with employees established for the company, as well as non-payment of wages or their significant delay (Andreeva, A.; Dimitrova, D., 2019). For this reason, the interaction with other control bodies is a basis for improving the efficiency and effectiveness of the control carried out by the Agency.

It should be noted that if the inspection is the first for the specific enterprise, the labour inspectors should make a more comprehensive assessment of the degree of compliance of the enterprise's activity with the relevant legislation. This assessment should focus on the compliance of the activity, in particular with labour legislation and health and safety legislation. Labour inspectors should also assess the employer's ability to comply with these provisions. In carrying out this assessment, it is good for the inspector, as far as possible, to interact with all representatives of the employees or trade unions in the company, as well as with the employer. Such interaction is crucial for solving specific problems affecting the health and safety conditions at work, as well as for avoiding possible conflicts.

Another direction, which the choice of the object for the inspection depends on, is related to the structure of the economy. Given the peculiarities of our economy, the largest relative share is owned by the micro-enterprises (9), which will most often fall within the scope of the inspections.

2.2. Selection of the Scope of the Performed Inspection

In this case, the scope is of dual importance - being a period to which the inspection should relate and being control activities to be included in this inspection. The scope of the inspection may be limited depending on the purpose of the inspection. This scope may also be affected by the control activities carried out by the state bodies, cooperating with the General Labour Inspectorate Executive Agency. The scope of the inspection also includes the period for which it is carried out. This period may be limited by the period of a delayed payment of wages or the period for which it has been established that people without employment contracts work at the object of the inspection.

In determining the scope of the inspection, all previous inspections of the company, if any, should be examined. When it comes to the results of these inspections, it should be established to what extent the mandatory instructions given in them have been fulfilled and implemented. Attention should be paid to compulsory compliance, especially in the field of health and safety at work. This will ensure the existence of a favourable work and social environment for the workers, which will lead to an improvement in the result of the work that employees do.

2.3. Preparation and Performance of the Inspection

Once the subject of the inspection has been identified, all results of previous inspections of the specific object, if any, should be reviewed. At the next stage, the normative acts and documents applicable to the object of the inspection should be determined. It should be foreseen whether special means will be used to carry out control measurements related to the inspection. This procedure can also be implemented during the inspection, as it is possible, certain circumstances, that were not known during its preparation, to be found in the course of the inspection. At the next stage, the members of the inspection team are determined, taking into account all the circumstances known at the time of determining the team of inspectors.

When carrying out the inspection, attention should be paid to certain procedures to improve the effectiveness of inspections as a tool to improve the performance of the companies. When performing the inspection in the object of control, certain factual circumstances are found, and if they are in contradiction with the effective normative acts, they can be characterized as violations. For example, when certain infringements are identified, the control bodies of the General Labour Inspectorate Executive Agency should not immediately impose coercive administrative measures, as they can lead to significant unpleasant economic consequences, especially for micro-enterprises. Usually these coercive measures are related to the suspension of the activity, the shutdown of a specific machine or facility, the suspension of illegal orders or orders of the employer, etc.

In this sense, the Agency's inspectors should be extremely prudent in applying these more extreme measures from an economical point of view. In the case of protection of the lives and health of the employees, this soft approach to imposing such coercive administrative measures should not be encouraged. In cases where it is found that there are workers and employees who are not familiar with the rules of healthy and safe working conditions, especially in hazardous work environments, they can be suspended from work until the completion of their training. This can also be done by prescribing the introduction of a special routine for safe work.

2.4. Completion, Documentation and Reporting of the Inspection Results

In this regard, if the violations found during the inspection are not serious and if the inspector considers that there is a high probability the employer will correct his activity, as well as that he will cooperate, then the use of the prescriptions should be applied. This form of impact on the controlled object is the most economical and administrative one from an economic point of view. At the same time, this approach is effective and the results that can be achieved will be the most lasting. Thus, we have prescriptions, in the form of a mandatory recommendation, accompanied by clear written instructions on how to make the necessary changes so that the activity of the object meets the regulatory requirements directly related to labour legislation and health and safety at work legislation.

The prescriptions should be justified and based on the legal obligations of the employer. Prescriptions, as an approach to completing the ongoing inspection, should be a top priority when carrying out controls in micro-enterprises. Surely, the prescriptions should have a deadline for implementation, and it is mandatory to check their compliance. In this case, a more flexible approach can be applied with regard to micro-enterprises.

Where possible, the inspection bodies carrying out the inspection should inform all representatives of the employees or trade unions in the company about the results of the inspection. This can be done by informing them of any breaches of labour law they have encountered, as well as of the further actions they intend to take. This approach is extremely effective and allows the control authorities to get acquainted in advance with the possible effects of the actions they will take as a result of the performed inspection. On this basis, an impact system can be built that achieves real and effective results for businesses, rather than pursuing only internal goals for the Agency.

In the case of established violations, which also are a violation of the current legislation, the control bodies should seek administrative liability, through which to force the employer to fulfil his obligations. In exceptional cases, when the employer gives objective reasons, including those which he proves with documents, the control body should analyze these circumstances and, if they are of an extraordinary nature, it should not seek administrative liability. The behavior of the employer should also be taken into account. If the employer behaves in accordance with the law, it is appropriate in these cases to use the mechanism of mandatory prescriptions, the implementation of which should be subsequently checked.

Upon completion of the inspection, the control bodies should document in writing all established facts, circumstances and actions, which they have taken during its performance. When no violations are found during the inspection, it may end with a description of the actions taken and performed in connection with it.

The reporting of the results of the inspection in the General Labour Inspectorate Executive Agency should be in accordance with the established reporting system in the Agency.

The control activity of the Agency is realized through planned and unplanned inspection. The planned inspection shall be carried out in accordance with the annual activity plans of the directorates, in implementation of the programs and measures set out in the annual activity plan of the Agency. The plans of the directorates also take into account the territorial structure of the economy, the degree of risk in enterprises, the severity and type of violations of labor legislation, the level of occupational injuries and occupational diseases.

The unplanned inspection is carried out:

1. by order of the Minister of Labor and Social Policy, of the executive director, the chief secretary or of the directors of the specialized administration, as well as of other state bodies, explicitly determined by law, as well as at the discretion of the inspectors;
2. by order of the court, of the bodies of the prosecution and of the bodies, carrying out pre-trial criminal proceedings;
3. upon requests and signals from workers and employees under labor legal relations, from organizations of the workers and employees, as well as in connection with information from the mass media;
4. upon requests and signals from the bodies for appointment, by the heads of the inspectorates in the administrative structures and of the trade unions or upon complaints from civil servants;
5. for establishing the reasons for occurred accidents during and on the occasion of performance of work.

3. PROBLEMS AND FACTORS INFLUENCING THE FINANCIAL - CONTROL PRACTICE IN COMPLIANCE WITH THE LABOUR LEGISLATION

There are three main control institutions in Bulgaria, which are authorized to control the observance and application of the labour insurance legislation by companies, enterprises and citizens, namely - National Revenue Agency / NRA /, General Labour Inspectorate Executive Agency and the National Social Security Institute / NSSI /. Each control institution has its own scope of action in control proceedings. Due to the specific nature of the control activities, we turn our attention to the General Labor Inspectorate Executive Agency (10).

The implementation of the control function of the General Labour Inspectorate Executive Agency is carried out through 28 territorial directorates, namely: Varna, Dobrich, Burgas, Silistra, Shumen, Razgrad, Targovishte, Ruse, Veliko Tarnovo, Sliven, Yambol, Haskovo, Kardzhali, Smolyan, Asenovgrad, Stara Zagora, Gabrovo, Lovech, Pleven, Vratsa, Montana, Vidin, Sofia, Sofia region, Pernik, Kyustendil and Blagoevgrad. The survey covers the 28 territorial directorates, and each inspectorate has surveyed 15 inspectors who monitor the observance of the labour legislation. The survey was conducted through pre-prepared questionnaires. Each questionnaire contains 16 questions.

The General Labor Inspectorate Executive Agency carries out its activity in the following manner (11):

1. It exercises comprehensive control over the observance of the labour legislation in all branches and activities.
2. It exercises specialized control over the observance of the Health and Safety at Work Act, the Employment Promotion Act, the Labour Migration and Labour Mobility Act, the legislation related to the performance of the civil service, and the rights and obligations of the parties to the employment relationship, and other normative acts when this is assigned by law.
3. It provides information and technical advice to employers and employees on the most effective methods for the observance of the labour legislation, as well as the legislation governing the health and safety at work, and other regulations, the control of which is entrusted to the Agency by law.
4. It exercises the right, provided for in the Commercial Law, to file a claim for initiating the insolvency proceedings of a trader with due and unfulfilled for more than two months wage obligations to at least one-third of the employees of the trader.

The control inspectors, who carry out both the overall control over the observance of the labour legislation and the specialized control, have powers "established in the Labour Code, in the Health and Safety at Work Act, in the Employment Promotion Act, in the Labour Migration and Labour Mobility Act, in the Civil Servant Act and in other normative acts, which assign control to the Agency" (11). When violations are found, the inspector has the following rights (11):

1. To apply coercive administrative measures, defined in the normative acts, under which the Agency carries out control activity
2. To issue a decree under Art. 405a of the Labour Code for declaring the existence of an employment relationship
3. To draw up an act for ascertaining an administrative violation and initiate administrative penal proceedings
4. To gives oral orders

3.1. Research Approach and Research Methodology

The control practice of the General Labour Inspectorate Executive Agency is influenced by various external factors that affect the inspection procedures and actions of the inspectors. In order to examine the relevant main factors, a questionnaire with 16 questions was created, which was provided to each territorial directorate for questioning of 15 inspectors from the respective directorate. Descriptive, factorial and correspondent analysis was applied to analyze the results. A total of 420 questionnaires were processed, which is a good representative survey for the control activity of the General Labour Inspectorate Executive Agency. Respondents assess (on a scale of 1-5) the extent to which they consider the following seven factors, having been tested, affect the quality of the control activity carried out by the inspectors of the General Labour Inspectorate Executive Agency: regulations (f1), political and economic factors (f2), social factors (f3), corruption factors (f4), staff qualifications (f5), specifics of the controlled object (f6) and administrative - organizational capacity of the respective directorate (f7).

The legal framework as a factor is studied in detail and presented in the first part of the study. Here we mainly focus on the impact that this legislation has on achieving the goals and objectives of the controllers. The active dynamics of the regulatory framework is also a prerequisite for changing internal procedures regulating the control activities for carrying out inspection activities (Nedyalkova, 2019). Most of the changes in the normative acts require additional explanations and clarifications from higher institutions / persons regarding the manner of application of the respective legal requirements in practice. These regulations are not always displayed and provided immediately. In most cases, the issues or questions of practice are explained through various letters and inquiries to the relevant institutions - the Ministry of Labour and Social Policy, the National Revenue Agency / NRA /, the National Social Security Institute or the Labour Inspection General Agency. The institutions in Bulgaria assist legal entities and individuals with questions and written inquiries, sent to them, regarding the legal interpretation and application of the regulations (Nedyalkova, 2019), but not always the relevant stakeholders benefit from this opportunity. This, in turn, gives rise to a number of violations in the observance and application of labour laws.

The political - economic factor (Aslaksen, 2020) is the next factor that is studied in the present study. The economic situation in which the business organizational units and enterprises develop, with its favourable and unfavourable changes, give a different impetus to the development of their activity. When this type of change is combined with the changes in the political environment, the impact is not only on the respective companies but also on the adaptive change of the control institutions I regard to the imposed organizational and structural changes.

The social factors (Kothe, 2013), influencing through the implementation and strengthening of the relevant social policy, have an impact on life expectancy and human health. The application and observance of the labour insurance legislation is a prerequisite for the establishment of a partnership between the citizens, the businesses, the non-profit organizations, the social partners and the state in the observance of the social policy. A policy, which aimed at “social inclusion and personal realization” (12). Bulgaria’s common social policy has changed on the basis of the restrictive measures imposed to combat the COVID-19 pandemic and the subsequent economic and social challenges. The announced pandemic of COVID-19, as well as the imposed restrictive measures against the various industries, caused a number of serious socio-economic problems for both ordinary citizens and businesses. The priority of the control institutions is to preserve the health of the people, by observing not only the labour legislation but also the various prescriptions and instructions given by the Ministry of Health. The focus of the inspections in 2020 has expanded, as also has the scope of the inspections. In 2020, the joint inspections of the Regional Health Inspectorates / RHI / and the Labour Inspection Territorial Directorates increased by 35%, compared to 2019. The actions of the control institutions are complex and cover both the establishment of the labour legislation and the observance of the hygienic and health norms. Also in 2020, the joint inspections between the structural units of the MIA / Ministry of Interior /, the National Revenue Agency / NRA /, the Regional Health Inspectorate and the Labour Inspection Territorial Directorates “increased by 45%. The scope of these inspections is aimed at establishing crimes, violations of labour and tax legislation and compliance with hygiene and health standards. For identified deficiencies, “acts have been drawn up by the competent institutions, mainly related to the lack of cash registers, inaccurate reporting of cash turnover and actual availability, lack of employment contracts of employees, lack of issued or uncertified health insurance books, non-compliance with sanitary hygiene standards. Where necessary, statements of findings have been issued and acts are to be drawn up by the owners or persons in charge of the sites for the identified irregularities" (13).

The corruption factor (Salinas-Jiménez, 2011), always with its negative effect, without which it is impossible to achieve gradation. Similar to the natural laws of nature, in which we see good and evil, positive and negative, the same is found in all other units / administrative-territorial units, centres of government, organizations, communities, etc., in which the impact of corruption cannot but manifest itself. The corruption factor is a prerequisite for the adoption and amendment of a number of normative acts in order to impose adequate prevention, applied as a way to reduce the crime caused by corruption.

The qualification of staff (Aouhassi § Hanoune, 2019) is also a significant factor in the implementation of the inspection activities by the General Labour Inspectorate Executive Agency. The general administration of the executive agency consists of the following directorates: Human Resources Management Directorate; Financial and Economic Activities; Public Procurement and Property Management; Administrative Services and Information Technologies; and Human Resources Management Directorate. The Human Resources Management Directorate is engaged and responsible for planning and organizing the training of the employees of the Labour Agency in order to increase the qualification and career development.

The Specifics of the controlled object factor influences the implementation of the inspection activity by the Labour Agency. The specifics of the site determine the approaches and methods by which the inspection activity will be carried out. The practical control activity starts from the stage of planning the inspection activity, passes through the preparation for the inspection, and the next stage is the implementation of the inspection itself. It is possible, depending on the specifics of the controlled object and according to the specifics of the inspection scope, to perform some subsequent inspection actions. Whether there is a follow-up inspection or not, any inspection activity should be completed with a report. It is common practice for the report to be kept by the inspectorate and for the company and the other parties concerned to be notified by letter of the relevant problems. In this way, the confidentiality of the information collected by the companies is preserved.

Administrative-organizational capacity (Orr § Burchill, 2016) is the next factor that has been explored. This factor considers the administrative structure of the Labour Agency, as well as the interaction between the individual structural organizational units and territorial directorates. The interaction should be both vertical (from top to bottom - from the top management to the individual employee) and horizontal - according to the individual organizational units.

The study is based on factor analysis, and accordingly the following basic requirements are met:

1. The output data is random.
2. The observations and research made are independent.
3. The variables involved are in a mutual correlation.
4. The data have a multidimensional normal distribution. The adequacy condition is met by a preliminary check of the data, using the Kaizer-Mayer-Olkin test, and the data must be> 0.5. The result of the verification is presented using Table 1

Table 1. Kaizer-Mayer-Olkin and Bartlett`s Test

KMO and Bartlett's Test		
Kaiser-Meyer-Olkin Measure of Sampling Adequacy.		,913
Bartlett's Test of Sphericity	Approx. Chi-Square	2896,353
	df	21
	Sig.	,000

5. Hypothesis testing, i.e. testing whether the tested seven factors - regulations, political and economic factors, social factors, corruption factors, staff qualifications, specifics of the controlled site and administrative - organizational capacity of the directorate - affect the quality of control activities carried out by the inspectors of the General Labour Inspectorate Executive Agency. Testing is performed using the Bartlett test. With its help, it is necessary to check whether the correlation matrix is identical, i.e. to find out whether the variables are not related, which will mean they are inappropriate because they lie on the same line. In the studied case, the examined data are "spherical" because Sig is 0.000 (see Table 1), i.e. KMO = 0.913> 0.5 and the Bartlett test has Sig. = 0.000 <0.05, i.e. the significance level is Sig. = 0.000 and is less than the critical risk level of 0.05. Therefore, the null hypothesis is rejected, i.e. there is a significant correlation between the primary variables, and in that case, the factor analysis is applicable.

3.2. Analysis of Results and Testing

The descriptive analysis of the data shows that the studied factors have a strong impact on the inspection activity of the General Labour Inspectorate Executive

Agency in all the surveyed 28 territorial directorates. The predominant estimates of the tested factors are over 3, i.e. the median is over 3, which means that they have a significant impact. The strongest influence is exerted by the factors: normative regulation (f1), political-economic factors (f2), social factors (f3) and the corruption factor (f4). The other factors - staff qualification (f5), specifics of the controlled site (f6) and the administrative - organizational capacity of the respective directorate (f7) have a lesser impact on the inspection activity carried out by the inspectors of the General Labour Inspectorate Executive Agency.

The study of the relation between the factors and their grouping required to determine their correlation and dependence and the data are presented using the correlation matrix. The corresponding distribution of the data from the correlation matrix is given in Table 2.

Table 2. Distribution of the values of the correlation matrix

Total Variance Explained						
Component	Initial Eigenvalues			Extraction Sums of Squared Loadings		
	Total	% of Variance	Cumulative %	Total	% of Variance	Cumulative %
1	5,583	79,750	79,750	5,583	79,750	79,750
2	,490	7,001	86,751	,490	7,001	86,751
3	,341	4,867	91,618	,341	4,867	91,618
4	,191	2,722	94,340	,191	2,722	94,340
5	,144	2,059	96,400			
6	,132	1,891	98,290			
7	,120	1,710	100,000			
Extraction Method: Principal Component Analysis.						

From the data presented in Table 2, it is found that only with the compilation of the first four factors (regulatory framework (f1), political-economic factors (f2), social factors (f3) and the corruption factor (f4) their impact on the inspection activity reaches 94%. Therefore, it can be assumed that they have the strongest impact and influence on the control activity of the inspectors. The other factors affect only 6% in total, which means that their severity is less and it can be assumed that these factors are not so significant and important for control practice.

When testing the four variables (*regulations* (f1), *political-economic factors* (f2), *social factors* (f3) and *the corruption factor* (f4)), the concentration of these variables was actually tested. A variable is a separate factor. For this reason, the variances of these variables ($\sigma 2 = 1.00$) are treated as inclusion coefficients, the

Table 3. Concentration of variables

Component Matrix[a]				
	Component			
	1	2	3	4
VAR00001	,854	,185	,462	-,027
VAR00002	,860	-,413	,187	,037
VAR00003	,911	-,243	-,091	,172
VAR00004	,844	,475	-,058	,121
VAR00005	,913	-,011	-,137	-,363
VAR00006	,937	,020	-,085	-,035
VAR00007	,926	,010	-,235	,104
Extraction Method: Principal Component Analysis.				
a. 4 components extracted.				

data of which are presented in Table 3.

From the data in Table 3, it is found that the concentration of the components of the first variable is the highest (f1), i.e. this is the regulatory framework, and the other factors contribute to the achievement of this high concentration, i.e. the change

Figure 1. Composition of factors

KMO and Bartlett's Test

Kaiser-Meyer-Olkin Measure of Sampling Adequacy.		,913
Bartlett's Test of Sphericity	Approx. Chi-Square	2896,353
	df	21
	Sig.	,000

of the regulatory framework is a result of the political and economic events, social events and the fight against corruption.

Taking into account all the data presented so far, and after the analysis of the main components (principal component analysis), we have grouped the factors that affect the inspection activity of the General Labour Inspectorate Executive Agency. The grouping of these factors is presented in FIG. 1:

Therefore, based on all the above, it can be assumed that the two main factors X1 and X2 consist of the following variables, namely X1 - the regulatory framework, political-economic variables, social variables and corruption variables. The main factor X2 is composed of the following variables qualification of the staff, specifics of the controlled site and the administrative organizational capacity of the respective territorial directorate of the General Labour Inspectorate Executive Agency.

CONCLUSION

The overall study is a comprehensive study on the impact of various variables on control practices in the application of labour law. The object of study is the activity of one of the main control institutions in Bulgaria, namely the General Labour Inspectorate Executive Agency.

Firstly, the new features in the legal framework of the control for the observance of the labour legislation in the context of the membership of Bulgaria in the EU are analyzed, because the legal regulation sets the framework in which the public relations in the field of the state control for the observance of the labour legislation are being developed. Bulgaria's membership in the EU has a significant impact on the development of the national law in the field of control over the observance of labour rights. Accordingly, the legislation is one of the main factors influencing the financial control practice for compliance with labour legislation.

Secondly, based on an analysis of the control practice of the General Labour Inspectorate Executive Agency, some guidelines are given for improving the performed inspections.

Thirdly, as a result of the factor analysis, it was found that the seven main variables that influence control practice, namely: legislation (f1), political-economic (f2), social (f3), corruption (f4), qualifications of the staff (f5), the specifics of the controlled site (f6) and the administrative-organizational capacity of the respective directorate (f7) are the main components of two main factors X1 and X2. Both factors have an equal impact on the control activity of the General Labour Inspectorate Executive Agency.

In conclusion, it should be emphasized that there is a clear relation between the legal framework and the efficiency of financial control practices for compliance with labour legislation. This conclusion is reached, firstly, through the legal analysis of the current legislation, made in the first part; secondly, through the analysis of the control practice of the General Labour Inspectorate Executive Agency, made in the second part; and thirdly, through the analysis of the factors influencing the inspection activity, made in the third final part of the research.

REFERENCES

Andreeva, A. (2020). Digitalization as a Factor for the Development of the Modern Labour Legislation. In *Digital Economy: Azerbaijan at the New Stage of Economic Development: Conference Proceedings of the International Scientific-Practical Conference*. Baku Business University.

Andreeva, A., & Dimitrova, D. (2019). *Spetsifiki na kontrola na izpalnitelna agentsia glavna inspektsia po truda, v konteksta na garantsiite za izplashtane na trudovoto vaznagrazhdenie*. Burgaski svoboden universitet.

Andreeva, A., & Yolova, G. (2019). The Right to Work in a Digital Society: Evolution and Trends. Mezhdunarodni klasterni politiki: Balgaro-kitayski forum: Sbornik s dokladi ot mezhdunarodna konferentsia. Varna: Nauka i ikonomika.

Andreeva, A., & Yolova, G. (2020). Liability in Labour Legislation: New Challenges Related to the Use of Artificial Intelligence. In Responsible AI and Ethical Issues for Businesses and Governments (pp. 214-232). IGI Global.

Andreeva, A., & Yolova, G. (2020). *Trudovo i osiguritelno pravo*. Nauka i ikonomika.

Andreeva, A., & Yolova, G. (2017). Tendentsii i predizvikatelstva pred trudovoto i osiguritelnoto zakonodatelstvo - deset godini sled chlenstvoto na R. Bulgaria v ES. *Nauchni trudove na Instituta za darzhavata i pravoto, 16*, 251 - 261.

Aouhassi, S., & Hanoune, M. (2019). Specific Qualification for Information System Components from Managers and Technical Staff Perspective. In Y. Farhaoui & L. Moussaid (Eds.), *Big Data and Smart Digital Environment. ICBDSDE 2018. Studies in Big Data* (Vol. 53). Springer. doi:10.1007/978-3-030-12048-1_6

Aslaksen, E. W. (2020). Political and Economic Factors. In *The Stability of Society. Lecture Notes in Networks and Systems* (Vol. 113). Springer. doi:10.1007/978-3-030-40226-6_7

Blagoycheva, H. (2016). Employment and the "Working Poor" Phenomenon in the EU. *International Journal of Economics and Business Administration, 4*(3), 3 - 18.

Blagoycheva, H., Andreeva, A., & Yolova, G. (2018). Legal Framework of Occupational Health Servicesin the EU and in Bulgaria. Izvestiya Journal of Varna University of Economics, 62(3-4), 250 - 264.

Dimitrova, D. (2019). Savremenni tendentsii v administrativnoto zakonodatelstvo na Bulgaria. In Pravoto i biznesat v savremennoto obshtestvo: Sbornik s dokladi ot 2-ra Natsionalna nauchna konferentsia. Nauka i ikonomika.

Dimitrova, D. (2020). Po nyakoi vaprosi na administrativnopravnata zashtita na pravoto na trud. In Pravoto i biznesat v savremennoto obshtestvo: Sbornik s dokladi ot 3-ta Natsionalna nauchna konferentsia. Nauka i ikonomika.

Kim & Mueller. (1978). Factor Analysis: Statistical Methods and Practical Issues (Quantitative Applications in the Social Sciences). SAGE Publications.

Kothe, E. (2013). Social Factors. In M. D. Gellman & J. R. Turner (Eds.), *Encyclopedia of Behavioral Medicine*. Springer. doi:10.1007/978-1-4419-1005-9_1179

Nedyalkova, P. (2019). Government Supervision – A Factor for Business Development. Journal of Management Policy and Practice, 20(2), 114 – 120.

Nedyalkova, P. (2019). Quality of Internal Auditing in the Public Sector. Perspectives from the Bulgarian and International Context. *Springer International Publishing*.

Orr, J., Smith, M., Burchill, C., Katz, A., & Fransoo, R. (2016). Outcomes of an investment in administrative data infrastructure: An example of capacity building at the Manitoba Centre for Health Policy. *Canadian Journal of Public Health*, *107*(4-5), e480–e481. doi:10.17269/CJPH.107.5659 PMID:28026717

Popova, Zh. (2011). *Pravo na Evropeyskia sayuz*. Siela.

Salinas-Jiménez, M. M., & Salinas-Jiménez, J. (2011). Corruption and total factor productivity: Level or growth effects? *Portuguese Economic Journal*, *10*(2), 109–128. doi:10.100710258-010-0059-3

ENDNOTES

1. https://ec.europa.eu/social/main.jsp?catId=157&langId=bg, seen on 27th Dec 2020
2. According to Art. 162, para. 7 of the Tax and Social Insurance Procedure Code: Public claims are claims for financial administrative sanctions and/ or fines, including fees and charges, imposed by the competent authorities or confirmed by the administrative or judicial authorities of EU member

states, or, where applicable, by the labour courts of the EU member states in connection with non-compliance with Directive 96/71 / EC of the European Parliament and of the Council of 16th December 1996 concerning the sending of workers in the framework of the provision of services (OB, L 18/1 of 21st Jan 1997) or Directive 2014/67 / EU of the European Parliament and of the Council of 15th May 2014 to ensure the implementation of Directive 96/71 / EC on the sending of workers in the framework of the provision of services and amending Regulation (EU) No 1024/2012 on administrative cooperation through the Internal Market Information System (IMI Regulation) (OB, L 159/11 of 28th May 2014)

3. Art. 121a, para. 1, item 2 of the Labour Code: Sending of employees in the framework of the provision of services is present when an employer, registered under the legislation of another EU member state, a member state under the Agreement on the European Economic Area, of the Swiss Confederation, or a third country, sends a worker or employee to the territory of the Republic of Bulgaria: (a) at its own expense and under its own direction on the basis of a contract between the employer and the service user; (b) a company in the same group of companies.

4. Reasons for the Draft Law for amendment and supplement of the Labour Code (602-01-60 / 20.10.2016); published at: https://www.parliament.bg/bg/bills/ID/66447/, seen on 27th Dec 2020

5. For example, Council Directive 2001/23 / EC of 12 March 2001 on the approximation of the laws of the member states relating to the guaranteeing of employees' rights in the event of transfers of companies, businesses or parts of companies or businesses; Council Directive 98/59 / EC of 20 July 1998 on the approximation of the laws of the member states relating to collective redundancies; Council Directive 94/33 / EC of 22 June 1994 on the protection of young people at work; Council Directive 89/656 / EEC of 30 November 1989 on the minimum safety and health requirements for the use of personal protective equipment at work (Third individual Directive within the meaning of Article 16 (1) of Directive 89/391 / EEC)); Council Directive 89/391 / EEC of 12 June 1989 on the introduction of measures to encourage improvements in the safety and health of workers at work, etc.

6. Draft Law on Amendments to the Labour Code (002-01-32/03.08.2020); published at: https://www.parliament.bg/bg/bills/ID/163309/, seen on 27th Dec 2020

7. https://ec.europa.eu/social/main.jsp?catId=157&langId=bg, seen on 27th Dec 2020

8. This term is used, but in different cases, it has a different scope. It is used in this statement to maximize the scope of organizationally, administratively and

economically differentiated entities, where the General Labour Inspectorate Executive Agency can exercise control.

9. Law on Small and Medium Enterprises, published in Official Gazette issue 84/September 24, 1999, last edited in issue 21/March 13, 2020.
10. General Labour Inspectorate Executive Agency - https://www.gli.government.bg/bg/node/6364, seen on 27th Dec 2020
11. Rules of Procedure of the General Labor Inspectorate Executive Agency, (published in Official Gazette issue 6/21st Jan 2014, ed. and sup. in issue 28/ 29th Mar 2018)
12. Social Policy. Management priorities 2017-2021. Council of Ministers of the Republic of Bulgaria - https://www.gov.bg/bg/pravitelstvo/programa-na-pravitelstvoto/sotsialna-politika, seen on 27th Dec 2020
13. Joint inspections of the police, NRA, RHI and the Labor Inspectorate of commercial objects in the area - https://oborishte.bg/съвместни-проверки-на-полиция-нап-рзи/, seen on 27th Dec 2020

Chapter 4
Sharing Economy: Conceptualization, Motivators and Barriers, and Avenues for Research in Bangladesh

Md. Oliur Rahman Tarek
Center for Enterprise and Society, University of Liberal Arts Bangladesh (ULAB), Dhanmondi, Bangladesh

Sajid Amit
Center for Enterprise and Society, University of Liberal Arts Bangladesh (ULAB), Dhanmondi, Bangladesh

Abdulla- Al Kafy
https://orcid.org/0000-0002-7544-5165
ICLEI South Asia, Rajshahi City Corporation, Rajshahi, Bangladesh

ABSTRACT

Globally, prominent sharing-based services include Uber, Lyft, and Airbnb, which have become behemoths in terms of their valuation, revenue, and number of users. Uber is reported to have over 100 million users globally. Bangladesh has also witnessed a rise in sharing-based services of both global and local origins. Sharing services have severely disrupted traditional business models and the economy they collectively encompass is referred to as the "sharing economy." Based on a systematic literature review of top management journals and other scholarly works, the authors present the most overarching conceptualization of sharing-based services. Taking this knowledge forward, this chapter not only conceptualizes and compares sharing-based services in Bangladesh but also identifies "collaborative consumption" as the most dominant type of sharing-based services among them. This chapter also presents scholarly works on the customers' motivators and barriers, which creates grounds for future research efforts in Bangladesh concerning collaborative consumption services.

DOI: 10.4018/978-1-7998-8258-9.ch004

1. INTRODUCTION

The advancement in information technologies has transformed the primitive nature of sharing activities restricted to friends, family, and neighbors into the software-aided exchanges among strangers. Technology-enabled sharing activities can be traced back to 1999 when Napster facilitated the sharing of digital music among peers as a form of peer-to-peer (P2P) file sharing (Belk, 2014). Over the years, start-up companies, with the help of their web-based platforms accessible from mobile applications, have created a bridge between the owners and interested people to ensure the shared consumption of limited resources. From pet-sitting (e.g. DogVacay) to parking-space sharing (e.g. JustPark), there are hundreds of web-based platforms (i.e. services) powering the so-called ''sharing economy'' by connecting people both locally and globally. Although there are definitional disputes among the scholars, one definition of sharing economy could be- consumers granting each other temporary access to under-utilized physical assets (“idle capacity”), possibly for money (Frenken & Schor, 2017).

These services have disrupted several industries and the growth potential of the sharing economy is astonishing. According to the forecast made by PricewaterhouseCoopers (PwC), five sectors of sharing economy will increase global revenues from $15 billion in 2015 to $335 billion in 2025 (PricewaterhouseCoopers LLP, 2015). Each night, on an average 2 million people are sleeping in the beds of strangers through Airbnb- a peer-to-peer accommodation renting platform (Airbnb, Inc., 2019). However, there are also failure instances of these services across the globe. For example, two of the most valued Unicorn Companies (valued at $1 billion or more) in the US have lost significant share values recently and are not expected to be profitable in near future (Monica, 2019). Due to its inability to attract users, Stayzilla (an Indian peer-to-peer accommodation sharing platform) closed its operation in 2017 (Täuscher & Kietzmann, 2017).

Academic scholars from diverging academic disciplines have attempted to unravel various aspects of this novel phenomenon (Sutherland & Jarrahi, 2018). The earlier cohorts of academic works focused mostly on the conceptualizations of sharing economy, the conceptualizations of the associated business models, and the motivators and barriers to users’ participation in these models. In these efforts, academic works have produced fragmented results. The dizzying level of terms (e.g. sharing economy platform economy, two-sided markets, collaborative consumption, access-based consumption, etc.) produced by the scholars bears the evidence of such fragmented results (Benoit, et al., 2017; Sutherland & Jarrahi, 2018). Furthermore, most of the conceptual and empirical research does not distinguish among various sharing-based services (Davidson, et al., 2017). Although there are already hundreds of works existing in the academic sphere, there is a dearth of works that have proposed an overarching conceptualization of this novel phenomenon.

We observe that there is a striking contrast between the number of academic works focusing on the western sharing economies and the Bangladeshi one, although Bangladesh, too, has seen the rise of sharing-based services over the past years. In Bangladesh, the ride-sharing has become a $260 million (22 billion taka) industry (Rahman, 2019) with 6 million rides each month (Kader, 2018) in less than 5 years. However, like other western markets, sharing-based services in Bangladesh are facing tough times with respect to achieving sustainable revenue growth and user acquisition. For example, one ride-sharing start-up valued at $100 million recently had to downsize nearly 300 mid to top-level employees due to slow revenue growth (Islam, 2019). This incident has shaken the country's entire start-up community and is feared to have long-term consequences. Although few scholarly works have addressed the limited aspects of sharing economy in Bangladesh, the need for academic works that attempt to conceptualize sharing-based services in an overarching manner and unravel the users' motivators and barriers is deeply felt.

Built upon a broader research study, this paper aims to close the above research gaps. More specifically, using a Systematic Literature Review method, we have attempted to contribute in the following ways.

First, we present and compare the existing seminal conceptualizations of the sharing-based services to find the most overarching conceptualization that well-explains the services' boundaries. We take this conceptualization forward to differentiate among the sharing-based services operating in Bangladesh. This is the first paper that has attempted to conceptualize the sharing-based services in Bangladesh to the best of our knowledge.

Second, we present the customers' motivators for and barriers to participation in the sharing-based services based on the existing academic works. With the aim to assist the practitioners (i.e. managers) of sharing-based services in Bangladesh, we present the motivators and barriers for the most dominant type of services identified in the conceptualization phase.

Third, we propose future avenues for research that not only would help to close research gaps but also would help the practitioners in moving the sharing-based services forward.

The structure of this paper is as follows. The next section describes the methodology used to search, identify, and scan the academic works. The 3rd section discusses overall findings from the search and identification activities. The 4th section presents the seminal conceptualizations and finds the most overarching conceptualization. Furthermore, this section analyzes Bangladesh's sharing-based services and differentiates among them, based on the conceptualization identified in the previous section. In the same section, we present the existing scholarly works on the customers' motivators and barriers. The 5th section provides the conclusion in which we discuss this paper's contribution. In the last section, we identify the limitations of this paper and suggest future research avenues.

2. MATERIALS AND METHODS

While there are already at least two high-quality works (Cheng, 2016; Sutherland & Jarrahi, 2018) that have used Systematic Literature Review as the method to review extensive agenda of sharing economy literature, we have used similar method to pursue more specific agenda- 1) conceptualization of sharing-based services, and 2) customers' motivators and barriers.

To tackle the searching and identifying the relevant academic works, we followed a multi-step process which we briefly describe below.

First, in order to search for the academic works on the sharing-based services, we have utilized the search terms discovered by Sutherland & Jarrahi (2018). These terms were ''sharing economy'', ''shareconomy'', ''collaborative consumption'', ''collaborative economy'', ''gig economy'', ''access-based consumption'', ''platform economy'', ''peer-to-peer economy'', and ''on-demand economy''.

In the second step, we attempted to identify high-quality journals that could potentially deal with topics related to sharing-based services. The rationale behind focusing primarily on high-quality journals is that major contributions in the field are like to come from these journals (Webster & Watson, 2002). In order to find out the high-quality journals, we consulted with the Erasmus Research Institute of Management (ERIM) Journals List, as suggested by Block, et al., (2016). Using this list, we could identify the best management journals (expressed as STAR) and the second-best management journals (expressed as P).

In the third step, we used the Advanced Search option of Google Scholar to run searches using the search terms identified in the first step. We indicated the time frame between 2010-2019 since research suggests that majority of the works were published after 2013 (Sutherland & Jarrahi, 2018). To limit the irrelevant results, we used the ''exact phrase'' field to input the search terms. We also indicated the specific journal names in the ''return articles published in'' field.

Running searches using the terms as phrases one by one, indicating one specific journal, and setting the time frame resulted in articles covering a wide range of agenda related to sharing-based services. We scanned and skimmed through the articles to sort out only those that have either proposed any conceptualization or presented the motivators/barriers of sharing-based services. After this process, we finally had the first set of academic works from high-quality journals that served our research aims.

We still needed to address two more concerns. Examining the prior review efforts, we observe that sharing economy has attracted many academic disciplines (e.g. transportation, science & technology, etc.) beyond the management discipline (Cheng, 2016; Sutherland & Jarrahi, 2018). Therefore, it is necessary that we take into consideration academic works beyond the management disciplines to see if these works have conceptualized the sharing-based services or explored the customers' motivators/barriers. To do that, we have followed somewhat similar to a snowball method through which we examined the citations produced by the first set of the academic works (Webster & Watson, 2002). In this way, we were able to include academic works that came from outside the management discipline and which have either proposed any conceptualization or presented the motivators/barriers of sharing-based services. Employing this method also facilitated the inclusion of other works (e.g. books, conference proceedings) beyond journal articles.

3. FINDINGS

At the end of the above process, we were able to identify academic works from a wide range of journals. These journals were, but not limited to, Journal of Consumer Behaviour, Journal of Consumer Research, Journal of Business Research, Journal of Marketing, International Journal of Hospitality Management, Managing Service, International Journal of Information Management, etc. This paper builds on 16 scholarly works (e.g. journal articles, book, conference proceedings) on sharing economy.

4. DISCUSSION

We observe that the conceptualizations we have identified are few in numbers but distinct in nature. Although often criticized by scholars (Webster & Watson, 2002), we have followed an author-centric approach for the conceptualizations so that we can review them (by author) individually to capture their propositions fully.

In our review, we have avoided reporting all the available works in the sharing economy literature. Instead, we have considered and elaborately described only the academic works that purposefully serve to the overall aims of this paper. This review approach is also in line with the suggestions put forwarded by the scholars (Fisch & Block, 2018; Short, 2009).

As cited before, scholars differ in their use of the terms (sharing economy, collaborative consumption, access-based consumption, etc.) in order to explain the same or similar sharing-based services. Additionally, we observe that scholars have cited various examples of sharing-based services to complement their conceptualizations. Before we start presenting the works, we provide brief descriptions of these services covered in the conceptualizations.

Couchsurfing is an online platform that connects people with spare spaces in their homes to people who need a place to stay for a short duration (peer-to-peer). Neither the hosts nor Couchsurfing charges the guests any kind of fee in return.

Airbnb is an online peer-to-peer platform that connects people who want to rent out the unused space on a short-term basis (e.g. one night, one week, etc.) to the people who are looking for such accommodation. Airbnb takes a commission for matching the hosts with guests and the guests need to pay the rent for the accommodation.

Uber is an online peer-to-peer platform that connects drivers with passengers for short-distance trips. Like in Airbnb, Uber takes a commission for matching the drivers with the passengers and the passengers need to pay the fare for the trips.

Zipcar is a platform in which the platform users get temporary access to the cars owned by the platform based on membership fees. One of the key differences between Uber and Zipcar is that while Uber is a peer-to-peer platform, Zipcar is not.

We believe the above descriptions of the sharing-based services would be helpful for the readership of this paper. Now, we move on to present the conceptualizations.

4.1. Conceptualization of Sharing-Based Services

According to Belk (2014), sharing is derived from both functional reasons and altruistic acts. According to his conceptualization, collaborative consumption is ''people coordinating the acquisition and distribution of a resource for a fee or other compensation''. Since Airbnb and Zipcar promote such coordination of acquisition and distribution of resources, Belk (2014) cites Airbnb and Zipcar as examples of collaborative consumption and labels them as ''pseudo sharing'' due to the presence of transaction. However, since Couchsurfing runs on altruism without any compensation involved, it is a true sharing service. We observe that Airbnb and Zipcar do not have the same business model. While Airbnb is a peer-to-peer platform where peers own the resources (i.e. space), Zipcar itself owns the resources (i.e. cars) to facilitate the sharing among users based on fees. Hence further distinction between their business models is needed which Belk (2014) did not offer.

Lamberton & Rose (2012) extend the classification of shared goods by illustrating Typology of Sharing Systems based on two considerations- rivalry and exclusivity. They try to sort out different sharing contexts by assigning them to 4 distinct quadrants. Quadrant 1 (public goods sharing) holds for lower exclusivity and lower rivalry with the examples of public parks, roads, and schools. Quadrant 2 (access/club goods sharing) accounts for lower rivalry and higher exclusivity with the examples of private clubs or investment clubs. Quadrant 3 (open commercial good sharing) explains lower exclusivity and higher rivalry with the examples of car sharing, bike sharing, etc. Quadrant 4 (closed commercial goods sharing) accounts for higher exclusivity and higher rivalry with the examples of cell phone sharing, health co-operatives. We observe that this typology, too, does not provide sufficient distinction between various types of sharing-based services.

Bardhi & Eckhardt (2012) coins the term ''access-based consumption'' in their work with the definition ''transactions that may be market mediated in which no transfer of ownership takes place''. Access-based consumption is different from Belk (2014)'s sharing based on the rationale that, while sharing is motivated by altruistic or prosocial acts, access is derived from economic exchanges and reciprocal benefits (Bardhi & Eckhardt, 2012). This conceptualization has been a seminal work due to its conceptualization of Zipcar-alike services where the platform itself owns the resources and the access is market mediated. However, this conceptualization, too, does not provide any distinct means to differentiate among sharing-based services.

Hamari, et al., (2015) define collaborative consumption as ''the peer-to-peer-based activity of obtaining, giving, or sharing the access to goods and services, coordinated through community based online services''. They consider sharing economy as an umbrella concept that encompasses other phenomena including collaborative consumption. To understand the scopes of collaborative consumption, Hamari, et al., (2015) mapped 254 collaborative consumption websites. According to the exchange mode, they have separated these 254 websites into two categories: access over ownership and transfer of ownership. Access over ownership accounts for renting, and lending while transfer of ownership accounts for swapping, donating, and purchasing of used goods. We find this mapping contradictory to the works of other scholars. First, transfer of ownership (169 of 254 websites mapped) is not considered as a characteristic of either sharing or access-based consumption. Hence, this mapping directly contradicts Belk's (2014) works and Bardhi & Eckhardt (2012). Second, Hamari, et al., (2015) cite Zipcar and Airbnb as examples of collaborative consumption. However, we already know that Airbnb and Zipcar differ significantly with respect to their business models.

According to Botsman & Rogers (2010), social lending, swap trading, car sharing, bartering, co-working, peer-to-peer rental, tool exchange- all of them are examples of collaborative consumption. Botsman & Rogers (2010) classify them into three systems- product service systems, redistributed markets, and collaborative lifestyles. Product Service Systems (PSS) encompasses the services ''that enable multiple products owned by a company to be shared, or products that are privately owned to be shared or rented peer-to-peer''. PSS thus resembles access-based consumption conceptualized by Bardhi and Eckhardt (2012). On the other hand, collaborative lifestyles encompass sharing less tangible assets (e.g. space, skills). We support (Belk, 2014)'s criticism about Botsman & Rogers (2010)'s conceptualization of collaborative consumption as "too broad" since this conceptualization does not make any distinction among marketplace exchange, gift giving, and sharing. This conceptualization also considers both Zipcar and Airbnb as examples of collaborative consumption, although they differ significantly with respect to their business models.

Habibi, et al., (2016) offer a Sharing-Exchange Continuum has two extreme points- exchange and sharing. While sharing contains characteristics such as nonreciprocal, money irrelevant, etc., the exchange contains reciprocal, balanced exchange, monetary, calculation, etc. as characteristics. According to this continuum, Couchsurfing is positioned more to the sharing side since it has dominant sharing characteristics. On the other hand, Zipcar is positioned more to the exchange side since balanced exchanges and high calculation are involved. Echoing to Belk (2014), Habibi, et al., (2016) state that collaborative consumption occupies the middle ground between true sharing and true exchange (**Figure 1**). We observe that this conceptualization distinguishes sharing-based services only based on the notion of sharing and exchange. We think that making further distinction among the services taking into consideration the ownership of resources (i.e. platform owned or peer-owned) would make this conceptualization better.

Figure 1. Sharing-exchange continuum, adapted from Habibi, et al., (2016)

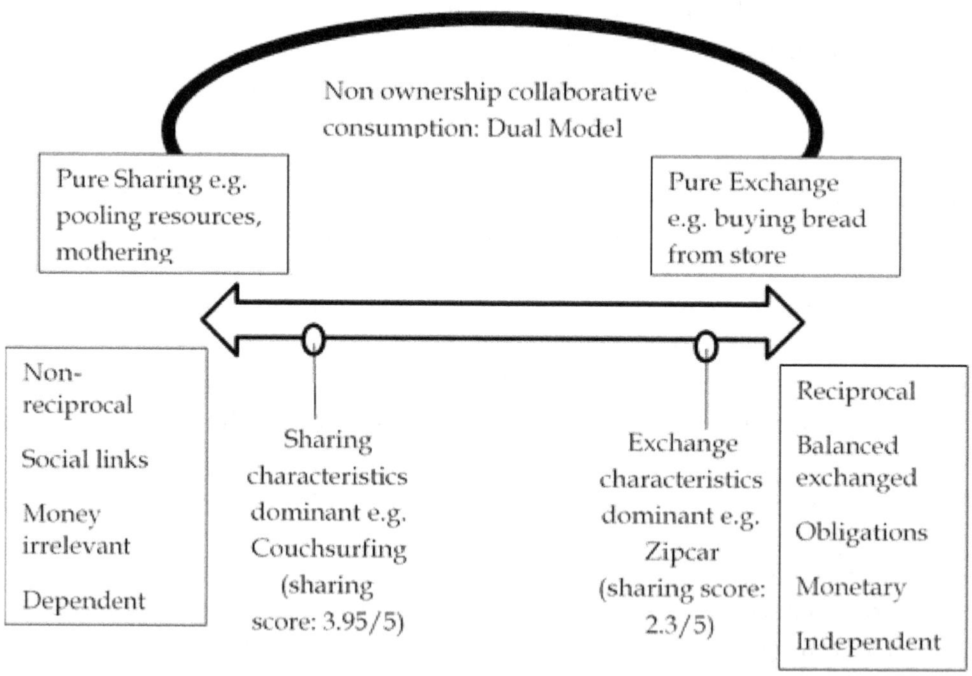

Benoit, et al., (2017) provide a framework that helps to conceptualize sharing-based services based on 3 considerations (**Table 1**). These are the number and type of actors (dyadic or triadic), the nature of the exchange (i.e. transfer of ownership), and the directness of exchange (i.e. market mediation). We observe that using these considerations, different sharing-based services can be distinguished clearly among themselves.

Table 1. Collaborative consumption and related phenomenon, slightly adapted from Benoit, et al., (2017)

Parameters	Non-ownership/ access-based services	Collaborative Consumption	Sharing/co-owning
Number and type of actors	Dyadic, between provider and customer	Triadic, between a platform provider, a peer service provider and a customer	Two or more individuals, e.g. within families or friends
Nature of exchange	No ownership transfer, shorter periods of agreed consumption time, sequential use	No ownership transfer, shorter periods of agreed consumption time of underutilized assets from the peer service provider, sequential use	No ownership transfer, Often shared ownerships, therefore simultaneous or sequential use
Directness of exchange	Mediated through market mechanisms	Mediated through market mechanisms	Not mediated through market, but social mechanisms

For example, Zipcar corresponds to access-based services since it satisfies all the conditions of the same. On Zipcar, the cars are owned by the platform and shared by customers. Here, the relationship between the actors is dyadic. Zipcar does not involve ownership transfer, rather merely facilitates access to the cars. Additionally, the exchange is market mediated since the customers pay fees to the platform. On the other hand, Airbnb corresponds to collaborative consumption. There are three types of actor on Airbnb. The customer rent the accommodation, the peer service provider rents out his/her space to the customer, and the platform facilitates this renting. Here, the relationship is triadic. Additionally, there is no ownership transfer involved on Airbnb. Lastly, the exchange is market mediated since the platform takes a commission and the peer service provider receives the rent from the customer. Uber, too, corresponds to collaborative consumption based on the above considerations. According to this framework, we may identify Couchsurfing as sharing since Couchsurfing runs on altruism and thus lacks any kind of market mediation.

Table 2 summarizes all the conceptualizations, related definitions, examples, and their weaknesses and contradictions. After reviewing the seminal conceptualizations, we identify that the framework provided by Benoit, et al., (2017) explains sharing, collaborative consumption, and access-based services better than any other conceptualizations covered in this paper. Based on our literature review, this conceptualization provides the most overarching instrument to date to distinguish among the sharing-based services.

Table 2. Summary of conceptualizations, definitions, examples, and weaknesses

Author	Definition/ Theory	Example	Contradiction/ Lacking
Belk (2014)	Collaborative consumption is people coordinating the acquisition and distribution of a resource for a fee or other compensation	Airbnb, Zipcar	Airbnb and Zipcar do not have the same business model
Lamberton & Rose (2012)	Commercial Sharing System is marketer-managed systems that provide customers with the opportunity to enjoy product benefits without ownership	Zipcar	A distinction among the services is lacking
Bardhi & Eckhardt (2012)	Access-based consumption	Zipcar, Airbnb	A distinction among the services is lacking
Hamari, et al., (2015)	Collaborative Consumption is the peer-to-peer-based activity of obtaining, giving, or sharing the access to goods and services, coordinated through community based online services	Zipcar, Airbnb	Contradicts with Belk (2014) and Bardhi & Eckhardt (2012)
Botsman & Rogers (2010)	Product Service Systems (PSS) Redistribution Markets Collaborative Lifestyles	Airbnb	Contradicts with Belk (2014), conceptualization is 'too broad''
Habibi, et al., (2016)	Sharing-Exchange Continuum	Airbnb- Collaborative Consumption 2. Couchsurfing- sharing dominant 3. Zipcar-exchange dominant	A distinction among the services is lacking
Benoit, et al., (2017)	Triadic Framework of Collaborative Consumption	Uber	No Lacking

4.2. Conceptualizing Sharing-Based Services in Bangladesh

In Bangladesh, ride-sharing dominates the sharing-based services in terms of adoption, growth, and fund raised. With only a few listings, Airbnb represents an insignificant presence in Bangladesh, if anything at all. Among all other cities in the country, Dhaka has been the breeding ground for ride-sharing services. High traffic congestion and high internet penetration rate have made Dhaka a lucrative city to launch and grow these services (Kamal & Ahsan, 2018). In stark contrast to the western cities where car-based ride-sharing services initially throve, Dhaka has seen the boom of motorbike-based ride-sharing services (Ahmed, 2018). This has been true for other Asian cities (e.g. Jakarta) as well with one thing in common among them, the unbearable traffic congestion. Bangladesh's ride-sharing market is currently dominated by four services- Uber, Pathao, Shohoz, and OBHAI. Most of them are active in motorbike-based and car-based ride-sharing services but they differ in their strengths, investment raised, and penetration in the market. Pathao and Shohoz have raised $10 million and $15 million in funding in 2018 (Kader, 2019). Both Uber and Shohoz have challenged Pathao's domination in motorbike-based ridesharing service with the introduction of UberMOTO and Shohoz Ride. Uber has been an unbeaten champion in the car-based sharing services and according to unconfirmed data, Uber has around 70% market share in the same. OBHAI is still unchallenged in CNG auto-rickshaw space. Additionally, JoBike- a bicycle sharing service, which is the first of its kind in Bangladesh, has started its operation in Dhaka earlier this year.

In Bangladesh, Uber, Shohoz, Pathao, and OBHAI connect the drivers with the passengers willing to take short trips based on the mutually-agreed, pre-determined fares. Based on similar mobile applications, and regardless of car or motorbike-based, these platforms have essentially replicated the business model of Uber ride-sharing services available in other countries.

On the other hand, Airbnb in Bangladesh follows the business model similar to its global model. It connects the people who want to rent out their under-utilized spaces (i.e. hosts) with the people who are looking for a short-term accommodation (i.e. guests). Based on the pre-determined rent set by the hosts, the guests pay the rent. Airbnb charges a commission for facilitating the exchange.

JoBike facilitates renting a bicycle for a short period of time from the nearby docking station. The users can top-up the credit, locate the nearby docking station, and unlock the bicycle through a QR code scanning based on the mobile application. Jobike bills the users based on a ''pay per minute occupied'' model.

Based on the conceptualization of sharing-based services suggested by (Benoit, et al., 2017), it is possible to distinguish among the services operating in Bangladesh. According to their framework, Uber in Bangladesh, Shohoz, Pathao, and OBHAI are examples of collaborative consumption. All of these services have 3 actors (e.g. a Pathao

driver, a passenger, and the platform Pathao itself) and hence the relationship among them is triadic. Also, there is no ownership transfer involved, the resource is owned by the peer service provider (e.g. bike is owned by Shohoz driver), and the consumption is short-term. Additionally, the exchange is market mediated in which the driver charges the customer and the platform charges the commission for facilitating the exchange. Airbnb in Bangladesh, too, satisfies the above criteria and hence is an example of collaborative consumption.

According to Benoit, et al., (2017)'s conceptualization, JoBike follows the business model of access-based consumption. JoBike has two actors (e.g. the customer and the platform itself) and hence the relationship is dyadic in nature. In contrast to the collaborative consumption, the resource (i.e. bicycle) is owned by the platform (i.e. JoBike) itself. Additionally, the consumption is short-term and the exchange is mediated through market mediation since the customer pays to the platform on a ''pay per minute occupied'' basis.

4.3. Motivators for and Barriers to Using Sharing-Based Services

Scholars have been studying the reasons behind people's acceptance and rejection of sharing-based services. Although our review effort has identified academic works investigating almost all forms of sharing-based services, we present here only the works that have investigated collaborative consumption services. Now that we have identified the most dominant type of sharing-based services prevailing in Bangladesh (i.e., collaborative consumption), presenting the barriers and motivators for the same bears significant relevance. In contrast to our review of conceptualization where we adopted an author-centric approach, we have followed a concept-centric approach for the motivators and barriers (Fisch & Block, 2018; Webster & Watson, 2002; Short, 2009) so that we can review them as constructs that have been explored by more than one author.

4.3.1. Customers' Motivators in Collaborative Consumption

Our review finds that **perceived utility or cost savings** play as strong motivators for the customers to use collaborative consumption services (Hamari, et al., 2015; Habibi, et al., 2016; Tussyadiah & Pesonen, 2018; Möhlmann, 2015). Furthermore, perceived utility or cost savings can have geographical and demographic implications too. For example, a study administered among Indian customers reveals the mediating effect of perceived utility in adopting collaborative consumption services (Hamari, et al., 2015). On the other hand, a study administered among American customers shows that cost savings play as a motivator for the young American travellers in their adoption of collaborative consumption services (Tussyadiah & Pesonen, 2018).

Hedonic experience may act as motivators for the people as Habibi, et al., (2016) find that American customers are willing to adopt these services due to the hedonic experience (i.e. having more fun, enjoying life more, etc.) some of these services provide.

Our review finds that **convenience** and **efficacy** positively affect the customers' adoption of collaborative consumption services. Customers may find ownership of resources as burdensome and prefer collaborative consumption services instead (Moeller & Wittkowski, 2010). On the other hand, customers' perception that collaborative consumption services make them more effective in daily life (efficacy) may also motivate them in their adoption (Habibi, et al., 2016).

Social appeals have been found as a determinant of customers' adoption of collaborative consumption services. Habibi, et al., (2016)'s study finds that American customers put forward social appeal (e.g. better relationships with others) as a reason for their adoption of collaborative consumption services. Furthermore, Tussyadiah & Pesonen, (2018)'s study reveals that older Finnish customers put forward social appeal as a motivator for their adoption of collaborative consumption services, especially for the adoption of Airbnb-like short-term accommodation renting services.

Trust may act as a strong motivator for the customers in their adoption. Trust not only determines customers' satisfaction with a collaborative consumption service but also affects the likelihood of using that service again (Möhlmann, 2015).

4.3.2. Customers' Barriers to Collaborative Consumption

Process risk/efficacy has been found as Customers' barriers in collaborative consumption. While process risk may refer to risks of sharing with others (Hawlitschek, et al., 2016), efficacy barrier refers to customers' inability to understand how the platform-based peer-to-peer sharing works (Tussyadiah & Pesonen, 2018).

Our review finds that customers may reject to adopt collaborative consumption services due to the perceived importance they put on owning resources compared to not owning, rather sharing. Moeller & Wittkowski, (2010)'s work provides evidence that **importance of possession** has significant negative effects on customers' adoption. On the other hand, Hawlitschek, et al. (2016)'s work posits that customers are less likely to adopt collaborative consumption services due to their independence from owning resources (**independence through ownership**).

Distrust/Lack of Privacy has been heavily cited as a strong barrier for the customers in collaborative consumption. Distrust towards the platform and the peer service provider (e.g. Airbnb host) may hinder customers' participation in the exchange activities (Tussyadiah & Pesonen, 2018; So, et al., 2018).

While the perceived cost savings have been found as the customers' motivators in collaborative consumption, **perceived cost savings** can also hinder the adoption. Tussyadiah & Pesonen, (2018)'s work bears such evidence where American customers did not adopt collaborative consumption services due to their perception that the cost savings were not convincing enough.

5. CONCLUSION

The pervasive nature of sharing economy and its services has disrupted many established industries and business models over the last few years. Additionally, strong growth forecast and a fair share of skepticism about its sustainability have put the sharing-based services at the centre of debates among practitioners, scholars, general public, and policymakers. We observe that, while hundreds of scholarly works have emerged on this new phenomenon, there is a dearth of works that have proposed an overarching conceptualization of sharing-based services. Furthermore, in stark contrast to the level of attention given to the sharing-based services in the developed countries, services operating in Bangladesh have received insignificant scholarly attention.

This paper addresses the above research gaps keeping the sharing-based services in Bangladesh as the focal point. This paper presents the seminal conceptualizations on the sharing-based services and identifies the most overarching conceptualization through a systematic literature review. With the help of this conceptualization developed by Benoit, et al., (2017), this paper not only conceptualizes and differentiates the sharing-based services operating in Bangladesh but also identifies collaborative consumption as the most dominant type of sharing-based services among them.

Taking the above findings forward, this paper reviews existing scholarly works and presents customers' motivators for and barriers to participation in collaborative consumption services. This paper discusses cost savings, hedonic experience, convenience, efficacy, social appeals, trust as the motivators; process risk, importance of possession, distrust, and perceived cost savings as the barriers to customers' adoption. In this way, this paper creates grounds for future scholarly works, which would help the managers of the collaborative consumption services operating in Bangladesh.

6. LIMITATIONS AND AVENUES FOR FUTURE RESEARCH

This paper is not without any limitations. While our literature review has been limited to only a sub-set of top journals, we believe that future review works should include more scholarly resources. The inclusion of more scholarly works regardless of the disciplines, would shed more light on the customers' motivators for and barriers to participation in the sharing-based services. On the other hand, to limit this paper's scope, we have not covered the peer service providers' (e.g. Uber driver) motivators and barriers. Collaborative consumption services are built on peers and thus both the customers and peer service providers bear equal significance. Future efforts could address this gap and present an extensive review of the peer service providers' motivators and barriers in collaborative consumption services.

Furthermore, future research efforts should include empirical studies focusing on both the customers' and peer service providers' motivators and barriers in Bangladesh. Most of the existing scholarly works on these issues are based on developed/other country's collaborative consumption services, which might not be relevant to Bangladesh's contexts. Unravelling customers' and peer service providers' motivators and barriers could significantly assist the practitioners in Bangladesh and may become instrumental for the sustainability of these services.

DECLARATION OF INTERESTS

The authors declare that they have no known competing financial interests or personal relationships that could have influenced the work reported in this paper.

REFERENCES

Ahmed, S. (2018). *Bike makers ride into booming market.* Available at: https://www.theindependentbd.com/printversion/details/155994

Airbnb, Inc. (2019). *Airbnb Newsroom.* Available at: https://news.airbnb.com/fast-facts/

Bardhi, F., & Eckhardt, G. M. (2012). Access-Based Consumption: The Case of Car Sharing. *The Journal of Consumer Research, 39*(4), 881–898. doi:10.1086/666376

Belk, R. (2014). You are what you can access: Sharing and collaborative consumption online. *Journal of Business Research, 67*(8), 1595–1600. doi:10.1016/j.jbusres.2013.10.001

Benoit, S., Baker, T. L., Bolton, R. N., Gruber, T., & Kandampully, J. (2017). A triadic framework for collaborative consumption (CC): Motives, activities and resources & capabilities of actors. *Journal of Business Research*, *79*, 219–227. doi:10.1016/j.jbusres.2017.05.004

Block, J. H., Fisch, C. O., & Praag, M. (2016). The Schumpeterian entrepreneur: A review of the empirical evidence on the antecedents, behaviour and consequences of innovative entrepreneurship. *Industry and Innovation*, *24*(1), 61–95. doi:10.1080/13662716.2016.1216397

Botsman, R., & Rogers, R. (2010). *What's Mine Is Yours: The Rise of Collaborative Consumption*. Harper Collins.

Cheng, M. (2016). Sharing economy: A review and agenda for future research. *International Journal of Hospitality Management*, *57*, 60–70. doi:10.1016/j.ijhm.2016.06.003

Couchsurfing International, Inc. (2017). *About Couchsurfing*. Available at: https://www.couchsurfing.com/about/about-us/

Davidson, A., Habibi, M. R., & Laroche, M. (2017). Materialism and the sharing economy: A cross-cultural study of American and Indian consumers. *Journal of Business Research*, *82*, 364–372. doi:10.1016/j.jbusres.2015.07.045

Fisch, C., & Block, J. (2018). Six tips for your (systematic) literature review in business and management research. *Management Review Quarterly*, *68*(2), 103–106. doi:10.100711301-018-0142-x

Frenken, K., & Schor, J. (2017). Putting the sharing economy into perspective. *Environmental Innovation and Societal Transitions*, *23*, 3–10. doi:10.1016/j.eist.2017.01.003

Habibi, M. R., Davidson, A., & Laroche, M. L. (2016). What managers should know about the sharing economy. *Business Horizons. Journal of the Association for Information Science and Technology*, *60*(1), 113–121.

Hamari, J., Sjöklint, M., & Ukkonen, A. (2015). The Sharing Economy. *Why People Participate in Collaborative Consumption.*, *67*(9), 2047–2059.

Hawlitschek, F., Teubner, T., & Gimpel, H. (2016). *Understanding the Sharing Economy—Drivers and Impediments for Participation in Peer-to-Peer Rental. 49th Hawaii International Conference on System Sciences.*

Islam, Z. (2019, July 6). Where is Pathao headed? *Star Weekend*.

Kader, R. (2018). *The Fascinating Story Of Shohoz: An Interview With Maliha M Quadir, Founder and MD, Shohoz.* Available at: https://futurestartup.com/2018/12/17/shohoz-story-maliha-m-quadir/

Kader, R. (2019). *Intelligence Brief: The Ride-hailing Market Updates.* Available at: https://futurestartup.com/2019/01/27/the-ride-hailing-market-updates-2019/

Kamal, S. M., & Ahsan, N. A. (2018). *'Uber-Pathao' ride-share's impact on Dhaka.* Available at: https://thefinancialexpress.com.bd/views/uber-pathao-ride-shares-impact-on-dhaka-1524842540

Lamberton, C. P., & Rose, R. L. (2012). When Is Ours Better Than Mine? A Framework for Understanding and Altering Participation in Commercial Sharing Systems. *Journal of Marketing*, *76*(4), 109–125. doi:10.1509/jm.10.0368

Moeller, S., & Wittkowski, K. (2010). The burdens of ownership: Reasons for preferring renting. *Managing Service Quality*, *20*(2), 176–191. doi:10.1108/09604521011027598

Möhlmann, M. (2015). Collaborative consumption: Determinants of satisfaction and the likelihood of using a sharing economy option again. *Journal of Consumer Behaviour*, *14*(3), 193–207. doi:10.1002/cb.1512

Monica, P. R. L. (2019). *Uber and Lyft both hit all-time lows and continue to struggle since their IPOs.* Available at: https://edition.cnn.com/2019/09/04/investing/uber-lyft-ipo-market/index.html

PricewaterhouseCoopers LLP. (2015). *The Sharing Economy.* Author.

Rahman, R. (2019). *Motorbike ride-sharing alleviates Dhaka traffic chaos.* Available at: https://www.reuters.com/article/us-bangladesh-ridesharing/motorbike-ride-sharing-a-panacea-for-dhaka-traffic-chaos-idUSKBN1WC098

Short, J. (2009). The Art of Writing a Review Article. *Journal of Management*, *35*(6), 1312–1317. doi:10.1177/0149206309337489

So, K. K. F., Oh, H., & Min, S. (2018). Motivations and constraints of Airbnb consumers: Findings from a mixed-methods approach. *Tourism Management*, *67*, 224–236. doi:10.1016/j.tourman.2018.01.009

Sutherland, W., & Jarrahi, M. H. (2018). The sharing economy and digital platforms: A review and research agenda. *International Journal of Information Management*, *43*, 328–341. doi:10.1016/j.ijinfomgt.2018.07.004

Täuscher, K., & Kietzmann, J. (2017). Learning from Failures in the Sharing Economy. *Management Information Systems Quarterly Executive*, *16*(4), 253–263.

Tussyadiah, I. P., & Pesonen, J. (2018). Drivers and barriers of peer-to-peer accommodation stay – an exploratory study with American and Finnish travellers. *Current Issues in Tourism*, *21*(6), 703–720. doi:10.1080/13683500.2016.1141180

Uber Technologies Inc. (2019). *Uber Newsroom.* Available at: https://www.uber.com/newsroom/company-info/

Webster, J., & Watson, R. T. (2002). Analyzing the Past to Prepare for the Future: Writing a Literature Review. *Management Information Systems Quarterly*, *26*(2), xiii–xxiii.

Chapter 5
Sustainable Development Through the Circular Economy:
Experience From Emerging Economies

Quazi Tafsirul Islam
https://orcid.org/0000-0003-3451-1346
North South University, Bangladesh

Md. Shamim Talukder
North South University, Bangladesh

Kazi Lamia Haque
North South University, Bangladesh

ABSTRACT

Linear economic models have led us to a point where our planet can no longer sustain itself and heal its natural resources. Thus, circular economy has provided us the opportunity to hope for increasing resource value, extending its life as a means to put waste back into the consumption chain. In emerging economies, circular economy-based business models are not as pertinent. However, in the past decade, the Sustainable Development Goals (SDGs) have provided a guideline for businesses, legislators, and academics. It has been witnessed that a few notable initiatives in the field of the circular economy have taken place in emerging economies which has led to achieving different SDGs to a certain extent. This chapter discusses the potential circular economy-based business models held in the attainment of different sustainable development goals.

DOI: 10.4018/978-1-7998-8258-9.ch005

SUSTAINABILITY

Sustainable development is based on the idea that societies must live and meet their needs with regard to and without putting at risk the future generations to meet their own needs (Brundtland et al., 1987). Sustainable development refers to development focusing on economic prosperity in their sight and a concrete resolution towards the planet and the society. In the last four decades, sustainable development has received much attention from policymakers, academics, researchers, and consumers. Sustainable development considerations are more important today than at any other point in time. The world has not reached the point of no return, beyond which the planet we live in will no longer be able to regenerate itself and its resources for us, but we are heading towards the line. In the coming years, several researchers both from the field of science and economics made the same argument that if we did not make changes to our conventional consumption habits, economic models, and made significant changes to the rapidly growing industrialization, then many of the non-renewable resources will be depleted by the late twenty-first century.

The first UN conference on Environment and Sustainable Development took place in 1972 in Stockholm, where for the first time the world leaders met, acknowledged, and discussed the possible impact human lives had on this planet. In 1994, the concept of sustainability was first directly associated with business models as the concept of the triple bottom line was first coined in (Elkington, 2004). The concept proposed was that businesses should not only consider the financial gains and losses when making critical business decisions that impact the society and environment, instead they should take into consideration the impact it has on all three ends, profit, people, and the planet.

In 2015, the United Nations General Assembly adopted the 17 agendas that they wish to achieve by the year 2030 termed as the Sustainable Development Goals (SDGs) or Global Goals which are a collection of 17 interlinked global goals designed to be a guideline for a better and more sustainable tomorrow. The 17 SDGs are (1) No Poverty, (2) Zero Hunger, (3) Good Health and Well-being, (4) Quality Education, (5) Gender Equality, (6) Clean Water and Sanitation, (7) Affordable and Clean Energy, (8) Decent Work and Economic Growth, (9) Industry, Innovation and Infrastructure, (10) Reducing Inequality, (11) Sustainable Cities and Communities, (12) Responsible Consumption and Production, (13) Climate Action, (14) Life Below Water, (15) Life On Land, (16) Peace, Justice, and Strong Institutions, (17) Partnerships for the Goals.

Today, raised awareness in many sectors has led to businesses and consumers adopting various new business models and products that support the environment. Organizations like Ellen MacArthur Foundation have opened doors to funding business models based on the circular economy, which support the planet in a non-conventional consumption model and product cycle.

CIRCULAR ECONOMY (CE)

Circular economy (CE) is not a recent concept. However, it has resonated a lot in recent years as consumer consideration towards leaving a habitable planet behind has exponentially increased. Studying a total of 114 definitions of the circular economy, Kirchherr, Reike & Hekkert (2017) explains that the Circular Economy (CE) business models significantly differ from conventional linear models as the idea is to replace the end of product life concept with a recycle, reduce, and reuse of material resources at micro, meso, and macro-level.

In a linear economy, initially, resources are mined, following that the material is sourced for further processing, then converted into finished goods; lastly, at the end of the cycle, the goods become trash and lose their resource value. In contrast, a circular economy refers to an economic model where resources are given new life by reusing, repairing, remanufacturing, or refurbishing (Awan et al., 2020). However, the idea lies on the same principles that the planet we live on can only sustain a limited amount of life and resource at a single point in time. For example, according to forecasts, all the critical resources like Antimony, Lead, and Indium on this planet used extensively to create renewable energy solutions will only last another decade or so (Desjardins, 2014).

Globally there is a trend of transitioning from linear towards CE as more firms express interest in CE business models and reap the benefits of growth, market share, and increased profits for firms utilizing CE business models (Hopkinson et al., 2018). In contrast to the linear economy, the products do not easily reach the end of life, and a cradle-to-cradle model of reusing the same resources to the creation of new products and regenerates value from the same resources.

CIRCULAR ECONOMY BUSINESS MODELS

The chapter discusses the 5 (five), contemporary business models, through a case study approach to understanding how sustainable development is achieved through circular economy business models. These organizations from developing and transitional economies better understand how these organizations are applying circular economy approached in their businesses through supply chain circularity, recovery, product life extension, sharing platforms, and offering products as services. All these different aspects of CE give us a unique opportunity to study and understand the feasibility of achieving real sustainable development through CE.

1. Paperman Foundation, India

The Paperman Foundation started its journey in 2010 in Chennai, India, with its main objective to implement the widely known 3Rs of the waste management hierarchy. The founder of this nonprofit organization, Matthew Jose, established the organization with the motive to reduce, recycle and reuse paper. As the implications of plastic pollution on the environment became prominent, they shifted towards plastic recycling. With Paperman, Jose has the vision to create social awareness about the environment and recycling while simultaneously create a sustainable waste management system.

Background and Timeline

According to The World Bank, India generates the maximum amount of waste globally ("In 30 years, India tipped to double the amount of waste it generates", 2020). As a result, the concept of the circular economy is still novel in emerging countries like India. Introducing circular economy can be done by changing the behavior of the population to be less wasteful. The process of awareness, however, proves to be very time-consuming.

To start this behavioral reform from the very roots, the organization began its work by working with various schools around Chennai, promoting paper recycling, and teaching the importance of sustainability on the way. Jose understood the monetary treasure present in the waste management system. As a result, to promote a positive attitude towards recycling, the organization started using incentives to reinforce the desired behavioral change.

The strategy of rewarding the positive behavior through cash incentives or donations to a partner organization proved extremely successful for Paperman. Their initiative to instill the spirit of recycling for a cause did not only present education but also societal value as they used the earnings generated to sponsor the education of underprivileged girls ("Ashoka Fellow Mathew Jose", 2015). They partnered up with the Nanhi Kali, an NGO. As more organizations joined the cause, and in 2012 they were actively supporting the education of 100 girls. By 2013, they had successfully established momentum and reached 200 schools and over 3,00,000 children.

In 2012, they started a new initiative to include the local trash buyers into their system. By 2013, they had integrated them into the system and had established an app that connected the trash buyers straight to the households where it is generated. In 2015, they introduced a new trash funding" program which allows small and medium trash collectors to raise money for local nonprofit organizations. Their doorstep recycling program proved to be a massive success as by 2017 they had included 270 trash collectors or "kabadiwallahs" from the city of Chennai in their system and simultaneously reached a milestone of 5000 touchpoints. In addition, through this program, they were able to raise 2.5 million Indian rupees to donate to 40 different nonprofits.

Through their progression in the past decade, they have made great contributions to the environment and society. Now having been involved in 20 different projects, they have successfully recycled 1 million kilograms of waste and have reduced 50,000 kgs of carbon emission from the atmosphere.

Paperman Products and Services Closing the Loop

Paperman mainly acts as an intermediary by facilitating the transactions between the trash collectors and waste generating bodies like households, offices, hotels, commercial entities, etc. They have created an app directly connecting the two parties and equipped the local trash collectors with digital practices that significantly improve their business practices. 10% of the total volume is generated from this platform. Once registered with Paperman, the entity can choose if to recycle for value or for a cause; 90% being the latter.

Upon collection, the waste is transferred to one of the facilities of Paperman for processing. The main processing facilities are present in Chennai and Andaman & Nicobar Islands. In these locations, the plastic waste is accumulated from various locations and sorted. Eventually, it is separated and processed to put up with the end user's requirement. Out of the total processed plastic, 80% is processed into PET or most commonly known as polythene, LDPE is used to produce locally molded plastic products, and MLP in cement production.

Paperman tries to close the loop and minimize the carbon footprints through recycling the solid waste generated by the Chennai population and processing it into a range of products and services. This increases the value and lifetime of already used services. Besides this, the organization has developed a set of ancillary services through "reverse mining". However, their largest contribution in establishing a circular economy lies in the way they are making behavioral changes and establishing the mentality that the value of the resources can be extended. Since they are working from the primary level, the impact they create is greater as these children will take this to their households and take this mentality into adulthood. As a result, they are enabling "alter-globalization" via their mobilization of the circular economy. As per UNRISD, alter-globalization is defined as "deeper systemic and structural changes which can have major implications for patterns of growth, investment, asset distribution, trade and consumption, as well as power relations". Besides this, they focus on improving the waste management systems by providing consultancy regarding recycling-related causes with the legislators. Another responsibility that they fulfill is to aid large enterprises in fulfilling their extended producer responsibility (EPR) obligations, generating 20% of their total revenues from this sector. They have also helped by financing Self Help Groups (SHG), informally operating, which have been effective for those at the very bottom of the social strata to maintain their livelihood. Paperman had bridged the gap between the traditional trash collectors and the corporate giants while simultaneously limiting the wastage of resources.

2. Sampurn(e)arth Environment Solutions Ltd, India

Sampurn(e)arth Environment Solutions Ltd is a Mumbai based startup that has revolutionized the waste management system in India. Established in 2012, this social enterprise was founded by Debartha Banerjee, Jayanth Nataraju, and Ritvik Rao while pursuing their Master's degree at Tata Institute of Social Sciences (TISS) (Sullivan, 2017). The organization provides a range of optimum waste management solutions while keeping sustainability a priority. Their goal is to educate and encourage people to adopt the cyclical waste management processes that urban India truly requires.

Background and Timeline

India generates more than 150,000 Metric tonnes of waste every day (Shrivastava, 2019). However, the waste disposal and management section are severely mismanaged and disorganized, leading to 550,000 metric tonnes of solid waste being dumped in open areas every year worsening the country's already severe pollution problem (Shrivastava, 2019). For emerging countries, as a country's income increases, so does its waste (Kaza et al., 2018).

They took this problem of urban waste management and integrated it into a profitable business model. The underlying value that waste intrinsically possesses presents an untapped market with endless possibilities if extracted. With their triple bottom line approach, Sampurn(e)arth, began to provide case management solutions to the pulse generators. As a result, their zero-waste approach towards the cause of circular economy has attracted several investors and corporate clients who receive CSR advice from the organization.

Another issue that they identified was the treatment of waste collectors or ragpickers. Though their service is one of the most essential, these individuals are treated as social pariahs as the occupation is severely stigmatized. Their working conditions were dangerous and no protective gear was provided, leaving them susceptible to diseases. Sampurn(e)arth sought out to change this by employing them and providing an alternative livelihood to these individuals and turning them into waste managers.

Sampurn(e)arth started their operations from door to door collection of waste from households. The waste was then segregated into solids and biodegradable waste and treated accordingly. The solid waste was sent to processing for recycling, while for the biodegradable waste they set composting or biomethanation plants based on the volume of waste generated. They provided a far more sustainable alternative as most of the waste would have ended up in landfills or burned which would deteriorate the pollution. Now, they have covered more than 30,000 households and processed over 8300 Metric tons of waste having a considerable impact in reducing the carbon footprint contributing to the cause of circular economy ("Sampurn(e)arth", 2021).

Within 2015, they had handled more than 1000 tonnes of both dry and wet waste (Mukherjee, 2015). They received their first round of funding in late 2015 from Intellecap's Impact Investing Network. They achieved their break-even in 2016, in their 4th year of operation (Sullivan, 2017). In 2017, they secured yet another round of funding. The company's economic model mainly has three distinct revenue streams: waste management services, the second is the retail of recycled products, and the third being an energy provider from the sale of biogas and the maintenance of the plants. (Sullivan, 2017). Thus, they manage to bridge the gap in the gap in the cost of processing the waste and the revenue generated.

Sampurn(e) Arth's Services and Closing the Loop

Sampurn(e)arth provides end-to-end waste management solutions in the most environmentally sustainable way, where people in the informal sector are actively integrated, providing them an alternate livelihood. They use a decentralized process in waste management, reducing transportation costs and emission of harmful gases.

According to the World Bank's Urban Development department and the What a Waste report published in 2012, the volume of solid waste will increase from the current 1.3 billion tonnes per year to 2.2 billion tonnes per year by 2025: a staggering 70%, a majority of which is attributable to the developing countries ("Global Waste to Grow by 70 Percent by 2050 Unless Urgent Action is Taken: World Bank Report", 2018). This presents a severe problem to the establishment of a circular economy as waste is not recovered and reused. To solve this emerging from in urban India, these entrepreneurs have come up with a range of solutions depending on the client's needs, the volume, and the type of waste.

For the waste management system of households and housing societies, Sampurn(e) arth provides individual solutions depending on the number and the scope. Door-to-door collection of waste is done by the workers and eventually sorted and segregated. The biodegradable waste is sent to the compost pit managed by the company, and the dry waste is collected and sent for recycling. Presently, they maintain 50 housing societies and deal with 15 metric tonnes of waste regularly. ("Sampurn(e)arth", 2021). Doing this increases the lifetime of the recycled products while the compost can be used to either fuel biogas or for agriculture. This greatly reduces the waste which would have otherwise gone to landfills or incinerated.

For their venture to help the corporate, they start with an internal waste audit which allows them to understand the volume and the components present. Following this, personalized solutions like bio methanation, compost pits, tumblers, or OWC are suggested. If their biodegradable waste exceeds 200 kilograms a day, the organization suggests the installation of a biogas plant ("Global Waste to Grow by 70 Percent by 2050 Unless Urgent Action is Taken: World Bank Report", 2018). The biogas made from the plant is an alternative source of energy that can be used for cooking, generating electricity if 1000 kgs of waste are produced in a day. The paper waste from these corporate offices is collected and recycled, and turned into new stationery, increasing the lifetime of the paper. For the companies, this reduces the stationary cost and promotes sustainability within the organization. In addition, Sampurn(e)arth also performs CSR activities on behalf of their corporate clients. These CSR solutions help to highlight the importance of recycling and cleanliness. These impact entrepreneurs contribute to the circular economy through their zero-waste system and illustrate that it is feasible to implement this system in India despite the challenges it is feasible to implement.

Sampuran(e)arth is also involved in helping companies fulfill their EPR obligations. They are affiliated with several companies and have been EPR partners with Tetrapack for the past 5 years, helping them recycle and reduce the waste and thus the carbon footprint ("Sampurn(e)arth", 2021).

3. Rewoven, South Africa

Rewoven was established in 2018 as a startup. It was developed by three young entrepreneurs Tshepo Bhengu, Esethu Cenga, and Lonwabo Mgoduso in an attempt to bring sustainability and create an impact in the fashion and clothing industry. Their project is currently in the commercial pilot phase.

Background and Timeline

The Fashion Industry is currently valued at 2.5 million trillion dollars and employs nearly 75 million individuals ("UN Alliance aims to put fashion on the path to sustainability ", 2018). A McKinsey & Company research illustrates that in 2018, 4% of the world's total GHG emissions, or 2.1 billion tonnes, were generated by the fashion industry (Berg, Granskog, Lee & Magnus, 2020). A lot of it can be attributed to fast fashion, material production, preparation, and processing which significantly contribute to waste. As the fashion industry continues to grow, so do the GHG emissions. With estimations, the industry's GHG emissions will likely rise to around 2.7 billion tonnes a year by 2030 (Berg, Granskog, Lee & Magnus, 2020).

The young entrepreneurs realized this very problem and came up with a solution that will allow them to reuse the fabric contributing to the global waste. This will prevent the textile from going into the landfills and ultimately generating even more GHG emissions. This was a passion project for them that would allow them to create an impact as well as support their beliefs in development and sustainability.

Rewoven started as an idea in 2018 during the Validation Creation (IVC) program created by the Allan Gray Orbis Foundation. During this, the entrepreneurs found an opportunity to study and understand the intensity of textile waste in South Africa. This allowed them to form an idea to solve the problem and finally develop a market prototype. As they continued to move forward with their ideas, they entered the H&M Foundation Global Change Award, which aimed to bring the concept of circularity and encourage sustainability in the fashion industry. Rewoven successfully made it to the top 10 among 6000 applicants due to their dedication towards bringing tangible change into the fashion industry ("rewoven", 2021).

The concept of circular economy has been at the front and center for Rewoven as they are trying to establish this very concept at the heart of the South-African clothing industry. Rewoven creates recycled fabrics from pre-consumer textile waste. This allows them to upcycle and extend the lifetime of the textile. More importantly, they have successfully cast this into a business model, deriving monetary value from waste while at the same time creating employment in the sector.

After November 2018, the entrepreneurs began sourcing cuts of waste textile from different manufacturers in Cape Town. Using that in 2019, they made their first prototype of recycled yarn. In addition, in March 2019, they entered the E-Squared Accelerator program due to their potential to generate impact and creation of employment in South Africa. This allowed them to expand their pilot into a bigger project and produce prototypes for recycled knitted and woven fabrics. In 2020, they received their seed funding which enabled them to start their commercial pilot successfully and market the 100% recycled textile materials. Rewoven has already prevented 159 819 kilograms of textile off-cuts and 4 500 meters of end-of-roll fabric from being dumped into landfills by recycling them ("rewoven", 2021).

Rewoven's Products and Closing the Loop

Rewoven starts its process with the collection of fabric to be recycled. According to an Ellen MacArthur Foundation 2017 report, in 2015 1.2 billion tonnes of GHG were released just through textile production. Rewoven understands that producing fabric is a process that requires a huge about of resources that might not be sustainable in the long run. However, even after such a resource-consuming process, globally 92 million tonnes of textile waste ends up in landfills creating further GHG emissions into the atmosphere, which is detrimental to the environment. Instead of scrapping the unwanted fabric, they recycle it into the fiber to eventually produce a new fabric with minimum waste. Rewoven collects Offcut fabrics, End-of-roll fabric, Old clothes, Rejected and Unsold Inventory.

Upon collection of the offcut cotton fabric, it is separated based on colors. The offcut fabric is then shredded and processed into the cotton fiber. In the next step, the fiber is processed with plastic fiber in a blend of 60% being cotton and 40% recycled polyester. This reinforces the fibers of the processed fiber so it can create new clothing. The recycled and reprocessed fiber is then spun into new yarn which is woven and knitted into new fabrics ("rewoven", 2021).

End of the roll fabric refers to fabric leftover after orders. They usually remain unused or are dumped. Instead of doing that, Rewoven sources these fabrics and makes them available to people looking to purchase at a reasonable price. By promoting upcycling and reuse, they make the economy circular by bringing these previously unavailable resources into the consumer market.

4. Attero, India

Attero Recycling was founded in 2008 by the two brothers Nitin Gupta and Rohan Gupta as an end-to-end solution to manage and recycle the accumulating electronic waste in India. Where people saw discarding electronic waste as a growing crisis, the brothers saw this as an untapped economic opportunity. Their goal is to sustainbaly manage electronic assets.

Background and Timeline

As per the Global E-Waste Monitor 2020 publication, over 53.6 million tonnes of waste were generated worldwide. Out of this 3.23 million tonnes were generated in India, ranking third in the production of e-waste worldwide. Out of these worldwide, only 9.3 million tonnes were documented and recycled, while the rest probably were dumped (Forti, Baldé, Kuehr, & Bel, 2020).

In today's day and age, we all have numerous electronic devices, but no one could ever comprehend how difficult disposing of these would be. Not only is most of it not difficult and hazardous to the environment, but the data security of the disposed of devices also presents a huge problem. Nitin and Rohan Gupta were trying to dispose of their faulty laptop when the realization came onto them that this presented a great business opportunity.

The word "Attero" means trash in Latin. As the country develops, the nature of the trash that is disposed of is also changing. Electronic waste is also treated as normal waste and is dumped into landfills like others despite containing plastic (non-biodegradable) and other harmful chemicals like lead and mercury. In addition, they contain several precious metals like copper and gold, which are roughly recycled, dismantled, or burned for extraction ("The Index Project", 2013). This not only creates more pollution but also risks the health of the people dismantling the electronics.

Attero Recycling provides a solution to these problems offering the services of Recycling, Data Security, Take Back Operations, Upcycling, Reverse Logistics, and EPR compliance ("Attero", 2021). They were among the first institutions to get registered under the Central Pollution Control Board (CPCB) (Mathew & Balaji, 2020). Their contribution towards the circular economy field lies in the fact that through refurbishment and recycling of resources, they are increasing the lifetime of existing products and reducing the need for new raw materials. The refurbished devices can be reused, and the metals extracted can be recycled into newer products from the precious metals.

Besides their innovative approach towards recycling e-waste, they have a vital social mission to unify the disorganized waste collector network into a unified supply chain. To do this, they collaborated with the International Finance Corporation to launch the Clean E-India Initiative in 2013 (Witkin, 2013). Besides this, they carried on the social goal through events at educational institutions informing them about the hazards of e-waste. By 2015, Attero had become India's largest and the world's cheapest recycler of e-waste (Sachitanand & Aravind, 2015). Attero also a NASA recognized innovator using patented technology for the processing of e-waste and metals. Their operations have spread throughout entire India, with them collecting e-waste from over 500 cities. Their main state-of-the- art 100,000 sq. ft. recycling facility is in Roorkee. They recycle nearly 500 tonnes of e-waste monthly and are associated with over 350 corporate institutions to source it (Witkin, 2013). They envision turning today's scrap metal into resources for the future.

Attero Products and Services and Closing the Loop

Attero Recycling is the largest electronic asset management company that refurbishes, reuses, and recycles the waste generated. In the first step, due to the efficient reverse logistic system of Attero, e-waste can be easily collected from anywhere and sent to the warehouses countrywide and finally to the processing facilities. Upon collection, the products are cleaned and checked to determine if they should be dismantled or refurbished.

The company recycles mobile phones, display units, IT goods, PCBs, and Li-Lion Batteries. In mobile phone recycling, all components like the lithium-ion battery, the flat panel/LCD, PCBs, and plastics are separated and sent to the specific divisions to be recycled. The recycled material can then be used as a raw material in electronics, jewelry, plating, automotive, etc., extending the resources and contributing to a circular economy. In a traditional Cathode Ray Tube display, high amounts of glass and lead are present, which can be reprocessed and reused. Recycling flat panel display units involved dismantling the wires, cables, and PCBs are separated and recycled. Following this, ferrous and non-ferrous metals are separated through the Magnetic Separator and Eddy Current Separator, eventually refined to a 99.9% accuracy through electro-refining. This allows for recycling the ferrous metals into iron and others into purer forms of copper and aluminum, circulated back into the market. IT products like laptops computers are dismantled and separated. The separated components like wires and plastics are separated. The remaining material goes through a shredder, following which the metals are separated and refined for further use. PCBs contain metals like lead, nickel, and copper, which though valuable, are pollutants. In addition, Attero also efficiently recycles Li-ion batteries reducing GHG emissions. ("Attero", 2021)

Attero also enables efficient refurbishing of devices. Through data sanitization and destruction, they can effectively remove confidential data from being breached. In addition, their upcycling allows them to prolong the lifetime of an old device by increasing its functional lifetime.

5. AgriProtein, South Africa

AgriProtein was founded in 2008 with the mission to provide a substitute for aquaculture and livestock feed and close the loop in food production. As a subsidiary of the Insect Technology Group, their motive is to harness the organic waste in a sustainable, environmentally friendly manner. They do this by using insects as a sustainable substitute for protein.

Background and Timeline

According to FAO, one-third of food produced for consumption ends up in waste, which, when accumulated, leads to an astounding 1.3 billion tonnes per year in food waste. Therefore, reducing food wastage has become pertinent to achieve the goal of Sustainable Development Goal (SDG) 2, which focuses on eradicating hunger ("Food Loss and Food Waste", n.d.).

To solve this very problem of food waste, AgriProtein has developed an innovative approach that will allow them to upcycle the food waste and convert it into animal feed in a sustainable manner. Through this venture, they aspire to make the food industry circular and close the loop through the reuse of food waste to create another protein substitute. Through this nutrient- recycling process, they aspire to contribute to SDG 12, which is to ensure sustainable consumption and production patterns ("Food Loss and Food Waste", n.d.).

Their goal from the very beginning was built on the concept of closing the loop in the food industry, and they do this by producing insect-derived substitutes to original high resource proteins. In 2009 they started exploring the science behind the farming of flies, and by 2010, they had launched their first pilot program in Elsenburg in Stellenbosch in association with a few partner institutes. They experienced a big breakthrough in the following year where they achieved considerable success in the farming of the fly larvae with nearly 100 kgs of daily output. This proved that the insects could be farmed on an industrial scale.

In 2015, they took the first step towards commercialization of the venture through the construction of a 9000 meter square in Philippi, Cape Town, with a processing capability of up to 100 tonnes of organic food waste daily. Soon after, in November of 2016, AgriProtein raised an astounding $17.5 million for expansion which valued the company at 117 million, placing them at the pinnacle of the industry ("AgriProtein", 2021).

In 2017, they decided to expand globally, rolling their operations out in agreement with Christof Industries developing a standardized and engineered factory design. Due to their extensive research and emphasis on clean technology, they were awarded a technology award at the CleanEquity Monaco 2017 ("AgriProtein", 2021). Just following that in 2018, the company raised an additional105 million dollars for expansion. AgriProtein was named in TIME magazine as a Top 50 Genius Company that same year after acquiring the largest investment in the insect industry will date ("Genius Companies 2018", 2018). The company has continued to expand strategically and build factories in important locations. As of 2021, AgroProtein has received the accolade of being on the Global CleanTech 100 for the fifth year consecutively.

AgriProtein Closing the Loop

The world population is increasing and is expected to reach the 8 million milestone by 2023 (Chamie, 2020). As the population increases, so will the demand for food. Insects present a natural source of protein and often rich in nutrition. Though often overlooked as a food source for humans, with growing scarcity and high food waste, they present a sustainable substitute as animal feed. In addition, they are far more sustainable and eco-friendly. In the aquaculture industry, simply switching from fishmeal to insect feed would not only reduce the carbon impact by 80% but also preserve the unstable population of wild fish previously used as feed ("Saving our seas, one factory at a time", n.d.).

AgriProtein has utilized the potential nutrient recycling through the use of insects: more specifically, the black soldier fly. Flies have been known for thousands of years as integral agents important for the breakdown of organic waste. As omnivores, they consume both plant and meat waste making them the perfect candidate for a circular project.

AgriProtein is the pioneer of the "black soldier fly" technology after more than a decade of research. The flies are kept in digitalized and secure environments mimicking nature. They also control the breeding of the flies ensuring genetic diversity and simultaneously maximizing egg production ("AgriProtein", 2021). The soldier flies are brought to climate-optimized cages for reproduction, with the potential of every fly laying 500 eggs in the next five days ("Saving our seas, one factory at a time", n.d.). In addition, the newly hatched larvae can reach 200 times their initial weight as they are fed researched diets in optimal rearing conditions ("Saving our seas, one factory at a time", n.d.).

The process begins with the collection of organic food waste, which is used as a food source for the black soldier flies. AgriProtein factories are equipped to process up to 350 tonnes of food waste in a day ("AgriProtein", 2021). After a quality check, the organic waste is turned into a nutrient-rich substrate for the larvae allowing for upcycling the waste. The larvae are presented with the processed substrate, and they continue to grow till they reach approximately 200 times their mass.

After the larvae finish their growth phase, the larvae and the waste substrate are separated. This is the step at which they are processed into their three unique product streams through the processing of the larvae and frass. The larvae are dried and processed to remove the fat. This created a 55% insect-based protein feed rich in amino acid which can be fed to fish, poultry, and livestock called MagMeal ("AgriProtein", 2021). The fat which was extracted beforehand from larvae is highly concentrated in lauric acid. This product called MagOil is multifunctional and can be used as a supplement, in aquaculture, as a substitute for traditional oils, or as biofuel. The remnants of organic waste or compost can now be used as a fertilizer and soil conditioner as it is rich in nutrients and is marketed as MagSoil ("AgriProtein", 2021).

DISCUSSION

A circular economy creates and adds value to existing resources by utilizing different approaches. Usually, it is done by extending the lifecycle of products and arranging them to sustain further use and cycle in the economy. Contrary to the linear economy, the value here is created based on creating more usage out of the same materials as many times as possible. The basic idea of a circular economy is intertwined with the idea of sustainability as a key motivator, and the symbol of the CE business model is to lower waste and cycle materials more in a world that is quickly depleting its resources. In all cases, CE business models require innovation that creates and delivers value through resource efficiency, extending the lifetime of a product, increase usefulness, closing the loop by reflowing the materials. These circular strategies require the consideration of circular principles at all stages of the business model and product development. The literature identifies CE as an approach to improve the environmental performances of products, decrease resource depletion, and support sustainability while doing so. In a comprehensive study of circular economy business models, Reike et al. (2018) attributed the model with 3R to 10R model, ranging from Refuse, Reuse, Reduce, Repair, Refurbish, Remanufacture, Re-purpose, Re-mine, Recycle material, to Recover energy. Although different studies have associated Circular Economy with different labels and several different factors, most studies cover a few common attributes. These are basic requirements that are desirable outcomes from circular economic models. The basic validity requirements of a CE business model, according to Corona et al. (2019), are listed below in Table 1;

Table 1. CE Validity Requirements

1. Reducing input of resources, especially scarce ones
2. Reducing emission levels (pollutants and GHG emissions)
3. Reducing material losses/waste
4. Increasing input of renewable and recycled resources
5. Maximizing the utility and durability of products
6. Creating local jobs at all skill level
7. Value-added creation and distribution
8. Increase social wellbeing

Source: Corona et al., 2019

Based on the cases above, we have identified that all the cases in different emerging economies have the features that make them suitable for a representative study of circular economy business models. We have also identified the extent to which these models have assisted in the achievement of different Sustainable Development Goals (SDGs) in their economy, the summary of which has been compiled in Table 2.

Table 2. Five organizations achieving different SDGs through CE business models

Organization	SDGs achieved	Location
The Paperman Foundation	SDG 4 Quality Education SDG 9 Industry, Innovation, and Infrastructure SDG 11 Sustainable Cities and Communities SDG 12 Responsible Consumption and Production SDG 13 Climate Action	India
Sampurn(e)arth	SDG 7 Affordable and Clean Energy SDG 8 Decent Work and Economic Growth SDG 11 Sustainable Cities and Communities SDG 13 Climate Action	India
Attero	SDG 9 Industry, Innovation, and Infrastructure SDG 12 Responsible Consumption and Production SDG 13 Climate Action SDG 17 Partnership for the Goals	India
Rewoven	SDG 5 Gender Equality SDG 9 Industry, Innovation, and Infrastructure SDG 12 Responsible Consumption and Production	South Africa
AgriProtein	SDG 8 Decent Work and Economic Growth SDG 12 Responsible Consumption and Production SDG 14 Life below water SDG 15 Life on Land	South Africa

From this chapter through the five established business models, it has been discussed that different CE business models can effectively assist in the achievement of Sustainable Development Goals (SDGs). With proper government support, local community support, and legislative changes to sustain CE business models, CE holds unexplored potential in emerging economies across the globe (Ahmed et. al, 2020). These models, if effectively and innovatively implemented can result in successful implementation of innovative solutions to our linear consumption model problems and secure resources for tomorrow.

REFERENCES

Ahmed, J. U., Gazi, M. A., Iqbal, R., Islam, Q. T., & Talukder, N. (2020). Value co-creation through social innovation in healthcare: A case of WE CARE Solar. *World Journal of Entrepreneurship, Management and Sustainable Development, 16*(4), 341–357. doi:10.1108/WJEMSD-03-2020-0024

Awan, U., Kanwal, N., & Bhutta, M. (2020). A Literature Analysis of Definitions for a Circular Economy. *Ecoproduction*, 19-34. doi:10.1007/978-3-642-33857-1_2

Brundtland, G. H., Khalid, M., Agnelli, S., Al-Athel, S., & Chidzero, B. J. N. Y. (1987). Our common future. Academic Press.

Corona, B., Shen, L., Reike, D., Carreón, J. R., & Worrell, E. (2019). Towards sustainable development through the circular economy—A review and critical assessment on current circularity metrics. *Resources, Conservation and Recycling, 151*, 104498. doi:10.1016/j.resconrec.2019.104498

Elkington, J. (2004). Enter the triple bottom line. *The triple bottom line: Does it all add up, 11*(12), 1-16.

Forti, V., Baldé, C. P., Kuehr, R., & Bel, G. (2020). *The Global E-waste Monitor 2020. United Nations University (UNU), International Telecommunication Union (ITU) & International Solid Waste Association*. ISWA.

Hopkinson, P., Zils, M., Hawkins, P., & Roper, S. (2018). Managing a Complex Global Circular Economy Business Model: Opportunities and Challenges. *California Management Review, 60*(3), 71–94. doi:10.1177/0008125618764692

Kaza, S., Yao, L., Bhada-Tata, P., & Van Woerden, F. (2018). *What a waste 2.0: a global snapshot of solid waste management to 2050*. World Bank Publications. doi:10.1596/978-1-4648-1329-0

Kirchherr, J., Reike, D., & Hekkert, M. (2017). Conceptualizing the circular economy: An analysis of 114 definitions. *Resources, Conservation and Recycling, 127*, 221–232. doi:10.1016/j.resconrec.2017.09.005

Utting, P. (2018). *Achieving the Sustainable Development Goals through Social and Solidarity Economy: Incremental Versus Transformative Change*. UNRISD.

ADDITIONAL READING

A New Textiles Economy: Redesigning Fashion's Future. (2017). Available online: https://www.ellenmacarthurfoundation.org/publications/a-new-textiles-economy-redesigning-fashions-future

AgriProtein. (2021). Retrieved 1 March 2021, from https://www.agriprotein.com/

Ashoka Fellow Mathew Jose. (2015). Retrieved 10 February 2021, from https://www.ashoka.org/en-bd/fellow/mathew-jose

Attero. (2021). Retrieved 8 March 2021, from http://www.attero.in/

Berg, A., Granskog, A., Lee, L., & Magnus, K. (2020). Fashion on Climate. Retrieved 25 February 2021, from https://www.mckinsey.com/industries/retail/our-insights/fashion-on-climate

Chamie, J. (2020). World Population: 2020 Overview. Retrieved 1 March 2021, from https://yaleglobal.yale.edu/content/world-population-2020-overview

Desjardins, J. (2014). A Forecast of When We'll run out of Each Metal. available at: https://www.visualcapitalist.com/forecast-when-well-run-out-of-each-metal/

Global Waste to Grow by 70 Percent by 2050 Unless Urgent Action is Taken: World Bank Report. (2018). Retrieved 15 February 2021, from https://www.worldbank.org/en/news/press-release/2018/09/20/global-waste-to-grow-by-70-percent-by-2050-unless-urgent-action-is-taken-world-bank-report

In 30 years, India tipped to double the amount of waste it generates - Times of India. (2020). Retrieved 10 February 2021, from https://timesofindia.indiatimes.com/india/in-30-years-india-tipped-to-double-the-amount-of-waste-it-generates/articleshow/74454382.cms

Mathew, A., & Balaji, R. (2020). Managing e-waste effectively: how these companies are helping India recycle electronic waste. Retrieved 20 February 2021, from https://yourstory.com/socialstory/2020/10/india-companies-managing-international-ewaste-day-recycle

Mukherjee, P. (2015). Debartha Banerjee, Jayanth Nataraju, Ritvik Rao: Won't be wasting away. Retrieved 15 February 2021, from https://mumbaimirror.indiatimes.com/2015-heroes/city-improvement/Debartha-Banerjee-Jayanth-Nataraju-Ritvik-Rao-Wont-be-wasting-away/mumbaihero/48990957.cms

Rewoven. (2021). Retrieved 8 March 2021, from https://www.rewoven.africa

Sachitanand, R., & Aravind, I. (2015). How startups like Attero Recycling, Karma Recycling are making money out of garbage. Retrieved 20 February 2021, from https://economictimes.indiatimes.com/small-biz/startups/how-startups-like-attero-recycling-karma-recycling-are-making-money-out-of-garbage/articleshow/49963439.cms?from=mdr

Sampurn(e)arth. (2021). Retrieved 8 March 2021, from http://sampurnearth.com/index.html

Saving our seas, one factory at a time. Retrieved 1 March 2021, from https://www.ellenmacarthurfoundation.org/case-studies/saving-our-seas-one-factory-at-a-time

Shrivastava, R. (2019). India's Trash Bomb: 80% of 1.5 lakh metric tonne daily garbage remains exposed, untreated. *India Today*. Retrieved from https://www.indiatoday.in/india/story/india-s-trash-bomb-80-of-1-5-lakh-metric-tonne-daily-garbage-remains-exposed-untreated-1571769-2019-07-21

Sullivan, K. (2017). For this environmental solutions company, Mumbai's trash is treasure. *Forbes India*. Retrieved from https://www.forbesindia.com/article/special/for-this-environmental-solutions-company-mumbais-trash-is-treasure/47677/1

The Index Project. (2013). Retrieved 20 February 2021, from https://theindexproject.org/post/attero-recycling

UN Alliance aims to put fashion on path to sustainability. (2018). Retrieved 25 February 2021, from https://unece.org/forestry/press/un-alliance-aims-put-fashion-path-sustainability

Witkin, J. (2013). Cleantech 100 case study: Attero waste management. *The Guardian*. Retrieved from https://www.theguardian.com/sustainable-business/attero-recycling-waste-global-cleantech-100

KEY TERMS AND DEFINITIONS

Business Model: A plan or infrastructure that generates and delivers value.

Circular Economy: A sustainable economic model based on reuse, recycling, and extending the useful life of existing resources.

Closing the Loop: To retain the maximum value of a resource by reusing, recycling and increasing the lifetime of waste in a circular economy model.

Cradle to Cradle (C2C): When a product reaches the end of its life cycle, the constituting resources are reused to produce a new product.

Emerging Economy: The growing economy of developing countries as they transition from low to middle income.

Linear Economy: An economic model where resources are used to make a product and then discarded after its useful life.

Recycling: Treatment and recovery of the materials contained in collected waste.

Remanufacturing: Manufacturing, Recovering, or Repair of a product from materials derived from waste.

Sustainability: To prevent the depletion of natural resources and protect and maintain balance in the environment.

Sustainable Development Goals: Goals set by the United Nations for the betterment of the world as a whole.

Chapter 6
The Correlation Between Income Inequality and Population Health:
An Empirical Study

Betül Inam
Bilecik Seyh Edebali University, Turkey

Dilek Murat
Bursa Uludag University, Turkey

ABSTRACT

Today, despite the increase in global wealth, the income gap between the rich and the poor gradually widens. This gap is significant in both developed and developing nations. Thus, increasing income inequality adversely affects several socio-economic indicators. Previous studies demonstrated that one of the socio-economic indicators that were negatively affected by income inequality is population health. The income inequality experienced by the individuals or throughout life adversely affects several populations' health outputs, especially life expectancy at birth. The present study aimed to test the correlation between income inequality and population health output indicators with canonical correlation method and based on the most current data available for several nations. To determine the correlation between the two datasets, the 2017 data for 29 European countries and Turkey were analyzed. Canonical correlation analysis revealed a significant correlation between the income inequality and population health indicator datasets.

DOI: 10.4018/978-1-7998-8258-9.ch006

INTRODUCTION

Income and wealth inequality was quite high a century ago; however, these figures dropped in the 20th century but started to rise at different rates across nations after the 1980s. The 2008 financial crisis did not reverse this trend. The inequalities between the nations mattered more in the 1980s when compared to in-country inequalities globally, today, it is the opposite. The rise in inequality has not been counterbalanced by the increase in social mobility. The reduction in gender pay gap tempered the rise of inequality in recent decades; however, gender inequality remains particularly high among higher income and wealth groups. Racial inequalities remain significant. Evidence suggested that trade and technology alone could not explain significant differences in inequality across developed countries. Changes in taxation and wage policies, as well as differences in education and health systems are significant (Chancel,2019). The wealth of the richest 388 people in the world was equal to the wealth of 3.6 billion people in 2010, and the wealth of the richest 62 people was equal to the wealth of 3.6 billion people in 2015. During the last 25 years, the average annual income of the poorest 10% of the world population increased by less than 3 dollars each year (OXFAM, 2016, p. 2). Despite the increase in global wealth, the difference between the rich and poor has increased every day. The richest 10% earn 40% of the global income, while the poorest 10% earn between 2-7% of the global income. High income inequality threatens social harmony, slows economic growth, and negates efforts to alleviate poverty (EU, 2017, p. 197). Since 1980, the rapid global increase in income inequality as observed in the USA, the global richest 1% would earn 28% of the global income in 2050, while the global poorest 50% would earn 6% share of the global income. If the increase in income inequality would be relatively slow as observed in European nations, it was estimated that the share of the richest 1% will decrease to 19% of the global income, and the share of the poorest 50% will increase to 13% in 2050 (Alvaredo et.al, 2018, p.250). Poverty, one of the significant consequences of income inequality, has also been an important global problem. Especially the extreme levels of poverty during the pandemic and several resulting problems exacerbated this problem. Poverty that increases due to income inequality could lead to further loss of income and negatively affect population health. It was estimated that the severity of the consequences caused by COVID would increase due to the increase in both domestic and international inequalities (OXFAM, 2020, p. 1).

Income inequality is involved in several social and economic problems. One of these problems is the health of individuals. Studies demonstrated that individual health is negatively affected by the income inequality in the society. Health is an important source of well-being. For example, it is possible to suggest several direct or indirect correlation between health and economy such as the production losses due to employee illness or the increase in productivity due to a better diet, the development of learning skills in healthy individuals, the employment of resources that could be used to treat diseases for various other objectives when the individuals are healthy, and high income potential of healthy individuals (WHO, 2004, p. 15). One of the reasons for the achievements of East Asian countries, which experienced high economic growth since the 1950s, was the rapid increase in per capita labor due to the developments in health. The reforms that aimed low cost in health were the key agent behind economic growth. The decrease in mortality and the prolongation of life increased the ratio of the active population in employment age between 1960 and 2000 and increased per capita production and revenues. Furthermore, prolonged human life led to high savings for retirement and led to a leap in economic development in East Asian countries where 30% of income was saved (Bloom, et.al., 2004, pp. 11-12). While income was a more significant factor in mortality rates previously within the context of the health-economy relations, today the impact of income inequality is more significant on mortality rate. In poor countries, income shields against poor health conditions, malnutrition and infectious diseases, while income inequality determines the course of social organization, stress and mortality in rich countries. It was suggested that income inequality will continue to affect the mortality rates and the health of the population until the nation is no longer poor (Deaton, 2003, p.151).

In the present study, first, the related literature is reviewed in the background section, then the main focus of the chapter is presented. Later, the issue of health and economy relationship from past to present is discussed. In the data and methodology section, the data employed in the analysis and methodology were discussed The future directions in research section included recommendations for future studies, the analysis findings are presented in the empirical findings section, and the conclusion section included comments and evaluations.

BACKGROUND

The correlations between the individual, regional and national health outcomes and socio-economic determinants has been the focus of interest in recent years. One of these determinants is income. Studies on the basic correlation between income and health focused on three theories. First theory was the absolute income hypothesis which associated the effect of income on health with the income level. The second was the relative income hypothesis which argued that personal health was affected by personal income level when compared to others in a reference group. When individual income is constant, higher average income in the reference group would translate to poorer health via psychosocial mechanisms. The third and final theory was the income inequality hypothesis. In this hypothesis, income inequality has a direct negative effect on personal health, independent of personal income. Several mechanisms may lead to this effect. One of these mechanisms is associated with trust and social capital, since inequality may lead to personal distrust, inducing antisocial behavior and lower civic participation in the society. Low social capital or lack of social connectedness may in turn lead to health consequences (Nilsson and Bergh, 2012, pp.4-5). The correlation between income inequality and health was researched in the 1970s. Roger (1979) reported that personal income is a powerful determinant of personal health and the correlation between personal income and health was concave and the positive impact of each additional income dollar on personal health decreases. Thus, this correlation is significant for the correlation between income distribution and mean health achievements. Income redistribution between the rich and the poor, in a country or among countries would improve population health.

While income was one of the important factors that determined the life span before the epidemiological transition, income inequality has become a significant determinant of life span after the transition. In poor countries, income inequality, poor sanitation, unhealthy working and living conditions, poor nutrition, and a plethora of infectious diseases are the major causes of death, as income inequality became the determinant of social regulations, stress and death in developed nations. Today, the correlation between income and death is determined by economic development (Deaton, 2003). Income inequality may reflect social harmony or social capital, and personal health may not respond simply to absolute income but also to social relativities such as relative deprivation, relative income, and relative social status. Income inequality in the society may be important since it accentuates these relativities, and hence has a negative impact on personal health (Wagstaff and Doorslaer, 2000, p.544). In a study conducted by Çukur and Bekmez (2011) with revenues, income inequality and infant mortality rates in 7 geographical regions in Turkey between 1975 and 2001, it was observed that the increase in income reduces infant mortality rate. Bozma et al. (2018) investigated the correlation between income inequality and life expectancy at birth for the 1995-2011 period in a study conducted on 87 countries and determined a negative correlation between the two variables for 35 OECD countries, and a positive correlation for other nations. Moore (2006) conducted a study on 107 nations and determined that the negative impact of income inequality was stronger in high-income countries. It was reported that income inequalities have strong negative effects on life expectancy. Wilkinson (1997) reported that mortality rate was lower in societies with a low income inequality level. Wilkinson associated the lower mortality rate in more egalitarian societies with the reduction in relative deprivation burden. Babones (2008) investigated the correlation between income inequality and population health in developed and developing nations between 1970 and 1995 and determined that there was a strong significant correlation between income inequality, life expectancy and infant mortality in over 100 countries over a period of 25 years. Pickett and Wilkinson (2007) found that there were correlations between income inequality and several infant and child outcomes such as infant mortality, low birth weight, child wellbeing and child mental health problems, which would not be expected to affect inequality. Ram (2005) investigated the impact of income inequality and poverty on population health in a study conducted with state-level US data between 2000 and 1990. When variables such as race, urbanization and education were included in income inequality parameters, it was observed that there was no decrease in the impact of income inequality on population health. An impact of poverty was determined on mortality rate, but the study concluded that income inequality had a stronger effect. In a study conducted in 2002, Rostila et al. (2012) reported that high and very high income inequality at the municipal level had a moderate impact on population health, however, this could be improved with social spending. Income inequality was not found to have a detrimental effect on health at the neighborhood level. It was found that high inequality affected the health of poor individuals more at the municipal level. Sun et al. (2012) identified a positive correlation between relative income inequality and general health in a study conducted with personal data collected from 12,449 students in 7 major cities in China in 2002; however, there was no significant correlation between depression, stress and smoking. Filho et al. (2013) investigated the correlation between income inequality, anxiety and mental disorders with a sample that included 3542 adults in Brazil. They reported that individuals living in locations with high income inequality exhibited higher mental disorder rates, albeit not always. Ray and Linden (2018), in a study conducted on 194 nations between 1990 and 2014, found that the increase in income inequality increased infant mortality in developed nations. In poor countries, however, they claimed that the possible Kuznet hypothesis could be improved by increasing health expenditures, GDP ratio and a cost-effective health technology. Aida et al. (2011) determined a significant correlation between income inequalities, poor health and poor dental health in Japan. The correlation between income inequality and health was partially explained by social capital, and it was found that social capital did not weaken the strong correlation between income inequality and dental health. Mellor & Milyo (2002) could not determine a consistent correlation between income inequality and health outcomes in a study conducted in the USA with the Current Census data for the 1995-1999 period. In a study conducted on 8 counties, Pickett et al. (2006) determined a correlation between the prevalence of any psychological disorder, income inequality and per capita income, in addition to severe psychological disorders and two economic variables. A study was conducted by Kim et al. (2018) based on 2015 American Community Survey and 2013 obesity estimates to investigate the correlations between national economic factors and obesity. Although higher income inequality was associated with lower obesity rates, a higher poverty rate was associated with higher obesity. Tweed et al. (2018) investigated the correlations between colorectal, lung, breast and prostate cancers and socioeconomic variables in West Scotland between 2001 and 2012. They determined that the strongest correlation was between the lung cancer incidence and socioeconomic conditions, since gender inequality worsened across the study period and there was a negative correlation between breast and prostate cancer incidences and socio-economic conditions, where the incidence was longer among individuals living in disenfranchised areas. Detonellenoere et al. (2018), in a study conducted on European countries to measure the correlation between income inequality and population health with basic health services data such as life expectancy, mental health and infant mortality, reported that primary healthcare services were extremely important in eliminating the negative correlation between income inequality and population health. Herzer & Nunnenkamp (2014) reported that income inequality increased life expectancy in developed countries. In contrast, the effect on life expectancy was significantly negative in developing countries.

MAIN FOCUS OF THE CHAPTER

The present study aimed to determine the correlation between income inequality and population health outcomes. For this purpose, datasets on income inequality and population health for European countries and Turkey were developed for 2017 and Canonical Correlation Analysis (CCA) was conducted on the data.

HISTORICAL CORRELATION BETWEEN HEALTH AND ECONOMY

Before the Industrial Revolution, it was not possible to talk about an upward trend even inputs such as per capita income, nutrition, clothing, heating, illumination and housing varied between the societies or the periods. In this era, the living conditions of an average individual were not much different from the conditions that prevailed hundreds of years before (Clark, 2013, p.1) The technological advances after the Industrial Revolution, increases in investments, manufacturing and income improved the economic and living conditions in several nations. Especially after World War II, the end of hot wars facilitated the upward trend. Economic development, which is one of the main determinants of the wealth or poverty of nations, led to an increase in average income, improved the diet of people and positively affected the citizens of several countries (Pamuk, 2017, p.3). In industrialized nations, a gradual decline has been observed in age-related mortality after the 1750-1800s. This date could be moved up to the 1920s for undeveloped countries, but especially After the World War II, mortality rates in undeveloped nations quickly caught the trend in developed countries. Furthermore, the decrease in fertility and child mortality rates followed the same trend with age-related mortality during the same period (Schultz, 2009, p. 6). Today, health is considered as a fundamental human right in the same category with quality of life, democracy, individual freedom and world peace (Belek, 2001, p.336). Health has become a broader concept that extends beyond the physical and mental well-being of individuals into population health, economy, management style, and the world peace. It is possible for individuals to live a long and healthy life, consistent with pop health level. Investments and expenditures in health improved the quality of life and productivity of the labor force, increased the life expectancy at birth, and developed countries increasingly invested in health services. These nations allocate a share of 10% or more of the national income to health services (Şener, 2006, p.385).

Health is an important concept that parallels the development level of the nations. In the 20th century, life expectancy has increased significantly, especially in Europe. Increasing income, improvement of sanitation and nutrition facilities were considered among the major factors for the decrease in mortality rates in the 19th century. In the 20th century, it was accepted that significant discoveries such as vaccines, antibiotics, and microbes were effective on the improvement of human health and lifespan (Bloom, 2004, p.10). Health is an important source of well-being. It is possible to argue that there are several indirect and direct correlations between health and economy such as higher productivity due to employee illnesses or better nutrition, improved learning skills among healthy individuals, allocation of the resources previously employed for the treatment of diseases for different areas for healthy individuals, and the increased income potential of healthy individuals (WHO, 2004, p.15). Individuals living in countries with high per capita income are expected to have a higher welfare levels and longer life span; however, individual well-being alone is not sufficient for health. No matter how high the income level, it is not possible for individuals to completely isolate themselves from the social conditions. Thus, even when the personal health conditions are good, living in an unhealthy society makes it difficult to experience the effects of welfare induced by an increase in personal income (Halisçelik, 2019, p.265). Today, the lowest income inequality is observed in European countries. After Japan, life expectancy is the longest in European countries. In the USA and Canada, despite the high per capita income, population health outcomes are poor and income inequality is extremely high (Alverado, 2018; World Bank). Income inequality is primarily a consequence of public policies that determine technological, market and social forces. However, inequality is not inevitable. A more efficient and equal income distribution could be realized by changing public policies. But it is difficult to reform the political processes that determine public policies. Any type of macro-level mismanagement could lead to inequality (Stiglitz, 2015, p.143). Thus, while income was a significant determinant of mortality in the history of health and economy, today, the impact of income inequality on mortality rate became significant. In poor countries, income shields the individuals against poor health conditions, malnutrition and infectious diseases, while income inequality determines the course of social organization, stress and mortality in rich nations. Income inequality will continue to affect mortality rate and population health until there are no poor people (Deaton, 2003, p.151). This correlation between global health and income inequality demonstrates the sagaciousness of empirical studies.

DATASET AND METHODOLOGY

The present study aimed to determine the correlation between income inequality and population health outcomes. CCA, a multivariate statistical method was employed to determine this correlation.

Dataset

The datasets analyzed in the study were obtained from The World Bank, Eurostat, and WHO databases. The study aimed to investigate the correlation between population health outcome indicators and income equality variable set. For this purpose, the 2017 data for 29 EU member nations, namely Austria, Belgium, Bulgaria, Croatia, Cyprus, Czech Republic, Denmark, Estonia, Finland, France, Germany, Greece, Hungary, Ireland, Italy, Latvia, Lithuania, Luxembourg, Malta, Netherland, Poland, Portugal, Romania, Slovenia, Spain, Sweden, Slovakia, Norway and United Kingdom, and Turkey, which were the most recent data available for all countries were analyzed. The study variables are presented below:

Life expectancy at birth (years) (LE): Life expectancy at birth indicates the number of years a newborn infant is expected live when prevailing mortality patterns at the time of birth were to stay the same throughout the life of the infant.

Global prevalence of cancer (% of population) (PC): The rate of the individuals with cancer within a population, measured as an age-standardized percentage. The rate is age-standardized with the assumption of a constant age structure to allow comparisons between the prevalence in various countries and periods.

Infant mortality rate (per 1000 live births) (IM): The number of infants who die within a year of birth per 1000 live births in a given year.

Maternal mortality ratio (per 100.000 live births) (MM): The maternal mortality ratio is the number of women who die due to causes associated with pregnancy or within 42 days of childbirth per 100.000 live births.

Mental health (MH) (% of population): The rate of the individuals with a mental health or substance use disorder in the general population. Mental health disorders include depression, anxiety, bipolar, eating disorders and schizophrenia, any substance abuse, or alcohol consumption disorder.

Gini coefficient (disposable income) (Gini): The Gini coefficient is based on the comparison of the cumulative rates of the population and the cumulative income rates they earn, and it varies between 0 in the case of perfect equality to 1 in the case of perfect inequality.

S80/S20 ratio (Income guintable share ratio) (%) (IGSR) (S80/S20) It is a measure of inequality in income distribution. It is the ratio of total income earned by the 20% of the population with the highest income (the top quintile_to the total income earned by the 20% of the population with the lowest income (the bottom quintile).

Poverty rate (%) (PR): The **at-risk-of-poverty rate** is the rate of individuals with an equivalized disposable income (after social transfer) below the **at-risk-of-poverty threshold**, which is set to 60% of the national median equivalized disposable income after social transfers.

Unemployment rate (annual %) (UR): The unemployment rate is the percentage of unemployed individuals in the labour force, where the labor force includes employed, unemployed and business owner individuals. Unemployed individuals are those who reported that they are out of work, available for work and have taken active steps to find a job within the pervious four weeks.

GDP per capita (current international dollars) (GDP): This indicator provides per capita gross domestic product (GDP) expressed in current international dollars converted by purchasing power parity (PPP) conversion factor.

METHODOLOGY

Canonical Correlation Analysis is an advanced and complex relational analysis method initially developed by Harold Hotelling (1935-1936). Simple correlation analysis determines the bivariate correlation between two variables (x, y). Multiple correlation analysis is a method that investigates the correlations between a dependent variable (y) and two or more independent variables (x_1, x_2, x_3,….., x_n). Inter-set or canonical correlation analysis is a multivariate technique that investigates the correlations between two variable sets of two or more variables (x_1, x_2, x_3,….., x_n; y_1, y_2, y_3,…..y_m) through linear components. (Özdamar, 2004, p. 419).

Canonical correlation is an adequate technique to determine the correlation between two variable sets. When based on a theory it is known that one set of variables is the predictor or independent set and the other set of variables is the criterion or dependent set, then the objective of canonical correlation analysis is to determine whether the predictor set of variables affects the criterion set of variables. However, it is not necessary to designate these two sets of variables as the dependent and independent sets. In such cases, the objective is simply to ascertain the correlation between the two sets of variables (Sharma, 1996, p. 391).
The objectives of canonic correlation analysis are listed below:

- To determine the weight vectors for each set of variables to allow maximal correlations between the linear combinations of the respective variables,
- To determine whether two sets of variables are statistically independent of each another linearly, or in contrast, to determine the magnitude of the correlations between two sets,
- To explain the nature of the correlations between sets of variables, generally by measuring the relative contribution of each variable to the calculated canonical correlations,
- To determine the degree that a set of variables explains the other set of variables,
- To determine the degree that a canonic variable contributes to the explanatory power of the set of variables that it is a member of,
- To determine the degree that a canonic variable contributes to the explanatory power of the set of variables that it is not a member of,
- To determine the relative power of various canonic functions to explain or predict the correlations (Alpert and Peterson, 1972, p. 187; Çankaya, 2005, pp. 24-25)

EMPIRICAL FINDINGS

The study aimed to determine the canonical correlation between the population health output indicators and income equality variable. The first set of variables called the income equality set included the Gini coefficient (Gini), income guintable share ratio (IGSR) (S80/S20), poverty rate (PR), GDP per capita (GDP), and unemployment rate (UR) variables. The second set of variables called the population health outcome indicators included life expectancy at birth (LE), global prevalence of cancer (PC), infant mortality rate (IM), maternal mortality rate (MM) and mental health (MH) variables. Certain descriptive statistics values for the analysis data are presented in Table 1.

Table 1. Descriptive statistics for the variables

Variable	Mean	Std. Dev.	Min.	Max.	Range
Gini	30,36	4,15	23,20	41,40	18,2
S80/S20	5,96	1,44	3,90	8,96	5,06
PR	16,83	4,03	9,10	23,60	14,50
GDP	43470	18284,63	21370,00	112822,00	91452,00
UR	7,60	4,01	2,90	21,50	18,60
LE	80,83	2,76	75,0	83,00	8,00
PC	2,10	0,43	0,95	3,15	2,20
IM	3,67	1,75	2,0	10,00	8,00
MM	6,93	4,57	2,0	19,00	17,00
MH	13,78	1,91	10,83	16,36	5,53

First, it would be proper to determine the Pearson correlation coefficients between the variables. The linear correlation coefficients calculated for these variables are presented in Table 2.

Table 2. The correlations between variables in the sets

	Gini	S80/ S20	PR	GDP	UR	LE	PC	IM	MM	MH
Gini	1,000									
S80/S20	0,900**	1,000								
PR	0,855**	0,902**	1,000							
GDP	-0,321	-0,352	-0,373*	1,000						
UR	0,332	0,366*	0,398*	-0,272	1,000					
LE	-0,400*	-0,423*	-0,441*	0,578**	0,183	1,000				
PC	-0,486**	-0,542**	-0,486**	0,625**	-0,278	0,578**	1,000			
IM	0,556**	0,492**	0,470**	-0,458*	0,066	-0,555**	-0,663**	1,000		
MM	0,514**	0,545**	0,559**	-0,398*	-0,071	-0,713**	-0,579**	0,627**	1,000	
MH	-0,023	-0,098	-0,174	0,521*	0,283	0,851**	0,438**	-0,288	-0,421*	1,000
**Correlation is significant at 0.01 level (2-tailed).										
*Correlation is significant at 0.05 level (2-tailed).										

The review of the coefficients presented in Table 2 demonstrated that there were statistically significant correlations between population health outcome indicators and the variables in the income equality variable set. In the income equality set of variables, it was observed that there were significant and strong correlations between Gini coefficient (Gini) and income guintable share ratio (IGSR)(S80/S20) and poverty rate (PR). Also, in the same variable set, it was determined that there was a significant and strong correlation between income guintable share ratio (IGSR) (S80/S20) and poverty rate (PR) variables. Significant and strong correlations were determined between life expectancy at birth (LE) and maternal mortality ratio (MM) and mental health (MH) variables in the set of population health outcome indicators.

The correlations between the population health outcome indicators and the income equality set of variables could be observed in the Table. There were negative and significant correlations between Gini coefficient (Gini) and life expectancy at birth (LE) and global prevalence of cancer (PC), and positive and significant correlations between Gini coefficient (Gini), infant mortality rate (IM), and maternal mortality rate (MM). The same was true for income guintable share ratio (IGSR) (S80/S20) and poverty rate (PR) variables. There were positive and significant correlations between the GDP per capita (GDP) and life expectancy at birth (LE), global prevalence of cancer (PC) and mental health (MH) variables. However, it was determined that there were negative and significant correlations between GDP per capita (GDP) and infant mortality rate (IM) and maternal mortality rate (MM) variables.

Table 3. Canonical correlations between the sets

Canonical Correlations	Wilk's Lambda	F	R^2	df	Sig.
0.818	0.089	2.779	0.669	25.000	0.000
0.757	0.269	2.174	0.573	16.000	0.015
0.527	0.631	1.242	0.278	9.000	0.290
0.338	0.874	0.802	0.114	4.000	0.530
0.115	0.987	0.324	0.013	1.000	0.575

The canonical correlation coefficients calculated between the variable sets and the Wilk's Lambda approximation are presented in Table 3. Since only statistically significant canonical correlation coefficients could be interpreted, the significance of these coefficients should be determined. Thus, based on the values presented in the table, it could be stated that the first and second canonical correlation coefficients were statistically significant at 0.01 and 0.05 significant levels, respectively. In the study, population health outcome indicators were considered as the dependent variable and income equality data set as independent variables. Thus, based on the first canonical variable pair presented in Table 3, it was determined that the income equality dataset could explain 66.9% of the variations in population health output indicators.

Table 4. The rate of explained variance

Canonical variable	Set 1 by self	Set 1 by set 2	Set 2 by self	Set 2 by set 1
1	0.496	0.331	0.541	0.362
2	0.136	0.078	0.215	0.123
3	0.148	0.041	0.086	0.024
4	0.134	0.015	0.066	0.008
5	0.087	0.001	0.091	0.001

Canonical correlation coefficients were analyzed for statistical significance based on the findings presented in Table 3. To interpret these variables, it would be beneficial to investigate the practical significance of the variables. Thus, the redundancy analysis findings for canonical correlations are presented in Table 4. As seen in the table, the first canonical variable of the first set of variables explained 49.60% of the total variance in the income equality set of variables and 36.20% of the total variance in the set of population health outcome indicators. The second canonical variable in the first variable set explained 13.60% of the total variance in the income equality set of variables and 12.30% of the total variance in the set of population health outcome indicators. The first canonical variable of the second set of variables explained 54.10% of the total variance in the income equality set of variables and 33.10% of the total variance in the set of population health outcome indicators. Similarly, the second canonical variable in the second set of variables explained 7.80% of the total variance in the income equality set of variables and 21.50% of the total variance in the set of population health outcome indicators. Consequently, it was determined that only the first canonical correlation coefficient and therefore the first canonical variable pair should be analyzed.

Table 5. Canonical and cross loads for set 1

	Canonical Loads					Cross Loads				
	1	2	3	4	5	1	2	3	4	5
Gini	-0.847	-0.375	-0.276	-0.175	0.188	-0.693	-0.284	-0.145	-0.059	0.022
S80/S20	-0.825	-0.265	-0.059	-0.496	-0.004	-0.674	-0.201	-0.031	-0.168	0.000
PR	-0.746	-0.074	-0.113	-0.528	0.383	-0.610	-0.056	-0.059	-0.178	0.044
GDP	0.708	-0.285	-0.577	-0.245	-0.158	0.578	-0.216	-0.304	-0.083	-0.018
UR	-0.148	-0.617	0.562	-0.232	0.477	-0.121	-0.467	0.296	-0.078	0.055

The canonical loads and cross loads calculated between the variables in set 1 and the canonical variables produced for the income equality set are presented in Table 5. The analysis revealed that the correlations between the first canonical variable derived for the income equality set and Gini, income guintable share ratio (IGSR) (S80/S20) and poverty rate (PR), GDP per capita (GDP), and unemployment rate (UR) variables were -0.847, -0.825, -0.746, 0.708 and -0.148, respectively. Based on these findings, it could be suggested that these two variables were the most important determinants of the first canonical variable, since there was a strong correlation between the first canonical variable and Gini and income guintable share ratio (IGSR) (S80/S20). The correlations between the first canonical variable derived for the population health output indicators set and Gini, income guintable share ratio (IGSR) (S80/S20), poverty rate (PR), GDP per capita (GDP), and unemployment rate (UR) were -0.693, -0.674, -0.610, 0.578 and -0.121, respectively.

Table 6. Canonical and cross loads for set 2

	Canonical Loads					**Cross Loads**				
	1	**2**	**3**	**4**	**5**	**1**	**2**	**3**	**4**	**5**
LE	0.808	-0.544	0.030	-0.079	0.211	0.660	-0.412	0.016	-0.027	0.024
PC	0.801	-0.004	-0.547	0.119	-0.213	0.655	-0.003	-0.288	0.040	-0.025
IM	-0.791	0.020	-0.108	0.238	0.553	-0.646	0.015	-0.057	0.080	0.064
MM	-0.767	0.299	-0.244	-0.478	0.184	-0.627	0.227	-0.128	-0.162	0.021
MH	0.444	-0.830	-0.245	-0.162	0.166	0.363	-0.629	-0.129	-0.055	0.019

The canonical loads and cross loads calculated between the variables in set 2 and the canonical variables produced for the set of population health output indicators are presented in Table 6. As seen in Table 6, the correlations between the first canonical variable derived for the set of population health outcome indicators and life expectancy at birth (LE), global prevalence of cancer (PC), infant mortality rate (IM), maternal mortality rare (MM), and mental health (MH) variables were 0.808, 0.801, -0.791, -0.767, and 0.444, respectively. There were strong correlations between the first canonical variable calculated for the set 2 and life expectancy at birth (LE) and global prevalence of cancer (PC). Thus, it could be argued that the significant determinants of the first canonical variable in the set 2 were the two above-mentioned variables. The correlations between the first canonical variable derived for the income equality set and life expectancy at birth (LE), global prevalence of cancer (PC), infant mortality rate (IM), maternal mortality rate (MM), and mental health (MH) variables were 0.660, 0.655, -0.646, -0.627 and 0.363, respectively.

The analysis of the findings presented in Tables 6 and 7 demonstrated that the first canonical variable derived for the income equality set should be renamed as Gini and the first canonical variable derived for the set of population health outcome indicators should be renamed as life expectancy at birth (LE).

FUTURE DIRECTIONS FOR RESEARCH

In the present study, it was observed that the population health data are unfortunately insufficient in several countries. In the future, especially if population health data could be available in developing countries or if government policies allow the employment of these data, it would be possible to conduct macro-level analyzes for these countries.

CONCLUSION

A healthy society is essential for the emergence of human capital required for economic development. Factors such as production losses due to diseases that individuals suffer or the increase in productivity due to better nutrition of individuals, high learning skills in healthy individuals, the allocation of healthcare resources to different goals when individuals are healthy, and the income potential of healthy individuals are extremely important for welfare. Although income level affects socio-economic variables, it is essential to ensure income equality for social welfare and a healthy society. In societies with high income inequality, both social and economic problems are common. Today, despite the increase in global wealth, the gap between the rich and the poor gradually widens. The income distribution in several developed nations is more unequal when compared to the past. Rising income inequality also negatively affects several socio-economic determinants. The reduction of the income inequality is extremely important to achieve and sustain social peace. High income inequality leads to significant obstacles to population health.

In the present study, the correlations between the income equality indicators, variables associated with income equality, and population health outcomes were determined in EU member countries and Turkey. The, the selected variable data were organized in two groups and a canonical correlation analysis was conducted. It was observed that only the first of the five canonical variables obtained in the analysis was statistically and practically significant. This canonic correlation coefficient was 0.818. Thus, the first canonical variable derived for the income equality set was named Gini and the first canonical variable derived for the set of population health outcome indicators was named life expectancy at birth (LE). In conclusion, it was determined that there was a significant and strong correlation between the income equality set and population health outcome indicators set. Furthermore, the analysis of the findings for the first canonical variable pair revealed that the income equality dataset could explain 66.9% of the variation in the population health outcome indicators. It was observed that the variables that contributed most to this significant correlation between the sets were Gini in the income equality set and life expectancy at birth (LE) in the population health outcome indicators set. It was also determined that the global prevalence of cancer, a population health outcome indicator, exhibited the second highest correlation with income inequality following the life expectancy at birth variable.

REFERENCES

Aida, J., Kondo, K., Kondo, N., Watt, R. G., Sheiham, A., & Tsakos, G. (2011). Income inequality, social capital and self-rated health and dental status in older Japanese. *Social Science & Medicine*, *73*(10), 1561–1568. doi:10.1016/j.socscimed.2011.09.005 PMID:21982631

Alpert, M. I., & Peterson, R. A. (1972). On the Interpretation of Canonical Analysis. *JMR, Journal of Marketing Research*, *9*(2), 187–192. doi:10.1177/002224377200900211

Alverado, F., & Cjancel, L. (2018). *World Inequality Report*. World Inequality Lab. Press. doi:10.4159/9780674984769

Babones, S. J. (2008). Income inequality and population health: Correlation and causality. *Social Science & Medicine*, *66*(7), 1614–1626. doi:10.1016/j.socscimed.2007.12.012 PMID:18222588

Belek, İ. (2001). *Sosyal Devletin Çöküşü ve Sağlığın Ekonomi Politiği*. Sorun Yayınları.

Bloom, D. E., Canning, D., & Jamison, D. T. (2004). *Health, Wealth and Welfare, Health and Development*. IMF Publishing.

Bozma, G., Eren, M., & Başar, S. (2018). Income distribution inequality and life expectancy relationships: Wilkinson hypothesis. *Atatürk Üniversitesi İktisadi ve İdari Bilimler Dergisi*, *32*(3), 793–805.

Çankaya, S. (2005). *Kanonik Korelasyon Analizi ve Hayvancılıkta Kullanımı* (Unpublished doctoral dissertation). Çukurova Üniversitesi Fen Bilimleri Enstitüsü, Adana, Turkey.

Chancel, L. (2019). *Ten facts about inequality in advanced economies*. WID Working Paper.

Clark, G. (2013). *Fukaralığa Veda Dünyanın Kısa İktisadi Tarihi* (Vol. 1). Baskı, Bilgi Üniversitesi Yayınları.

Çukur, A., & Bekmez, S. (2011). The Relationship between Income, Income Inequality and Health in Turkey: Evidence from Panel Data Analysis. *Gaziantep Üniversitesi Sosyal Bilimler Dergisi, 10*(1), 21–40.

Deaton, A. (2003). Health, Inequality, and Economic Development. *Journal of Economic Literature, 41*(1), 113–158. doi:10.1257/jel.41.1.113

Detollenaerea, J., Desmarest, A. S., Boeckxstaens, P., & Willems, W. (2018). The link between income inequality and health in Europe, adding strength dimensions of primary care to the equation. *Social Science & Medicine, 201*, 103–110. doi:10.1016/j.socscimed.2018.01.041 PMID:29471179

Eurostat. (2017). *Sustainable Development in the European Union 2017*. European Union Publishing.

Filho, A. D. P. C., Kawachi, I., Wang, Y. P., Viana, M. C., & Andrade, L. H. S. G. (2013). Does income inequality get under the skin? A multilevel analysis of depression, anxiety and mental disorders in Sao Paulo, Brazil. *Journal of Epidemiology and Community Health, 67*(11), 966–972. doi:10.1136/jech-2013-202626 PMID:23908459

Halisçelik, E., Acaravcı, A., & Güzel, A. S. (2019). Income Distribution, Health Expenditure and Life Expectancy Nexus in Turkey: ARDL Bounds Testing Analysis. *International Journal of Economics and Innovation, 5*(2), 263–275.

Herzer, D., & Nunnenkamp, P. (2014). *Income Inequality and health: evidence from developed and developing countries*. Helmut Schmidt Universität Hamburg, Working Paper No. 141.

Hotelling, H. (1935). The most predictable criterion. *Journal of Educational Psychology, 26*(2), 139–142. doi:10.1037/h0058165

Hotelling, H. (1936). Relations between two sets of variates. *Biometrika, 28*(3-4), 321–377. doi:10.1093/biomet/28.3-4.321

Kim, D., Wang, F., & Arcan, C. (2018). Geographic Association Between Income Inequality and Obesity Among Adults in New York State. *Preventing Chronic Disease, 15*, 180–217. doi:10.5888/pcd15.180217 PMID:30316306

Mellor, J. M., & Milyo, J. (2002). Income Inequality and health status in the United States, evidence from the current population survey. *The Journal of Human Resources, 37*(3), 510–539. doi:10.2307/3069680

Moore, S. (2006). Peripherality, income inequality, and life expectancy: Revisiting the income inequality hypothesis. *International Journal of Epidemiology, 35*(3), 623–632. doi:10.1093/ije/dyl026 PMID:16507644

Nilsson, T., & Bergh, A. (2012). *Income Inequality and Individual Health: Exploring the Association in a Developing Country*. IFN Working Paper No. 899.

Oxfam. (2016). *210 Oxfam Briefing Paper*. Oxfam.

Oxfam. (2020). *Why majority of the world's poor are woman*. https://www.oxfam.org/en/why-majority-worlds-poor-are-women

Özdamar, K. (2004). *Paket programlar ile istatistiksel veri analizi* (Vol. 5). Baskı, Kaan Kitabevi.

Pamuk, Ş. (2017). *Türkiye'nin 200 Yıllık İktisadi Tarihi* (Vol. 8). Baskı, Kültür Yayınları.

Pickett, K. E., James, O., & Wilkinson, R. G. (2006). Income inequality and the prevalence of mental illness: A preliminary international analysis. *Journal of Epidemiology and Community Health, 60*(7), 646–647. doi:10.1136/jech.2006.046631 PMID:16790839

Pickett, K. E., & Wilkinson, R. (2007). Child wellbeing and income inequality in rich societies: Ecological cross sectional study. *British Medical Journal, 335*(7629), 1080–1087. doi:10.1136/bmj.39377.580162.55 PMID:18024483

Ram, R. (2005). Income inequality, poverty, and population health: Evidence from recent data for the United States. *Social Science & Medicine, 61*(12), 2568–2576. doi:10.1016/j.socscimed.2005.04.038 PMID:15963618

Ray, D., & Linden, M. (2018). Health, inequality and income: A global study using simultaneous model. *Journal of Economic Structures, 7*(22), 1–28. doi:10.118640008-018-0121-3

Rodgers, G. B. (1979). Income and inequality as determinants of mortality: An international cross-section analysis. *Population Studies, 33*(2), 343–351. doi:10.1080/00324728.1979.10410449

Rostila, M., Kölegård, M. L., & Fritzell, J. (2012). Income inequality and self-rated health in Stockholm, Sweden: A test of the 'income inequality hypothesis' on two levels of aggregation. *Social Science & Medicine, 74*(7), 1091–1098. doi:10.1016/j.socscimed.2011.11.027 PMID:22336734

Schultz, T. P. (2009). *Population and Health Policies*. IZA Disccussion Paper Series, No: 4340.

Şener, O. (2006). *Teoride ve Uygulamada Kamu Ekonomisi*. Beta Yayınevi.

Sharma, S. (1996). *Applied Multivariate Techniques*. John Wiley & Sons, Inc.

Stiglitz, J. E. (2015). *Eşitsizliğin Bedeli. Bugünün Bölünmüş Toplumu Geleceğimizi Nasıl Tehlikeye Atıyor?* İletişim Yayınları.

Sun, P., Unger, J. B., Palmer, P., Ma, H., Xie, B., Sussman, S., & Johnson, C. A. (2012). Relative income inequality and selected health outcomes in urban Chinese youth. *Social Science & Medicine*, *74*(1), 84–91. doi:10.1016/j.socscimed.2011.10.010 PMID:22137733

Tweed, E. J., Allardic, G. M., McLoone, P., & Morrison, D. S. (2018). Socio-economic inequalities in the incidence of four common cancers: A population-based registry study. *Public Health*, *154*, 1–10. doi:10.1016/j.puhe.2017.10.005 PMID:29128730

Wagstaff, A., & Doorslaer, E. (2000). Income inequality and health: What does the literature tell us? *Annual Review of Public Health*, *21*(1), 543–567. doi:10.1146/annurev.publhealth.21.1.543 PMID:10884964

WHO. (2004). *Investing in Health for Economic Development*. WHO Publishing.

Wilkinson, R. G. (1997). Socioeconomic determinants of health Health inequalities: Relative or absolute material standards? *BMJ (Clinical Research Ed.)*, *314*(7080), 591–599. doi:10.1136/bmj.314.7080.591 PMID:9055723

ADDITIONAL READING

Eberstadt, N., & Satel, S. (2004). *Health and the income inequality hypothesis*. The AEI Press.

Fisher, G., & Strauss, R. (2021). *Europe's income, wealth, consumption and inequality*. Oxford University Press. doi:10.1093/oso/9780197545706.001.0001

Hojjat, T. A., & Hojjat, R. (2017). *The Economics of Obesity: Poverty, Income Inequality and Health*. Springer Publication. doi:10.1007/978-981-10-2911-0

Johnson, D. E. (1998). *Applied Multivariate Methods for Data Analysts*. Brooks/Cole Publishing Company.

Johnson, R. A., & Wichern, D. W. (1998). *Applied Multivariate Statistical Analysis* (4th ed.). Prentice-Hall Inc.

Kawachi, I., Kennedy, B. P., Lochner, K., & Prothrow-Stith, D. (1997). Social capital, income inequality, and mortality. *American Journal of Public Health, 87*(9), 1491–1498. doi:10.2105/AJPH.87.9.1491 PMID:9314802

Pickett, K. E., & Wilkinson, R. G. (2015). Income inequality and health: A causal review. *Social Science & Medicine, 128*, 316–326. doi:10.1016/j.socscimed.2014.12.031 PMID:25577953

Piketty, T. (2017). *Capital in the twenty first century*. The Belkknap Press of Harvard University Press. doi:10.4159/9780674982918

Tabachnick, B. G., & Fidell, L. S. (2019). *Using Multivariate Statistics* (7th ed.). Pearson.

Truesdale, B. C., & Jencks, C. (2016). The Health Effects of Income Inequality: Averages and Disparities. *Annual Review of Public Health, 37*(1), 413–430. doi:10.1146/annurev-publhealth-032315-021606 PMID:26735427

KEY TERMS AND DEFINITIONS

Developed Country: The countries with high development levels.
Developing Country: Those other than the developed countries.
European Countries: Countries located in Europe.
Income Inequality: Unequal distribution of income.
Mental Health: Not having any psychological or psychiatric problem.
Population Health: Physical, mental, and social well-being of individuals.
Poverty: Not having enough income.
Unemployment: Inability to find a job despite the desire for employment.

Chapter 7
The Effect of Net FDI Inflow on Economic Growth in Turkey:
An Application With Toda-Yamamoto Approach

Dilek Temiz Dinç
Çankaya University, Turkey

Aytaç Gökmen
Çankaya University, Turkey

ABSTRACT

Capital is one of the first and foremost requisites of economic development for every country in this world. However, not every country is given abundant capital. Foreign direct investment (FDI) occurs as a good cure to solve capital-related issues. In this study, the net FDI inflow and economic growth correlation was researched in Turkey for the period of 2010:1-2018:3 by employing quarterly data as well as applying the Augmented Dickey Fuller Test (ADF); Phillips-Perron (PP); Kwiatkowski, Phillips, Schmidt, Shin (KPSS); Elliott, Rothenberg, and Stock (ERS) Point Optimal; Ng-Perron Unit Root Tests; and Toda-Yamamoto Causality Tests. According to the findings of the study, there is a unidirectional causality running from net FDI to economic growth in Turkey.

INTRODUCTION

FDI inflows mostly have a positive effect on host country's economic activities and development activities by means of valuable technology and know-how which along

DOI: 10.4018/978-1-7998-8258-9.ch007

with the activities of the local firm can help the economy gain impetus. Moreover, international trade also acts as an impetus for economic growth by enabling more efficient production of goods and services, by offshoring production to states which have comparative advantage in manufacturing them. Resting upon specific parameters as human capital, local investment, infrastructural development of the host state, macroeconomic stability and commerce and institutional policies incepted by the government of the host state the effect of the FDI inflow and commerce on economic growth of the host state differentiates. FDI and commercial function act as catalysts of growth in nation states. It is expected that higher FDI ratio could lead to experiencing rapid economic growth. Therefore, FDI shall encourage in less developed countries to give impetus to accelerate technological change and economic growth (Battacharya, 2010).

Supposedly, enhancing the upgrading of domestic enterprise, the expansion of advanced research-development operations and participating in quality enhancement of domestic labor force, FDI shall play an important role in improving the productivity of the host countries and maintaining economic development. The practice has also demonstrated that any sustainable economic development requires more than an amenable economy to technological inflows of inputs. Thereby, to survive, businesses of different sizes are supposed to allocate significant sources in view of obtaining high technology and knowledge. With this respect and taking into consideration the lack of resources mainly in the least improved states, FDI inflows have the potential to enhance the quality of the existing manufacturing factors and to develop several competitive advantages rested on specialized factors. With regard to host countries, the technological transfer by FDI generates positive impacts, as for instance; increasing laborers' knowledge and abilities; the diffusion of technological and managerial practices, reflecting upon the costs and the quality of the merchandises and services, the development of the correlation among transnational corporations and the local institutions; starting local businesses to direct their efforts towards a technologies operations so as to face the growth of competition. Moreover, adopting current technologies by scientific and technological transfer could boost productivity in less advanced countries where businesses compete on the basis of price and productivity quality. Furthermore, from a certain point of economic development, manufacturing growth shall not be based on imported innovations as entails the development of new and unique products utilizing the most sophisticated manufacturing process. However, there is a diversity of exogenously determined traits which impact that investment improvement path of any given state, factors such as natural resources endowments, size and population density, the phase of industrialization, the state polices implemented, the degree of industrialization, the government policies implemented, economic and political infrastructure, and so on. Therefore, due to the fact that inward FDI impacts intermingle with those of the other economic growth factors and thus the correlation between FDI inflows and economic development is difficult to test by econometric models (Iacovoiu, 2015). As indicated in the introductory phase of this paper, FDI is very beneficial for recipient host countries. Yet, the aim of this paper is to review FDI literature, FDI and economic growth correlation and reveal the possible impact of net FDI in Turkey by considering some macroeconomic indicators based on credible national and international publications.

1. FDI & ECONOMIC GROWTH NEXUS

FDI could have positive growth impacts in territories and industries which are primarily close to the technological frontier, whereas the growth grade is left unchanged or even declined in backward regions and industries. Domestic enterprises that are far from the technological border have no incentive to innovate and invest in research and development (R&D) when foreign competitors enter the industry; even if they do so, such enterprises could have no chance to rival with multinational entrants. FDI should also widen income discrepancies if less advanced premises lack the absorptive capability to benefit from FDI-instigated spillover. It is argued that spillover is based on the absorptive capacity of domestic businesses, with small technological breaks stimulating spillovers and large breaks limiting them. Moreover, developing states are supposed to have reached a minimum level of economic development before they can attain the growth-enhancing impacts of FDI (Maye-Foulkes, Nunenkamp, 2009).

The current theoretical models state that FDI is advantageous for host state's economic growth. According to conventional economic theory, FDI would tend to focus on less developed states, where there exist numerous greater opportunities to accomplish higher returns. Nonetheless, there exist several preconditions in order for FDI to become productive in developing states. The presence of a minimum threshold grade of human capital, of enhanced local infrastructures, as well as developed domestic financial systems are regarded to be great significance in order FDI to flow in less advanced states and possess a measurable effect on economic growth. In essence, the lack of such prerequisites in numerous developing states has led to unequal distribution across states with numerous developing states facing issues to attract foreign investors. FDI is regarded as a significant means for direct technology diffusion. Especially, in developing states, FDI is probably the most significant channel for technology transfer because of the scarcity of financial sources and the immediate necessity of reconstruction. With respect to this, one could expect that FDI shall contribute to economic growth, indirectly, by accelerating the diffusion of general-purpose technologies (Dimelis, Papaioannou, 2010).

The correlation between FDI and economic growth has galvanized a numerous empirical literature based on both industrial and developing states. An important number of empirical studies on the role of FDI in host states imply that FDI is a considerable source of capital complements local private investments, is mostly associated with new job opportunities and improvement of technology transfer and boosts overall economic growth in host states. With respect to developing states in particular, macro-empirical work on the FDI-economic growth correlation has indicated that – being subject to a number of significant elements, such as human capital base in the host state, the commercial regime and the degree of openness in an economy – FDI would have a positive effect on overall economic growth. One shall also note that FDI has possibly desirable factors which impact the quality of growth important implications for poverty reduction. FDI could alleviate negative shocks to the poor which result from financial, instability and help to enhance corporate governance. A wide literature on the determinants of FDI in developing states clearly shows the significance of infrastructure, skills, macroeconomic stability and firm institutions for attracting more FDI (Chowdhury, Mavrotas, 2006).

From a theoretical respect, there could be numerous means in which FDI can stimulate economic growth. For instance, the standard neoclassical Solow growth model implies that FDI raises the capital stock and thereby growth in the host economy is instigated simply by capital accumulation. In the neoclassical growth model with decreasing return to capital, FDI has thereby only a short-run effect on growth, before each state spreads its new steady state. In endogenous growth models, FDI shall have a short effect on growth but, remarkably, they could also have a perpetual impact, particularly if they are more productive than local investment and may cause positive technological spillovers. This could be the instance mainly, if FDI instigates the incorporation of new technologies in the manufacturing function of the host state economy. The existence of foreign businesses could have an effect on receiver states beyond the impact of the increase in its total capital, by utilizing large positive externalities, potentially enhancing the state's technology, with positive impacts on total productivity and growth (Cipollina et al., 2012).

The causality between FDI and gross domestic product (GDP) growth may occur in either direction. FDI shall instigate GDP growth in the mode of the Solow growth model. This claims that by means of capital accumulation in the recipient states, FDI could have growth impacts on host economies for FDI is similar to domestic investment and FDI is estimated to create non-convex growth by stimulating the incorporation of new inputs and foreign technologies in the production function of the recipient state. One could state that in developing states, lack of technology is the crucial limitation to economic growth. Recent endogenous growth models have accentuated the significance of technology. Further studies imply that FDI could be able to improve economic growth of host states through knowledge and technology transfers as well as spillover effects. Moreover, multinational corporations have a significant role in the dissemination of global technologies and management applications into the domestic economy which could have positive reflections on the domestic economy, in turn which could have positive effect on economic growth. The causality may also go to the reverse way; quick GDP growth usually constitutes a high level of capital resource gap in the host state and the host state could hence demand more FDI by offering favorable terms to attract foreign investors, since FDI is a source of capital. More importantly, quick economic growth in the host state would constitute the confidence of foreign investors investing in the host state. In total, better economic growth in host states enables foreign investors with a better investment environment. Quick economic growth, coupling with an increasing high per capita income, would constitute great opportunities for making profits in the host state. In essence, output growth is regarded as one significant determinant for FDI inflows to a host state and this point of view is called the market size hypothesis or the growth driven hypothesis. It is possible that the causal connection between FDI and economic growth has firm correlation, and it is quite likely that the two variables move together through response. States with economic not only generate more demand for FDI, that is similar to domestic investment, but also may offer better opportunities which cause increased income for foreign investors and then invite a greater volume of FDI. Henceforth, FDI inflows may prompt economic growth of the host state by means of positive direct impacts and spillover effects. Moreover, FDI and economic growth are positively interdependent and may lead to a two-way causality (Zhao, Du, 2007).

FDI has a significant role in modernizing the economy and instigating economic growth in host states especially in developing countries. In the case of latter one, it is also critical to coordinate foreign aid with follow-up FDI to maximize its effect. Additionally, FDI can constitute an international network which optimizes the movement local products across frontiers, constitutes cost savings and related scale and scope economies for business organizations. Not all business organizations engage in FDI or choose to internationalize, there is a wide separate literature that investigate corporate motivations and rationale. Many state studies, which deal with the productivity impacts of FDI spillovers on businesses, or plants using micro level data, provide positive results on the role of FDI with respect to instigating economic growth. It is demonstrated that spillover effects increase significantly with the inclusion of FDI in standard model, therefore explaining the link to total factor productivity and hence economic growth. There is some evidence to support a positive relationship between an increase in commercial flows, FDI and higher growth rates. Moreover, there is the evidence to support a positive relationship between an increase in commercial volume, FDI and greater growth rates. If foreign investment generates towards more productive industries, the perceived positive relationship would overemphasize the positive effect of FDI on economic growth (Batten, Vo, 2009).

FDI might have eternal impact on the growth impact. FDI could only impact the level of income under its contribution to capital accumulation in the host state with impelling the long-term growth rate. In new endogenous growth models, there are a number of channels by means of which FDI permanently impacts the economic growth rate in the long run. As it is in the neoclassical models, FDI could affect the output directly by raising the stock of capital. Yet, this impact is likely to be small under the assumption of perfect sustainability. As new endogenous model's growth models regard long run growth as a function of technological progress and human capital enhancement, the main channel that FDI can increase the growth rate is by rising production by means of technology transfer, productivity spillovers and externalities. FDI is a combined composition of capital stock, know-how and technology and can raise the existing stock of knowledge in the recipient economy by way of labor training, skill acquisition and diffusion as well as through the introduction of alternative management applications and organizational arrangements. When FDI improves the economic growth by way of the magnitude of its effects depends positively on the level of human capital available, in the host state. This level of human capital is reflective of the absorptive capability of the host state to new technology. FDI improves growth in which the host state has accepted commercial liberalization policies. This indicates that FDI is more significant for economic growth and assists in export-promoting than import-substituting states. Moreover, FDI contributes to economic growth by means of direct effect such as an increase in productivity and instigating exports, as well as, positive externality impacts in terms of facilitating transmission and diffusion technology. FDI is positively correlated with economic growth but host states entail human capital, economic stability and liberalized markets in order to benefit from long-term FDI impacts. The positive influence of FDI on growth is expected to be higher than local savings in favor of the hypothesis that FDI inflows are more productive than local investments. Moreover, one can conclude that the spillover impact of knowledge embodied in FDI could enhance domestic productivity and thereby stimulate growth (Hoang et al., 2010). In accordance with the neoclassical growth theory, economic growth is mainly led by capital accumulation, up to the reasonable level of capital stock per labor, even though convergence could last for very long time. With respect to investment as a main determinant of economic growth, global capital flows, especially the FDI are expected to complete local capital supply, thereby enabling financing for domestic investment projects (Jude, 2019).

2. LITERATURE REVIEW

There are many studies in the literature that deal with the correlation between FDI and economic growth. The main of these studies are as follows: Şimşek and Behdioğlu (2006) researched the possible contribution of FDI to economic development whether positive or negative by using Cobb-Douglas production function. The findings of the research show that there is a positive effect of FDI on GDP in Turkey.

Afşar (2007) researched the correlation between FDI and economic growth for Turkey which was liberated foreign capital inflows specifically after 1980s. The Granger causality relation was utilized so as to investigate the hypothesis on the existence of the causality between FDI and economic growth. The study involves the period of 1992:1 and 2006:3, shows the causality correlation from FDI to economic growth to Turkey. Moreover, one could state that there is one-way correlation between FDI and economic growth and the causality of the correlation runs from FDI and economic growth.

Alagöz et al. (2008) investigated the correlation between foreign direct investment inflow and economic development by utilizing quarterly data for the period of 1992-2007. The aftermath of the Granger causality test did not show causality among variables.

Katırcıoğlu (2009) empirically analyzed the grade of relation and the direction of causality between net FDI inflows and economic growth for Turkey by using the bounds test for co-integration and Granger causality applications. The result of the study implies that both of the factors are in long-range equilibrium correlation only when FDI is dependent variable respecting to auto-regressive distributed lag modeling approach. Eventual research of the paper shows that economic growth in the Republic of Turkey stimulates expansion in net DI inflows.

According to Öztürk and Acaravcı (2010), their study researches the power of the foreign direct investment-export-growth and foreign direct investment-import-growth hypotheses for Turkey by utilizing quarterly time series data for 1998:1-2009:1 period. The ARDL bounds test indicates that there is a correlation of a long-run causality between the FDI, import (IM) and real GDP, but no indicator of a long-run relationship between the FDI, export (EX) and GDP in Turkey. According to the causality test stemming from GDP-IM-FDI equation, there is correlation of two-way (bidirectional) correlation between GDP and IM, evidence of one-way (unidirectional) causality from FDI to GDP and indicator of one way Granger causality from FDI to IM. The existence of unidirectional correlation relations indicates that FDI strategies shall be devised to instigate economic growth.

According to Bilgili et al. (2012), Turkish foreign direct investment growth equation has important structural changes in level and trend and that has important variable shifts in explanatory variables such as Turkish GDP growth, labor cost and the electricity price growth.

The main objective of Arısoy's (2012) investigation is to define the contributions of foreign direct investment to the total growth and whether foreign direct investment have had an effect on total factor productivity (TFP) of Turkey for the period 1960-2005 utilizing aggregate production function. This study investigates that the two fundamental channels through which foreign direct investment could impact host state economic growth are technology spillovers and physical capital accumulation. Further, it is inclined to identify the correlation linkage among foreign direct investment, TFP and economic growth and then assessing several channels by means of which foreign direct investment is correlated to TFP utilizing some recent econometric techniques. The empirical results show that foreign direct investment contributes positively to TFP and growth by means of capital accumulation and technological spillovers.

3. AN EMPIRICAL RESEARCH ON THE NET FDI INFLOW & ECONOMIC GROWTH CORRELATION IN TURKEY: THE DATA SET & METHOD

The relationship between net FDI inflow and economic growth in Turkey for this study was researched by employing Toda-Yamamoto (1995) causality test. The quarterly data was utilized in this study covering the period of 2010:1-2018:3. The related data set was acquired from the data bases of Turkish Statistical Institute (TUIK) and the Central Bank of the Republic of Turkey (TCMB). All of the econometric results were obtained by using Eviews9 program. The variables used in the entire analysis were seasonally adjusted and denoted in million Turkish Liras (TL).
The definitions of the variables used in the study are as follows:

FDI: Seasonally adjusted Net Foreign Direct Investment
GDP: Seasonally adjusted Real Income (Real income was used as to represent economic growth)
The time trace graphics of the variables used in this study is denoted in Figure 1.

Figure 1. Time Trace Graphics of FDI & GDP

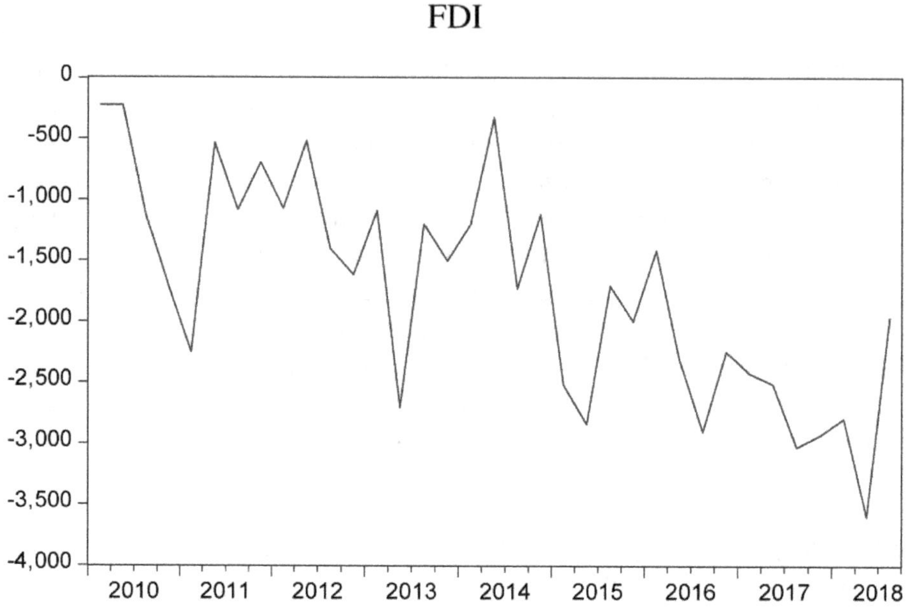

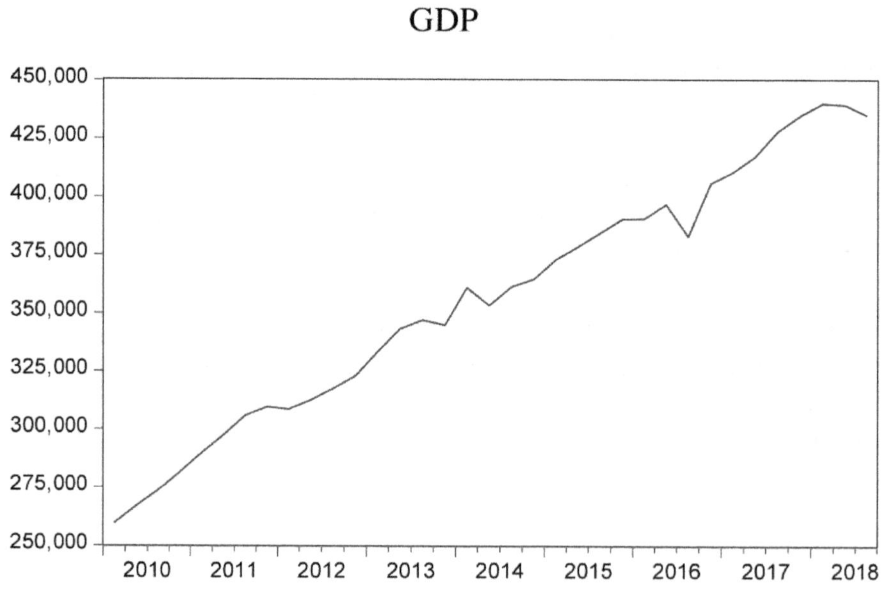

When the direction of the real income (GDP) is considered, the general trend increases for the period of 2010-2018. However, one can state that the net FDI series follow fluctuating course, yet the general trend decreases for them. This adversely correlated course in the series between the net FDI and real income constructed the main reasoning of this study to research the relation of causality.

The Granger (1969) causality test is mostly preferred in econometric studies for its high rate of applicability (Çalışkan et al., 2017). However, in order to apply the Granger causality test, it is expected that the series to be tested shall be stationary (Granger, 1969). If the variables are not stationary, the F Test cannot be valid since the test statistics do not have the standard distribution (Gujarati, 2003). Moreover, the Granger causality test is too sensitive to lag-length and according to the lag-length determined, the results may vary in the analysis (Çalışkan et al., 2017). Therefore, the determination of the lag-length is considerable with respect to Granger causality test. However, within the Toda-Yamamoto (1995) causality test, for the cointegrated series having the same degree or different degrees, the causality analysis can be made without the existence of cointegration (Büyükakın et al., 2015). Furthermore, the Toda-Yamamoto causality analysis is an approach that prevents disinformation that may results from differing degrees (Terzi & Yurtkuran, 2016). The Modified Wald Test (MWALD) that presents X^2 distribution is applied for the restricted parameters of vector autoregression (VAR) model which has the k lag-length in the Toda-Yamamoto analysis. This analysis is a two-stage method. Within the first stage of the analysis, the optimal lag-length (k) of the VAR model which leads to sensitive outcomes regarding lag-lengths and the maximum cointegration (d_{max}) levels of variables are determined. Moreover, in the second stage, the modified VAR model that has the lag-length of ($k+d_{max}$) is estimated.

4. EMPIRICAL ANALYSIS

4.1. Unit Root Tests

In order to analyze the stationarity of the series, the conventional unit root tests such as the Augmented Dickey Fuller Test (ADF) (1981); Phillips-Perron (PP) (1988); Kwiatkowski, Phillips, Schmidt, Shin (KPSS) (1992); Elliott, Rothenberg & Stock (ERS) Point Optimal (1996) and Ng-Perron (2001) were utilized. The ADF and PP unit root test results which are related to the variables used in this study are presented in Table 1. The figures in parenthesis indicate the lag-lengths which are estimated with the utilization of Schwarz (SC) information criterion.

Table 1. ADF & PP Unit Root Test Results

Variable	ADF test statistics		Constant (C), Trend (T)	Result
FDI	-3.415291 (4)	P=0.0682	C, T	not stationary
GDP	-1.198436 (1)	P=0.6633	C	not stationary
DFDI	-5.872205 (3)	P=0.0000	C	stationary
DGDP	-8.045579 (0)	P=0.0000	C	stationary
Variable	PP statistics		Constant (C), Trend (T)	Result
FDI	-3.425862 (4)	P=0.0603	C, T	not stationary
GDP	-1.310997 (2)	P=0.6131	C	not stationary
DFDI	-5.829641 (3)	P=0.0000	C	stationary
DGDP	-8.111661 (3)	P=0.0000	C	stationary

Note: A p-value > 0.05 indicates unit root is detected (not stationary); otherwise, it means there is no unit root (stationary). The "D" used in front of the variables indicates the first difference.

When the Table 1 is examined, at the 5% significance level and according to the ADF and PP test results, the series of FDI and GDP involve unit root and are not stationary. The difference of these series which are not stationary is taken and made stationary. Therefore, according to the ADF and PP unit root tests, the maximum cointegration degree (d_{max}) of the variables is estimated as 1.

In order to reinforce the stationarity of the difference of the series, the KPSS trend stationarity test was applied. The results of the KPSS test is presented in Table 2.

Table 2. KPSS Test Results

Variable	LM-Stat Constant (C), Trend (T)	Asymptotik Critical Value (5%)	Result
FDI	0.162521(C, T)	0.146000	not stationary
GDP	0.615237 (C)	0.463000	not stationary
DFDI	0.067730 (C, T)	0.146000	Stationary
DGDP	0.034896 (C, T)	0.146000	Stationary

According to Table 2, since, the LM test statistics related to the degrees of variables are absolutely higher than KPSS test critical values at the 5% significance level, it was decided that they are not stationary and involve unit roots. The findings obtained from the first-degree difference of the variables specify that the difference of the variables is stationary. The findings obtained from the KPSS test support the results acquired from ADF and PP unit root tests. According to the maximum cointegration degree of the KPSS test, (d_{max}) was estimated as 1.

After the ADF, PP and KPSS unit root tests, Ng-Perron (2001) unit root test was applied. The result of the Ng-Perron unit root test is presented in Table 3.

Table 3. Ng-Perron Test Results

	Constant				Constant+Trend			
Variable	MZ_a	MZ_t	MSB	MPT	MZ_a	MZ_t	MSB	MPT
FDI (3)	-6.61013	-1.78416	0.26991	3.82049	-16.2688	-2.77846	0.17078	6.03364
GDP (2)	-0.31550	-0.18807	0.59609	15.7353	-13.9585	-2.53056	0.18129	7.15147
DFDI (3)	-9.60061	-2.00675	0.20902	3.13529	-20.1085	-3.06605	0.15248	5.15195
DGDP (0)	-13.9630	-2.53346	0.18144	2.16110	-17.4782	-2.94218	0.16571	5.02104
Asymptotic critical value 5%	-8.10000	-1.98000	0.23300	3.17000	-17.3000	-2.91000	0.16800	5.48000

Note: () indicates lag length.

While the null hypothesis of the MSB and MPT tests indicate the stationarity of the series as it is in the KPSS test, the null hypothesis of the MZ_a and MZ_t tests indicate unit roots in series as it is in the PP and ADF tests. The Ng-Perron test was analyzed by means of "Spectral OLS-Detrented AR". In Table 3, since the first degree difference calculated with MZ_a and MZ_t values are higher than the table values as well as the values related to MSB and MPT are smaller than the table values, the series are stationary at the first difference of I(1). This result obtained from the Ng-Perron unit root test is consistent with the results obtained from ADF, PP and KPSS unit root tests.

Eventually, the ERS point optimal unit root test was applied in the study which was developed by Elliott, Rothenberg and Stock (1996). The results of the ERS unit root tests are presented in Table 4.

Table 4. ERS Point Optimal Unit Root Test results

Constant+Trend			
Variable	**P_t**	**Critical Value (%5)**	**Result**
FDI (0)	5.824882	5.720000	Unit root available
GDP (0)	8.088824	5.720000	Unit root available
DFDI (2)	5.344468	5.720000	Unit root does not exist
DGDP (1)	5.538066	5.720000	Unit root does not exist
Constant			
Variable	P_t	Critical Value (%5)	Result
FDI (3)	8.749225	2.970000	Unit root available
GDP (1)	6.884110	2.970000	Unit root available
DFDI (0)	2.663020	2.970000	Unit root does not exist
DGDP (0)	2.179258	2.970000	Unit root does not exist

Note: The values in parentheses are determined by the SIC, refers to lag lengths.

The result of the ERS unit root test indicates that the series are not stationary at the level and the difference indicates their stationarity. The result of the ERS test is consistent with the other conventional unit root tests. With respect to this, according to the entire unit root tests applied in this study, the maximum cointegration degree of variables (d_{max}) was estimated as 1.

4.2. Lag-Length

The second phase of the Toda-Yamamoto unit root test is to specify the lag-length. The adequate lag-length is supposed to be estimated by means of information criterions and defining tests. The lag-length to be used in the model is specified by VAR analysis and represented in Table 5.

The lag-length was estimated as 1 according to LR, FPE, AIC, SC and HQ information criterions. It is expected that the lag-length defined was tested by defining tests. The LM test was applied in order to test the existence of the autocorrelation issue within the first determined lag-length. When the probability values in Table 6 are reflected, the null hypothesis related to the nonexistence of autocorrelation problem was accepted in the 1st lag-length at the 5% significance level.

Table 5. Determination of VAR Lag Length

Lag	LR	FPE	AIC	SC	HQ
0	NA	6.39e+14	39.76690	39.86032	39.79679
1	**104.1914***	**1.76e+13***	**36.17463***	**36.45487***	**36.26428***
2	6.061848	1.81e+13	36.19882	36.66589	36.34824
3	1.409546	2.25e+13	36.40420	37.05809	36.61339
4	9.143774	1.94e+13	36.23545	37.07617	36.50440
5	2.998879	2.24e+13	36.34428	37.37183	36.67300

* indicates lag order selected by the criterion
LR: sequential modified LR test statistic (each test at 5% level)
FPE: Final prediction error, AIC: Akaike information criterion, SC: Schwarz information criterion
HQ: Hannan-Quinn information criterion

Table 6. Autocorrelation LM Test Results

Lags	LM-Stat	Prob
1	6.660551	0.1550
2	1.992528	0.7371
3	1.011507	0.9080
4	6.256724	0.1808
5	1.397163	0.8447

The White Heteroscedasticity Variance Test was applied in order to specify the heteroscedasticity problem after the autocorrelation test. The result of the test is presented in Table 7.

Table 7. White Heteroscedasticity Test Results

Lags	Test Statistics	Probability Value
1	15.17098	0.2322

Note: The H_0 hypothesis in the variance test is “there is no variance”.

According to this result, it is accepted that there is no heteroscedasticity problem in error terms at the 5% significance level. Eventually, it is estimated that there is no autocorrelation and heteroscedasticity problem in the VAR analysis which was made by considering 1 lag-length.

It is the next step in the study to research whether the 1 lag-length VAR model is stable or not. The location of the inverse roots of AR (Autoregressive) characteristic polynomial related to the estimated model in the unit circle offers information regarding to stationarity of the model.

Figure 2. Inverse Roots of AR Characteristic Polynomial

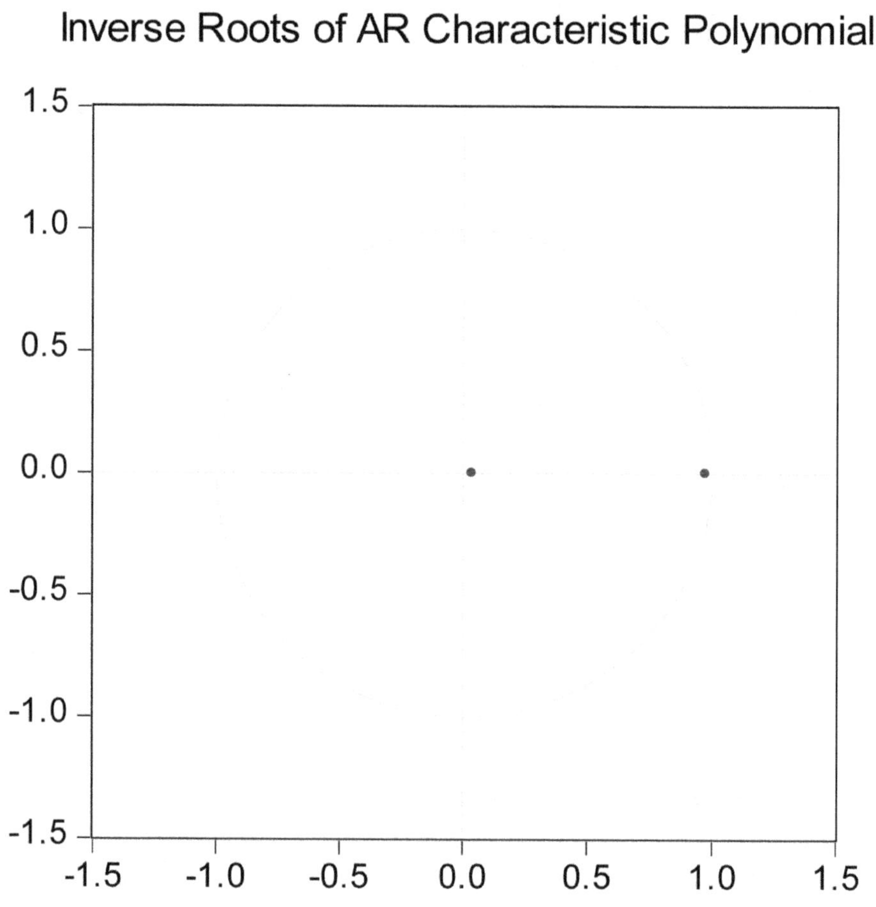

As it is evident in Figure 2 that the inverse roots of AR characteristic polynomial are not outside of the circle, thereby this specifies that the VAR model constructed is in a stable structure. According to the results obtained from Tables 5, 6, 7 and

Figure 1, one can state that the optimal lag-length is 1. In this vein, it could be decided that (k) optimal lag-length is 1.

4.3. Toda-Yamamoto Causality Test

It was concluded that the ($k + d_{max}$) level is 2 in order to make the Toda-Yamamoto causality test. The results related to this situation is presented in Table 8.

Table 8. Toda-Yamamoto Causality Test Results

Direction	X^2 test Statistics	Probability	Decision**
FDI →GDP	5.493600	0.0441	There is a causality running from net FDI to real income*
GDP →FDI	2.602314	0.2722	There is not a causality running from real income to net FDI

*The real income (GDP) is used to represent economic growth in the analysis. **According to %5 significance level.

As a result of the Toda-Yamamoto causality test, there is a unidirectional causality between the economic growth of Turkey and net foreign direct investment. This unidirectional causality runs from net FDI to economic growth.

RESULT

Not every country is bestowed with large natural resources, capital, information and know-how in this world. That's why, each and every state is in need of new capital formation either from domestic sources or from foreign sources. Moreover, foreign direct investment is a swift path to have access to new financial capital formation, acquisition of new technologies, knowledge and know-how. Therefore, foreign direct investment is beneficial for states in order to develop and flourish.

Furthermore, this is a paper to analyze the relationship between net FDI inflow to Turkey and economic growth by employing some econometric methods. The correlation between net foreign direct investment and economic growth was analyzed by employing Toda-Yamamoto (1995) causality test in this study. The study involves the period of 2010:1-2018:3. The quarterly data was used in the empirical analysis. As a result of the Toda-Yamamoto causality test, it was found that there is a unidirectional causality running from net foreign direct investment to economic growth in Turkey. The results obtained from this study support the results of the study of Afşar (2007).

REFERENCES

Afşar, M. (2007). *The Causality Relationship between Economic Growth & Foreign Direct Investment in Turkey*. Conference Paper, "Business & Economics Society International 2007 (B&ESI), Antibes, France.

Alagöz, M., Erdoğan, S., & Topallı, N. (2008). Foreign Direct Investment and Economic Growth: Evidence from Turkey 1992-2007. *Gaziantep University Journal of Social Sciences*, *7*(1), 79–89.

Arısoy, İ. (2012). The Impact of Foreign Direct Investment on Total Factor Productivity & Economic Growth in Turkey. *Journal of Developing Areas*, *46*(1), 17–29. doi:10.1353/jda.2012.0013

Battacharya, M. (2010). Causal Nexus Trade, FDI and Economic Growth -Evidence from India. *Paradigm*, *14*(1), 12–23. doi:10.1177/0971890720100104

Batten, J., & Vo, X. V. (2009). An analysis of the relationship between foreign direct investment and economic growth. *Applied Economics*, *41*(13), 1621–1641. doi:10.1080/00036840701493758

Bilgili, F., Tülüce, N. S. H., & Doğan, İ. (2012). The determinants of FDI in Turkey: A Markov Regime-Switching approach. *Economic Modelling*, *29*(4), 1161–1169. doi:10.1016/j.econmod.2012.04.009

Büyükakın, F., Bozkurt, H., & Cengiz, V. (2015). The Analysis of the Interest Channel of the Monetary Flows in Turkey with the Granger Causality and Toda-Yamamoto Methods. İİBF Journal of the Erciyes University, 33, 101-118.

Çalışkan, Ş., Karabacak, M., & Meçik, O. (2017). The Education Expenses in the Turkish Economy and its Correlation to Economic Growth. The Bootstrap Toda-Yamamoto Causality Test Approach. *KOSBED*, *33*(1), 45–56.

Chowdhury, A., & Mavrotas, G. (2006). FDI & Growth: What Causes What? *World Economy*, *29*(1), 9–19. doi:10.1111/j.1467-9701.2006.00755.x

Cipollina, M., Giovannetti, G., Pietrovito, F., & Pozzolo, A. (2012). FDI and Growth: What Cross-country Industry Data Say. *World Economy*, *35*(11), 1599–1629. doi:10.1111/j.1467-9701.2012.01478.x

Dicky, D., & Fuller, W. (1981). Likelihood Ratio Statistics for Autoregressive Time Series with A Unit Root. *Econometrica*, *49*(4), 1057–1072. doi:10.2307/1912517

Dimelis, S., & Papaioannou, S. (2010). FDI and ICT Effects on Productivity Growth: A Comparative Analysis of Developing and Developed Countries. *European Journal of Development Research*, *22*(1), 79–96. doi:10.1057/ejdr.2009.45

Elliot, G., Rothenberg, T., & Stock, J. (1996). Efficient Tests for An Autoregressive Unit Root. *Econometrica*, *64*(4), 813–836. doi:10.2307/2171846

Granger, C. W. J. (1969). Investigating Causal Relations by Econometric Models and Cross Spectral Methods. *Econometrica*, *37*(3), 424–438. doi:10.2307/1912791

Gujarati, D. (2003). *Basic Econometrics* (4th ed.). McGraw-Hill.

Hoang, T. T., Wiboonchutikula, P., & Tubtimtong, B. (2010). Does Foreign Direct Investment Promote Economic Growth in Vietnam? *ASEAN Economic Bulletin*, *27*(3), 295–303. doi:10.1355/ae27-3d

Jude, C. (2019). Does FDI crowd out domestic investment in transition countries? *Economics of Transition and Institutional Change*, *27*(1), 163–200. doi:10.1111/ecot.12184

Katırcıoğlu, S. (2009). Foreign Direct Investment & Economic Growth in Turkey: An Empirical Investigation by the Bounds Test for Co-Integration & Causality Tests. *Economic Research Journal*, *22*(3), 1–9.

Kwiatkowski, D., Phillips, P., Schmidt, P., & Shin, Y. (1992). Testing the Null Hypothesis of Stationarity Against the Alternative of A Unit Root: How Sure Are We That The Economic Time Series Have A Unit Root? *Journal of Econometrics*, *54*(1), 159–178. doi:10.1016/0304-4076(92)90104-Y

Maye-Foulkes, D., & Nunenkamp, P. (2009). Do Multinational Enterprises Contribute to Convergence or Divergence? A Disaggregated Analysis of US FDI. *Review of Development Economics*, *13*(2), 304–318. doi:10.1111/j.1467-9361.2009.00510.x

Ng, S., & Perron, P. (2001). Lag Length Selection and The Construction of Unit Root Tests with Good Size and Power. *Econometrica*, *69*(6), 1519–1554. doi:10.1111/1468-0262.00256

Öztürk, İ., & Acaravcı, A. (2010). FDI, Trade and Growth in Turkey: Evidence from ARDL Bounds Testing Approach. *Argumenta Oeconomica*, *25*(2), 95–115.

Phillips, P., & Peron, P. (1988). Testing for A Unit Root in Time Series Regression. *Biometrika*, *75*(2), 335–346. doi:10.1093/biomet/75.2.335

Şimşek; M. & Behdioğlu, S. (2006). The Impact of FDI on Economic Growth in Turkey: An Empirical Study. *İİBF Journal of the Atatürk University*, *20*(2), 47-65.

Terzi, H., & Yurtkuran, S. (2016). The correlation between education and economic growth in Turkey: Sims and Toda-Yamamoto Analysis. *Eskişehir Osmangazi University İİBF Journal*, *11*(2), 7–24.

Toda, H., & Yamamoto, T. (1995). Statistical inference in vector autoregressions with possibly integrated processes. *Journal of Econometrics*, *66*(1-2), 225–250. doi:10.1016/0304-4076(94)01616-8

Zhao, C., & Du, J. (2007). Causality Between FDI and Economic Growth in China. *Chinese Economy*, *40*(6), 68–82. doi:10.2753/CES1097-1475400604

Chapter 8
Impact of the Pandemic on the Indian Economy and Wellbeing

Chitra Krishnan
https://orcid.org/0000-0003-1135-8852
Amity University, Noida, India

Richa Goel
Amity University, Noida, India

Jasmine Mariappan
University of Technology and Applied Sciences, Oman

ABSTRACT

The goal of the study is to look at the impact of COVID-19 on major industries including automobiles, wellness, education, tourism, and many others, as well as migrant workers' status. COVID-19, a sudden epidemic, has had a devastating impact on the Indian economy. The migrant population was also affected by this situation. They were concerned about labor shortages, monthly rationing, and social insurance shortages. In this investigation, secondary data was gathered. The study focuses on the influence of COVID-19 on important industries such as automotive, wellness, education, tourism, and so on, as well as the position of migrant workers. Secondary data was acquired for this inquiry. Blogs, magazines, newspapers, news from foreign agencies, written academic papers, government materials, and websites are examples of secondary sources. Educational institutions, customers, legislators, the government, and the community will all profit from this research.

DOI: 10.4018/978-1-7998-8258-9.ch008

INTRODUCTION

The COVID-19 pandemic struck at the heart of human society over a year and a half ago, reminding us of mother nature's might. After the first wave, we felt we had regained control of the situation in India, but the second wave left us in severe need of basic necessities such as oxygen and medical supplies. COVID-19 has already claimed the lives of over 3.8 lakh individuals, despite the fact that the second wave appears to be winding down, with daily incidences reducing to around 60,000 from nearly 4 lakhs. With the expectation that the medical situation will substantially improve, it is now time to look at the macroeconomic implications of the second wave. After the first coronavirus case was reported in the southern state of Kerala in late January 2020, India implemented strict coronavirus testing at airports (COVID-19).

Over the next few weeks, a series of events developed, ending in the suspension of all inbound and outward travel on March 22, that year. Different countries' governments are hoping to "flatten the curve" by encouraging individuals to follow travel restrictions and "stay at home" instructions. To stop the virus from spreading further, some countries have even blocked their international borders (Nicole et al, 2020). The statement sparked widespread concern, particularly among the poorest members of society, such as farmers and migrant laborers, who were left stranded and jobless overnight after being forced to leave their homes due to a lack of transportation. Despite the government's announcement of a 1.7 trillion-rupee rescue package, it was clear that a sizable portion of the populace would be looking for alternatives. Due to the clear effect of the lockdown, economists lowered GDP rates for the foreseeable future. However, because of the country's industry composition, which is dominated by unorganized marketplaces, it was predicted that the country will bounce back swiftly. In late March, organized-sector losses were estimated to be about nine trillion rupees, with losses expected to rise if the lockdown continues. Services and manufacturing, in particular travel and tourism, financial services, mining, and construction, were unsurprisingly the most affected industries, with decline rates of up to 23% between April and June 2020 (The Economic Times, 2020). The pandemic brought with it a great deal of uncertainty and ramifications for businesses all over the world. Despite the fact that India is ahead of the majority of countries in terms of its ability to adopt work-from-home policies, particularly in white collar jobs, job and earnings shortages, as well as pricing volatility, were expected. During the months of the lockdown, employment plummeted, eventually stabilizing as the economy in most sections of the country improved. Since March 2021, when the country was hit by the second wave of the pandemic, economic activity has been declining. As a result, GDP predictions were predicted to dwindle, resulting in losses of more than 38 billion dollars if local lockdowns were to last until June 2021 (Chandrasekhar, 2020. Unprecedented numbers of infections and deaths across the country prompted more lockdowns in some areas, putting a strain on the hospital system in the midst of political turmoil.

METHODOLOGY

Secondary data is used in this research work, such as blogs, newspaper articles, magazines, statements, journals, and so on. The usage of a thorough literature review procedure has been employed to carry out the current investigation. The literature review strategy is a well-established technique for secondary data base reviews. They provide as a firm foundation for future research. However, conducting a literature review and using the results for strategy purposes is always a challenge.

AS OF NOVEMBER 11, 2021, COVID-19 CASES WORLDWIDE

The coronavirus disease (COVID-19) outbreak had been confirmed in over 220 countries and territories as of November 11, 2021. The virus had infected about 252 million individuals globally, with five million people dying as a result. The United States, Brazil, and India are among the most badly afflicted countries. Peru experienced the most losses to COVID-19 up through November 11, 2021, based on a comparison of coronavirus mortality in 206 nations relative to their population. The virus has infected more than 251.4 million persons globally as of the same date, with more than five million deaths. COVID-19 test rates, on the other hand, can vary by country. Furthermore, when the number of deaths is compared to confirmed COVID-19 cases, significant disparities between nations emerge. The source appears to make no distinction between COVID-19's "Wuhan strain" (2019-nCOV), "the Kent mutation" (B.1.1.7), which first showed in the UK in late 2020, and the 2021 Delta variation (B.1.617.2) from India.

COVID-19'S ECONOMIC IMPACT IN INDIA

India's growth for FY2021 was initially revised downward by the World Bank (2016) and rating agencies, resulting in the lowest results India has seen in three decades since its economic liberalization in the 1990s. However, once the economic package was announced in mid-May, India's GDP predictions were revised downwards even further, signaling a deep recession. CRISIL predicted on May 26 that this will be India's worst recession since independence. According to State Bank of India analysis, the GDP contracted by more than 40% in Q1. The contraction will not be consistent; instead, it will vary depending on a variety of factors such as state and sector. The Ministry of Statistics announced GDP numbers for Q1 (April to June) FY21 on September 1, 2020, showing a decline of 24% compared to the same period the previous year. After the lockdown was imposed in 2020, an estimated 10 million migrant workers returned to their home countries. What was unexpected, however, was that neither the state nor the federal governments had any information about the migrant workers who lost their jobs and lives as a result of the lockdown. Apart from creating up a digital-centralized database system, the government offered assistance to migrant workers who returned to their homes during the second wave of the boom. The second wave of Covid-19 has highlighted and exacerbated existing economic vulnerabilities in India. Except for a few essential services and activities, India's $2.9 trillion economy stays closed throughout the lockdown. The lockdown had a disastrous effect on the economy by closing down stores, cafés, factories, transportation services, and business establishments. The global epidemic has had the greatest impact on the informal economy.

We had a protracted national lockdown and a substantially lower number of peak cases in the first wave. Manufacturing and the urban economy had ground to a halt, while the rural sector remained active due to less restrictions. As a result, agriculture, which employs 58 percent of our population and is the primary driver of our rural economy, has continued to develop. Agriculture gained even more from a good rainfall and cheaper and more readily available labour. In FY21, our agricultural economy increased by 3.4 percent while the entire economy decreased by 7.7 percent, according to GDP estimates. The Indian economy was already in trouble when the second wave arrived. The covid-19, when combined with the humanitarian situation and the government's silence, has revealed and exacerbated existing disparities in the Indian economy. The economy will continue to decline over the next four quarters, and a recession is unavoidable. According to studies performed by the Centre for Monitoring Indian Economy, jobless rates rose sharply during the April-June quarter of 2021, ranging from 7.9% to 13%. MSMEs are closing their doors as a result of the economy's effects. Millions of jobs have been lost permanently, reducing consumer spending.

In the third quarter of fiscal year 2021, India's quarterly GDP is expected to expand by 0.4 percent over the same quarter the previous fiscal year. This was a substantial improvement over the period between April and June 2020, when the country was put under lockdown to contain the epidemic and GDP growth fell by about 25% compared to the previous year.

WHAT IMPACT HAS COVID-19 HAD IN VARIOUS INDUSTRIES?

Most Indian enterprises are impacted by the new coronavirus (COVID-19), both directly and indirectly, with considerable financial reporting implications associated with increased economic uncertainty and risk. Many firms' activities may have been directly impacted by pandemic-prevention initiatives.

Automobile Sector

India's automakers are once again under pressure, as sales have plummeted. According to a research by Emkay Global Financial Services, the vehicle sector in India is projected to continue under pressure in the near term as a result of the Covid-19 crisis. Automobile sales will be heavily influenced by consumer sentiments because they are discretionary products. Citizens' consumer mood is currently low, and demand for non-essential items is likely to decrease much lower. The passenger vehicle segment may suffer as a result of this.

Manufacturing

During both the first and second waves, manufacturing was hit hard. The majority of the manufacturing sector had to work at a reduced capacity or shut down in order to control the spread of the coronavirus. Manufacturing of non-essentials was hurt harder and for a longer period of time. Fears of protracted lockdowns prompted a return to the communities. Furthermore, following the initial wave, the global and local supply networks had not entirely adjusted. This has resulted in increasing raw material costs for both small and large businesses.

Service Sector

The services sector has been the backbone of the Indian economy in the last two decades, accounting for more than half of the country's GDP. However, our service and knowledge-based industries are based on the 18th-century manufacturing industry notion that proximity and discipline of workers to the factory are vital in achieving good production. Our software engineers and telemarketing employees follow the same mindset. With the advent of the internet, this notion has shown to be an obsolete relic from the past. Now, until 4G internet is available, the workforce can be decentralized, and everyone can work from wherever. Due to the impact of the coronavirus, the service industry in India experienced the sharpest fall in growth rate compared to previous years (COVID-19). During the lockdown, trade, hotels, transportation, storage, and communication bore the brunt of the damage. The decrease eased in the first half of 2021, and the economy began to develop again. This segment grew by about 40% in the second quarter of 2021 compared to the same quarter in 2020 (India Today, 2021).

Oil and Gas

The Indian oil and gas business is important in the global perspective; it is the world's third-largest energy user, trailing only the United States and China, and accounts for 5.2 percent of global oil demand. The nationwide lockdown reduced demand for transportation fuels (which represent for two-thirds of total demand in the oil and gas sector), as car and industrial manufacture plummeted and goods and passenger mobility (both bulk and personal) fell. Despite the fact that crude prices fell during this time, the government increased excise and special excise tax to compensate for the revenue loss, as well as the road cess.

Pharmaceuticals

Since the onset of the Covid-19 pandemic, the pharmaceutical sector has been on the increase, particularly in India, the world's largest producer of generic pharmaceuticals. It has been booming in India, exporting Hydroxychloroquine around the world, especially to the US, UK, Canada, and the Middle East, with a market size of $55 billion by the start of 2020. Prices of raw materials imported from China have recently risen as a result of the pandemic. Because of the industry's strong reliance on imports, a broken supply chain, and labour shortages caused by social alienation, generic medications have been hit the worst. Simultaneously, the pharmaceutical business is struggling due to government-imposed export limits on vital pharmaceuticals, equipment, and PPE kits in order to secure adequate supplies for the country. The rising demand for these treatments, combined with their limited availability, makes matters more difficult. In such a difficult time, easing the financial load on pharmaceutical businesses, reducing tax burdens, and addressing the labour shortage could be the deciding factors.

Fiscal Deficit

The Covid-19 pandemic has had little impact on our deficit and disinvestment targets. Finance Minister Nirmala Sitharaman established a fiscal deficit target of 6.8% for 2021-2022 in this year's government budget. India's fiscal deficit for 2020-21 has risen to 9.5 percent of GDP, up from 3.5 percent previously forecast. Our finance minister has stated that by 2025-26, he will achieve a fiscal deficit of 4.5 percent of GDP by boosting tax collections through higher tax compliance and asset monetization. The fiscal deficit for 2021-22 and 2022-23 was 3.3 percent and 3.1 percent, respectively, according to the government's medium-term fiscal policy statement released in February 2020.

Stock Markets

India's stock markets suffered their greatest losses in history on March 23, 2020. The SENSEX dropped 4000 points (13.15 percent), while the NSE NIFTY dropped 1150 points (12.98 percent). However, on March 25, one day after the Prime Minister ordered a complete 21-day lock-down, the SENSEX achieved its largest gains in 11 years, adding a value of 4.7 lakh crore (US$62 billion) to investors' portfolios. The financial markets in India soared sharply again on April 8, following optimistic indications from Wall Street that the pandemic may have hit its peak in the United States.

Education Sector

The Covid-19 Pandemic has caught up with the worldwide education system. The Indian Education sector has demonstrated remarkable resilience, including 33 crore students, 1,000 colleges, 45,000 colleges, over 15 lakh schools, and more than one crore teacher. The Pandemic of Covid-19 has restricted classroom teaching and learning history in schools, colleges, and other educational institutions and has turned into digital education. This crisis, on the other hand, has fostered creativity in the education sector. The Covid 19 times has brought in a new wave – a digital boom in the whole education sector. The crisis exacerbates existing education differences, limiting opportunities for many of the most disadvantaged children, young people and adult's girls, migrants, people with disabilities, and displaced persons living in rural and poor areas - to continue their education. An additional 23.8 million children and youth (pre-primary to tertiary) will drop out or fail to attend school due solely to the economic effects of the Pandemic. The disruption was necessary for the higher education sector, as many Indians study second only to China, studying abroad, particularly in the worst-affected countries, the USA, UK, Australia, and China.

Food and Agriculture

The Covid-19 pandemic has had little impact on our fiscal deficit and disinvestment goals. Finance Minister Nirmala Sitharaman declared a 6.8% fiscal deficit target for 2021-2022 in this year's government budget. India's fiscal deficit for 2020-21 has increased to 9.5 percent of GDP, up from 3.5 percent previously forecast. Our finance minister has pledged that by 2025-26, we would have a fiscal deficit of 4.5 percent of GDP, thanks to increased tax compliance and asset monetization. According to the government's medium-term fiscal policy announcement, the fiscal deficits for 2021-22 and 2022-23 were 3.3 percent and 3.1 percent, respectively, in February 2020.

Power Sector

The Indian economy is expected to lose 10–31 percent of its GDP depending on how long the lockdown lasts. This method can also be used to estimate economic losses in other places. COVID-19's effects on electricity consumption, supply, and CO2 emissions from the power industry. Daily supply from coal-fired power plants decreased by 26% during the lockdown, resulting in a possible emissions reduction of 15–65 MtCO2 depending on the duration of the lockdown (Kanitkar, 2020).

Real Estate and Construction Sector

During the second wave, real estate and construction industries began to be disrupted as a huge number of migrant workers departed urban regions. As of 2020, the situation for this industry has not been dire (ILO, (2021).

ECONOMIC PACKAGE

In a speech to the country on May 12, the Prime Minister suggested that the coronavirus issue should be viewed as an opportunity, emphasizing domestic products and "economic self-reliance," or an Atmanirbhar Bharat (self-reliant India) through the Atmanirbhar Bharat Abhiyaan (self-reliant India Mission). The Finance Minister began setting out the details of the Prime Minister's vision the next day, and this would continue for the next few days. The goal, according to the Finance Minister, is to "spur growth" and "self-reliance," but "self-reliant India does not imply shutting off from the rest of the world."

The economic package included a mix of reforms, infrastructure development, corporate support, and a small amount of direct monetary assistance (Yadav, S. (2020). The package's "collateral-free loans" were designed to "resume corporate activity and protect jobs." Changes to FDI policy, power sector privatization, provident fund contributions, and steps to make doing business easier were also announced. State-level land reforms, which were not included in the economic package, are also part of the overall changes (Sharma, R, (2020).

WHAT IMPACT HAS COVID-19 HAD ON INDIA'S INCOME, CONSUMPTION, POVERTY, AND UNEMPLOYMENT?

The COVID-19 epidemic triggered a global economic downturn, with millions of people losing their jobs and livelihoods. COVID-19 has highlighted and amplified societal imbalances (Corak, 2020). The epidemic put the world into survival mode in less than three months, with countries battling to keep the coronavirus out of their country and from spreading among people (Baker et al, (2020). The impact has been more negative for the people of all regions and groups, but for the poor and vulnerable. Efforts to monitor the spread of the virus have led governments worldwide to take measures that are necessary to promote social division, including the closing of economic activities. Indian migrant workers encountered numerous challenges (Sengupta et al (2020). Millions of migrant workers faced a loss of income, food shortages, and uncertainty about their future when companies and businesses were shut down due to the country's lockdown (Kapur, I. (2020). Many of them, as well as their families, went hungry as a result of this. Thousands of people then began walking home because they had no other option owing to the lockout. As a result, the federal and state governments took different steps to assist them, including arranging transportation for them. With the commencement of lockdowns in countries, states, and cities, existing inequities became more apparent, with freshly laid-off workers joining long lines for government assistance (Scheiber et al., 2020). Despite the fact that lockdown policies have altered everyone's lives in all countries that have implemented them, migrant workers have encountered greater obstacles than the native population since they have become more vulnerable to social, economic, and psychological hardship.

In India, an informal sector with little to no social security safeguards is rather vulnerable and unregulated. The COVID-19 crisis may have a long-term effect on informal sector jobs as they are the most marginalized groups and are more likely to be subjected to the new world pandemic (International Labor Organisation 2020). The lives of women migrant workers and their families in India have borne significant burdens of COVID-19 (Choudhary, (2020).

According to the World Economic Forum, the country has a population of 139 million migrants. The International Labour Organization (ILO) estimated that 400 million employees will be displaced as a result of the pandemic and the lockdown. Lockdowns rendered them jobless, putting their lives in jeopardy. Uttar Pradesh and Bihar are the states with the most migrants, followed by Rajasthan and Madhya Pradesh. The cities of Mumbai and Delhi are the most popular destinations for migrants. Women move for marriage, while most males go for job. The majority of migrant workers are low-wage workers in the manufacturing and construction industries.

According to government reports, the FCI godowns had enough food grain to feed the impoverished for at least a year and a half. While government programmes promised that the impoverished would receive increased rations as a result of the lockdown, the distribution system failed since ration cards are area-specific and fair price shops were mostly inaccessible. As of mid-April, the 'One Nation, One Ration Card' scheme had only been deployed in a few states. While the programme permitted migratory workers to obtain free food grains wherever in the country, few people were aware of it.

Furthermore, the technique required biometric authentication, which was dropped due to concerns about the virus spreading through common fingerprint sensors. Many people in Telangana were unable to receive the ration due to a lack of Aadhaar cards. As a result of the lockdown, many people were left without food and money. According to a poll released by 'The Hindu,' 96 percent of migrant laborers did not receive government supplies, and 90 percent did not receive earnings during the lockdown.

Minister of Labour and Employment, revealed in Parliament on 14 September 2020 that data received from state governments suggested that an estimated 10 million migrants attempted to return home as a result of the COVID-19 epidemic and subsequent lockdown (Ganguly et al, (2020). On 15 September 2020, he declared in Parliament that no statistics was kept on the number of migrants in the country who had perished or become unemployed as a result of the pandemic. Despite the government's rollout of special trains and buses later in May, migrant laborer's preferred to travel in huge groups in the cargo compartments of trucks and containers, or on foot. Due to hunger, they did not wait for their time to board the government-provided transportation. They also believed that by returning to their hometowns, they would be able to resume farming and take up minor employment under the MGNREGA. In rural regions, the use of mobile and broadband data has more than doubled thanks to BharatNet.

Despite government promises and plans to provide jobs in rural areas, several migratory workers returned to the city after lockdown restrictions were eased as part of Unlock 1.0 in June, owing to a lack of work in their hometowns. A huge number of them were on their way back to Mumbai. The resumption of regular railway services contributed to this as well. Cities, too, reported severe labour shortages, particularly in the construction industry. According to a research performed in April–May, 77 percent of migrant workers were willing to return to cities in search of job. The return of migrants to cities is expected to aid in the recovery of the economy, which has been hit hard.

DISCUSSION AND CONCLUSION

This Pandemic delayed both private investment and consumption, causing job and economic disruption. By establishing a 5 trillion economies by 2025, the 2019-2020 Economic Survey proposes increasing network goods exports, incorporating "assemble in India for the world" into Make in India, and creating 40 million employments. (Economic Survey, 2020). India's economic and budgetary recovery will be jeopardized if the outbreak worsens over time or the number of patients increases drastically. The initial wave of infections, as well as the resulting lockdown measures, had a huge impact on commodities and the car industry. It made a major resurgence in the second half of 2021. This Pandemic delayed both private investment and consumption, causing job and economic disruption. By establishing a 5 trillion economies by 2025, the 2019-2020 Economic Survey proposes increasing network goods exports, incorporating "assemble in India for the world" into Make in India, and creating 40 million employments.

Half of Indian households are still dependent on agriculture, either directly or indirectly. Unemployment payments are not paid to people who work in the subsistence sector since they are not covered by social security. During difficult times, the government is required to priorities its essential necessities. They will bounce back if these needs are met. To alleviate the suffering of the poor and vulnerable, the government must concentrate on effective relief measures. Lifting a partial lockout in industrial homes and the building industry will allow production to begin. Workers must be able to put their trust in the government and industry by guaranteeing that their health and economic demands are met. India's labour regulations are antiquated, with some going back to the nineteenth century. Complicated labour legislation in India is responsible for keeping small manufacturers alive and preventing job growth.

Because of the complexities of the legislation, the industry employs workers unofficially, resulting in lower wages. In 2018, India's jobless rate reached a 45-year high of 8.1 percent. Prior to the contemporary state's existence, India's social protection was largely community-based. The old, sick, and defenseless have been taken care of in society (in towns and villages). Sharing food or donating food as charity was a regular occurrence. However, the government agreed to fund a substantial percentage of the assistance provided by local philanthropists who had already performed several charity acts for the crisis society. The formation of a new state halted population-based social security programmes. We need to create a social safety net for everybody who is supported by the government. Various social security programmes exist.

The global COVID-19 recession in 2020 and 2021 was widely expected, as it provided global proof of the impending closure of all economic operations – production, consumption, and business – in order to monitor COVID-19 spread.

The shutdown design is unique to COVID-19 because of a supply shock, a demand shock, and a market shock. The timing and size of government support, the level of corporate debt, and how low demand is fulfilled all play a role in an economy's recovery. All crises, on the other hand, provide a once-in-a-lifetime opportunity to reconsider how an individual, a group, or a society will develop. The Indian economy must adopt sustainable growth models that emphasize self-assurance, inclusive institutions, and ecologically responsible regulations.

REFERENCES

Baker, S. R., Bloom, N., Davis, S. J., Kost, K., Sammon, M., & Viratyosin, T. (2020). *The unprecedented stock market reaction to COVID-19*. National Bureau of Economic Research Working Paper, 26945. https://www.nber.org/papers/w26945

Chandrasekhar, C. P., & Ghosh, J. (2002). *The Market that Failed*. Leftword Books.

Choudhari, R. (2020). COVID 19 pandemic: Mental health challenges of internal migrant workers of India. *Asian Journal of Psychiatry*, *54*, 102254. doi:10.1016/j.ajp.2020.102254 PMID:32593122

Corak, M. (2020). COVID-19 is not the great leveller, it's the great revealer. *Economics for Public Policy, 13*. https://milescorak.com/2020/04/13/covid-19-is-not-the-great-leveller-its-the-great-revealer/

Ganguly, D., Misra, S., & Goli, S. (2020). *India's COVID-19 episode: resilience, response, impact and lessons*. https://www.nytimes.com/2020/05/30/opinion/sunday/india-coronavirus-lockdown-inequality.html

Kanitkar, T. (2020). The COVID-19 lockdown in India: Impacts on the economy and the power sector. *Global Transitions*, *2*, 150–156. doi:10.1016/j.glt.2020.07.005

Kapur, I. (2020). COVID 19 and Migration: A Case of Indian Unorganized Laborers. *COVID 19 and Migrant Health, 35*.

Krishnan, C., Baba, M. M., Singh, G., & Srivastava, A. (2021). COVID-19 and the Marginal People of India. Handbook of Research on the Impact of COVID-19 on Marginalized Populations and Support for the Future, 255.

Nicole, M., Alsafi, Z., Sohrabi, C., Kerwan, A., Al-Jabir, A., Losifidis, C., ... Agha, R. (2020). The socio-economic implications of the coronavirus and covid-19 pandemic: A review. *International Journal of Surgery*, *78*, 185–193. doi:10.1016/j.ijsu.2020.04.018 PMID:32305533

Sahoo, P., & Ashwani. (2020). COVID-19 and Indian Economy: Impact on Growth, Manufacturing, Trade and MSME Sector. *Global Business Review*, *21*(5), 1159–1183. doi:10.1177/0972150920945687

Scheiber, N., Schwartz, N., & Hsu, T. (2020). White-collar quarantine' over virus spotlights class divide. *The New York Times*. https://nyti.ms/2Jm2SVa

Sohini & Jha. (2020). Social Policy COVID 19 and impoverished migrants: Challenges and prospects in Locked Down India. *The International Journal of Community and Social Development, 2*(2).

Sharma, R. (2020, May 30). The rich love India's lockdown. For the poor it's another story. *The New York Times*.

Singh, B. P. (n.d.). Impact of COVID-19 on Rural Economy in India. *SSRN Electronic Journal*. doi:10.2139/ssrn.3609973

Yadav, S. (2020). Precarity as a coping strategy of the Gonds: A study of insecure and long-distance seasonal migration in Central India. *Indian Journal of Human Development*, *14*(1), 7–22. doi:10.1177/0973703020909328

India Today. (2021). *Covid derails economy: 5 sectors that have been hit hard.* https://www.indiatoday.in/business/story/5-sectors-hit-hard-as-covid-19-derails-economic-recovery-1796662-2021-04-30

The World Bank. (2016). *India's Poverty Profile*. https://www.worldbank.org/en/news/infographic/2016/05/27/india-s-poverty-profile

Chapter 9
Facets of the Gender Gap in Labour Force Participation and Economic Empowerment Disruption:
Study of the Competing Needs of Family and Work

S. K. Baral
https://orcid.org/0000-0003-2061-714X
Indira Gandhi National Tribal University, India

Durga Madhab Mahapatra
FM College (Autonomous), India

Soumendra Kumar Patra
Ravenshaw University, India

ABSTRACT

According to Centre for Monitoring Indian Economy (CMIE) data, the average employment for January 2019-March 2020 was 403 million, which declined to 282 million in April 2020 and recovered steadily thereafter to reach 393million by August 2020. In India, female labour force participation is abysmally poor and has declined over the years, despite a rise in education. The causes for this are complex and, aside from objective factors, include a whole variety of social and cultural aspects. One of the factors causing this is the social mentality of women becoming homemakers. Furthermore, the scarcity of schooling and work-oriented courses, the lack of mobility, and sexism in the workplace have been deterrents to women's access to the public workspace. Therefore, initiatives that aim to fix this void need to be holistic. Legislation alone is not enough, and to close this gap, all stakeholders should join hands. The chapter attempts to analyse facets of the gender gap in labour force participation and economic empowerment disruption through the pandemic.

DOI: 10.4018/978-1-7998-8258-9.ch009

INTRODUCTION

The corresponding numbers are 360, 256 and 353 million for men, and 43, 26 and 39 million for women, respectively. Male employment is thus 98% in August, and female employment is 91%, the respective pre-pandemic average. The normalisation of WFH, without concomitant changes that reduce the burden of domestic chores and care work, and an increase in paid work opportunities is unlikely to raise women's participation in the labour force. As the pandemic forces our economy to hit the "reset" button, paying attention to job creation with a gender equity lens is essential for India to realise it tremendous gender dividend. International Girls' Day is an international day of celebration proclaimed by the United Nations; it is sometimes referred to as Girls' Day and International Girls' Day. Progress for teenage girls has not kept pace with the realities they face today and many of these differences have been reinforced by COVID-19. Under the theme "My Voice, Our Equal Future" this year-2020, let's take the opportunity to be motivated by what teenage girls see as the shift they want, the strategies they are leading and demanding around the globe, big and small. The National Sample Survey Office's time-use survey report released last month reveals that Indian women spend nearly four hours more on unpaid work than men, with grim implications for women's workforce participation. In addition, the minimum first step in recognising that the joint duty of men and women is parenting and childcare. The paper aims to detail the involvement of work and gender sensitivity in the Gender Equality Index-2018.

In 2017, India's Gender Inequality Index scored 0.524, placing it in the bottom 20% of ranking countries for that year. In order to hold the family together, about 65 percent of Indian men believe women should tolerate abuse, and women often deserve to be beaten. The International Men and Gender Equality Survey (IMAGES) questionnaire stated in January 2011 that 24 percent of Indian men had committed sexual harassment during their lives at some point. Women are constitutionally entitled to equal rights in India's social context, but there is a great need to raise society's awareness of gender issues so that there is no problem. Women have the right to be free from sexism, abuse and violence. Removing the barriers of an unsafe atmosphere will help women, as individuals and contributors to employment, societies, and economies, fulfil their potential. In addition, for workers who became new fathers, Zomato rolled out 26 weeks of paid paternity leave. Many private corporations, too, give paternity leave, without the prodding of legislation. If more women are not to drop out of the job grid, the post COVID reality makes it much more important for workplaces to allow men to take more responsibilities at home. But the primary reason for encouraging more men to step up is not a utilitarian calculation. The advancement of equality has been evaluated for far too long by the number of women accommodated in productivity and performance systems. The hierarchy that devalues the function of treatment, which, despite its drudgery, is central to the messiness and sense of being human, has not been challenged. It is a hierarchy that gives rise to distant patriarchs and men who fear emotional life. For Indian men and women, paternity leave that gives them time to become fathers is a win-win for both. "As per New data released by the Centre for Disease Control and Prevention's National Centre for Health Statistics surveying nearly 32,000 adults and 6,800 children across more than 33,000 households reveals that in 2019 women were more likely to experience symptoms of depression and anxiety than men, and more likely to receive counselling or therapy, or take prescription medication, to promote their mental health" (Khatri, Tina 2020).

Table 1. Stated the status of Country wise Gap to reach Gender equality

Country	Men	Gap to reach Gender Equality
Sweden	44.70	5.30
Norway	43.90	6.10
US	43.40	6.60
France	38.90	11.10
UK	36.10	13.90
China	28.40	21.60
Ghana	23.60	26.40
India	9.50	40.50
Pakistan	8.90	41.10

Source: NSO Time Use Survey 2019; Care Work and Care Jobs for the future of decent work (ILO).

On average, women accounted for 39 per cent of the population worldwide during 2019-20, but holding just 28 per cent of managerial roles. In the two areas with the lowest number of women in managerial roles, Northern Africa and Western Asia, and Central and Southern Asia, women barely achieved less than half the global average of 13 percent of such positions.

Table 2. Stated the workforce worldwide as regards to women in managerial positions

Particulars	Percentage
WORLD	27.89%
LatAm & Caribbean	39.00%
Australia and NZ	38.06%
Europe & N America	37.75%
E & SE Asia	32.10%
Sub- Saharan Africa	30.06%
Oceania*	27.38%
C & Southern Asia	13.23%
N Africa & W Asia	11.75%

Lat-Am. Latin America Na Northern. E Eastern SE South-eastern C Central W: Western. "Excluding Australia and New Zealand Data refer to women under categories CEOs, senior officials and legislators, administrative and commercial managers and production and specialised services managers". (*Source: "UN Department of Economic and Social Affairs"*)

Table 3. Stated the Women Law Makers in Lower Houses

Rank	Country	Percentage of Women in Lower/single Houses	Number
1	Rwanda	63	49
2	Cuba	53.2	322
3	Bolivia	53.1	69
4	Mexico	48.2	241
5	Grenada	48.7	7
38	UK	32.2	209
75	US	23.5	102
96	Pakistan	20.2	69

Source: "World Economic Forum, Global Gender Gap Report 2018"

In western countries, the growth of women's political advancement over the past decade has reversed somewhat. (a) Chancellor Angela Merkel of Germany is the largest female head of government serving in Germany. (b) As her preferred heir, 'Annegret kramp-karrenbauer.' (c) Nancy Pelosi has become the most influential woman in American politics, and President Trump's de facto opposition leader. (d)

Zacinda Ardern, New Zealand's Prime Minister, has proven that motherhood is no obstacle to the top Job, becoming the second leading history to give birth while in office (The Economic Times Magazine, 17th to 23rd, 2019).

INDIA'S SUSTAINABLE GOAL AND GENDER EQUALITY: AN ASSESSMENT

As per IMF report 2017 found "that India has one of the lowest female labour force participation rates". "At around 33 percent at the national level in 2012, India's female labour force participation rate is well below the global average of around 50 percent and the East Asian average of around 63 percent". "Further, it has been on a declining trend in India, particularly since 2004-05" (Kochhar, Kalpana 2020). However, the concerns about inequality and injustice women face in various societies don't require a league consisting only of economists and policy-analysts. Both historically and contemporarily, philosophers and literary figures world over have reaffirmed their interest through their characters in these overwhelming problems. From Helsinki conference the world travelled through Millennium Development Goals and reached in2015 more comprehensive and inclusive Sustainable Development Goals (SDGs). "Goal 5 of Sustainable Development Goals 2015 aims to eliminate all forms of discrimination and violence against women in the public and private spheres and to undertake reforms to give women equal rights to economic resources and access to ownership of property". "Descent work, equal access to education, and representation in political and economic decision-making processes are the rights women must enjoy". "Investment in the empowerment of women results not only in making progress on Goal-5of the Sustainable Development Goals but also in fuelling sustainable economic development". The commitment of India to implement the Sustainable Development Goals was spelt out through the speech and commitment made by Prime Minister of India at the UN Summit for the adoption of post 2015 Development Agenda. The Government of India, Prime minister focussed "Today, much of India's development agenda is mirrored in the Sustainable Development Goals." Moreover, as the assault on poverty is more emphasised, empowerment requires not only extended traditional development programmes, but also a new age of inclusion and empowerment, turning remote aspirations into immediate possibilities. In addition, the new bank accounts for $180 million; direct transfer of benefits, micro-enterprises and micro-finance, building on the power of digital and mobile apps, with an emphasis on basics, accommodation, electricity, water and sanitation for all. This is not only essential for welfare, but also for human dignity. Development is intrinsically linked to women's empowerment and starts with a massive girl-child education programme that has become the mission of every family.

The Government of India has recognised, amid others, two important ways to empower women: Economic empowerment through participation in economic activities and opportunities and second through mitigation of educational deprivations. The schemes chalked out and implemented broadly address these requirements and thereby endeavour to ensure that women gain equal rights, opportunities and access to resources. The first and foremost thing is their safety, security and economic empowerment. Towards that end, schemes like "Mahila Police Volunteers (MPV) envisaging engagement of Mahila Police Volunteers in States/UTs who act as a link between police and community and facilitate women in distress"; Pradhan Mantri Ujjawala Yojana empowering women below poverty line and protecting their health by providing LPG cylinder free of cost, Pradhan Mantri Sukanya Samriddhi Yojna aims at economic empowerment of girls by opening their bank accounts and enabling their parents to save funds for their female child's education and marriage. Beti Bachao, Beti Padhao Yojana that came into being in January 2015, drives at generating awareness and improving the efficacy of welfare services for girl child. "Further, safe motherhood intervention under National Health Mission with the objective of reducing maternal and neo-natal mortality among poor pregnant women" (Srivastav, K.K. 2020).

GENDER SENSITIVITY: A LONG AWAY

To ensure this, gender awareness will go a long way. Gender sensitization is the shift in behaviour in order to build gender equity with greater understanding and empathy. Not only does abuse of any form affect women's physical, emotional, sexual, and reproductive health, but it also adversely affects decisions regarding their self-esteem, ability to work, and fertility. Abuse hinders women's inclusion in micro and macro-level growth and planning projects. Sensitive, ineffective, unethical and unacceptable justice processes and law enforcement machinery do not tackle different forms of crime (Satywan Saurabh, 2020). The National Family Health Survey indicates that 30 percent of women in India have witnessed physical abuse since the age of 15 in the 15 to 49 age range. Furthermore, the study shows that about 31 percent of married women have witnessed their husbands' physical, sexual, or emotional abuse. Not only in the womb and infancy, but in every field of life, women are discriminated against. Women are forced to face the pressures and constraints of their everyday lives, to ensure their capacity for personal growth and independence and gender equality, to live a better and more dignified life, to make society inclusive and safe. The first step. Gender sensitization will help to dissipate certain theories that we are male. "Gender sensitization and widespread social change are needed to end gender crimes" (Satywan Saurabh, 2020) Odisha has achieved the shady variance of claiming the 3rd place in the country as far as crime against women is concerned, as per the latest report of the National Crime Records Bureau (NCRB). According to the NCRB report, for every one lakh population in Odisha, 91.3 number of crimes are committed against women while the conviction rate stands at negligible 8.3 per cent. Similarly, cybercrime has also increased by nearly 76 percent in the state in 2019 as compared to 2018, the latest data released by the national crime records bureau (NCRB) revealed. Also, according to the Odisha government's Economic Survey report 2018-19, women earn nearly 3 times less than men in the state which is a worrying trend. Women are still not considered a skilled workforce. "According to WHO estimates, less than 40 percent of women experiencing violence seek the help of any kind". "Women who ask for help go to family and friends and see very few formal institutions and systems, such as police and health services". "Less than 10 percent of those women who sought help to experience the violence appealed to the police". "The latest data indicates that police file charge sheets in 86% of rape cases but trial courts are only able to settle 13% of pending rape cases with a reduced conviction rate of 32%". "In cases of child rape, the conviction rate is 34.2% and the pendency is 82.1%" (Satywan Saurabh, 2020).

'L'Oreal' Paris, a French cosmetics brand, has unveiled its standard intervention training programme against street harassment in India. As part of its "Stand Up" campaign, which has already been launched in various countries such as France, Spain, Italy and Mexico, the company linked up with NGO Breakthrough to provide on-the-ground training in the region. Singer Neha Bhasin will also come up with a song titled Kehnderehnde, which is against cyber bullying. The goal of the track is to highlight problems such as slut-shaming, misogyny, cyber bullying, and confining stereotypical Stan to women. One should lift his/her voice against misconduct. In addition, Laxmii bomb films a satire of sorts against outdated traditions and rituals, but due to the sheer plasticity of the plot, the attempt fails itself. The film also tries to make the noises about the transgender community politically right, as well as Hindu Muslim harmony (Deshpande, Ashwani, 2020).

The International Labour Organisation (ILO) estimates that two-third of the job lost globally due to Covid-19 belongs to Women. The survey finds that achieving Gender Parity at work can add 28 trillion dollars or 26 percent to global GDP by 2025. India alone could add 770 billion dollars or 18 percent to its GDP by 2025 if it enabled half of its productive workforce women. Further, the OECD estimates that in Denmark and Sweden increases in women's labour force participation accounts for 0.25 to 0.40 percent points of annual growth in per capita GDP over the last four decades; to put that into dollars. The current GDP per capita in Denmark and Sweden about $55,000 to 60000 would otherwise have been $5000 to 6000 lowers. However, there is significant cost to countries and firms from the gaps in economic empowerment between men and women. "The Gender gaps in labour force participation estimated by IMF; the result in income losses of 27 percent in the Middle East and North Africa, 23 percent in south Asia, 17 percent in Latin America and the Caribbean, 15 percent in East Asia and the Pacific, 14 percent in Europe and Central Asia and 12 percent in sub-Saharan Africa". Moreover, Society plays an important role in creating a safe environment for women. Giving birth to gender sensitive children will create a safe society. After the "Nirbhaya" incident, the UN human rights chief said against rape and violence, women in India have a "national problem" that would require a "national solution". Better policing, fast-track courts, speedy punishment of time. Needs because each can serve as one. Public places should be made safe for all. "Girls and girls should be raised in an atmosphere of freedom and a culture of mutual respect". "It is important to implement and implement and implement policies that promote gender equality by ending discrimination against women in marriage, divorce and custody laws, inheritance laws, and ownership of assets". "The focus should be on what can be done, what is currently lacking, and the constant effort to measure the results otherwise this outrage will pass without even meaningful change" (Satywan Saurabh, 2020). "The cruelly by husband and Relatives under Section 498 A of India Penal code constituted the biggest percentage of registered crimes against women 30.9 percentage followed by Assault 21.80 percentage and Kidnapping and Abduction 17.90 parentage respectively" (Shah, Ajay, 2020).

Table 4. Stated the Pending Cases as per Crime in India Report-2019

Time Period	Assault	Rape	Cruelty by Husband and Relatives
Up to 6 Months	14,866	6,161	24,235
6 Months to a Year	13,646	4,994	17,976
1 Year to 3 Years	5,632	3,060	10,290
More than 3 Years	944	746	1,941

Source: Crime in India Report-2019, NCRB

Table 5. Stated the Crime Against women as per Crime Report in India-2019

Sl.	Crimes	Number	Percentage of all registered crime against women
1	Cruelly by Husband and Relatives	1.25.298	30.9
2	Assault on women	88,367	21.80
3	Kidnapping and Abduction	72,780	17.8
4	Rape	32,033	7.90

Source: Crime Report in India-2019. NCRB

The Indian women increased their participation in paid work between April and July 2020 because the new normal of "work from home" (WFH) allowed them to combine their domestic and employment responsibilities. This sounded hopeful because women's (in)ability to work outside the nomocratically intertwined with their predominant responsibility for domestic chores and unpaid care work. "Historically, women's LFP has increased when the time cost of domestic /unpaid care work is reduced, or is shared more equally with men, or made more compatible with market work". "National-level data reveal that the pandemic has not succeeded in shifting the need of gender gaps in paid and unpaid work". The biggest contraction in employment was in April 2020.

The Time Use Survey- 2019 by the National Statistical office (NSO) reveals gender stereotypes continue to plague the country. Women still handle most of the unpaid domestic and caregiving work at home, both in rural and urban areas, while men continue to take up more employment and related activities outside the home. "An International Labour Organisation (ILO) report says that across the world, without exception, women perform three-fourth of the unpaid caregiving work-76.2 per cent of the total hours spent in such activity". Men in India and Pakistan handle the least amount of unpaid caregiving work. "Across the world, women continue to bear the burden of unpaid care work". "Women dedicate on average 3.2 times more time than men to unpaid care work: 4 hours and 25 minutes per day, against 1 hour and 23 minutes for men, according to ILO".

Table 6. Stated the most unpaid domestic work is done by women

Rural + Urban	Male	Female	Person*
Most unpaid domestic work is done by women (%)	26.1	81.2	53.2
Women also spend nearly thrice the time on such work (in mins)	97	299	248
Women do most of the unpaid caregiving work (%)	14	27.6	20.7
They spend more than twice the time on caregiving (in mins)	76	134	114

*person refers to the proportion in the overall population
Source: "NSO Time Use Survey 2019; Care Work and Care Jobs for the future of decent work (ILO)"

Table 7. Stated most Men continue to work outside the house

Rural + Urban	Male	Female	Person*
Employment and related activities (%)	57.3	18.4	38.2
Women lag behind learning	23.9	19.8	21.9
But socialising and communication are democratic activities (%)	91.4	91.3	91.3

*person refers to the proportion in the overall population
Source: NSO Time Use Survey 2019; Care Work and Care Jobs for the future of decent work (ILO)

India is committed to the divergence and inclusion of women in the sharing of pavers and to putting political power in place. Their rights are safer, and gender justice is greater. But in 2010, Rajya Sabha passed the bill in parliament and state legislatures for a 33 percent reservation for women. The Percentage of women ministers in 2014-15 (15.6%), 2015-16 (17.8%), 2016-17 (12.0%), 2017-18 (12.0%), 2018-19 (12.0%) and 2019-20(16.05%.) respectively. Women in India are hampered by (a) low level of Education (b) lack of access to health care (c) lack of employment and low social status, which manifest in crimes such as (a) rape (b) Female foeticide (c) dowry death and (d) domestic violence. However, As per NSO Time Use Survey 2019; Care Work and Care Jobs for the future of decent work(ILO).in both rural and urban areas, the pattern is the same – women provide most of the unpaid caregiving work(%) as in Rural(81.2 percent) and Urban (79.2 percent) respectively. The Gender equitable entrepreneurship development is the need of the recent time in realizing the true potential in India. It has been a thrilling journey, engaging with our extensive network of ground partners and friends to connect with the best women entrepreneurial talents.

OBJECTIVES OF THE STUDY

The study undertaken to fulfil the research objectives:

1. To explore the India's Sustainable Goal and Gender Equality.
2. To find the Gender Sensitivity as regards Global Gender equality Report-2019.

REVIEW OF LITERATURE

Srivastav, K.K. (2020) stated that The Government of India has recognised, amid others, two important ways to empower women: Economic empowerment through participation in economic activities and opportunities and second through mitigation of educational deprivations. The commitment of India to implement the Sustainable Development Goals was spelt out through the speech and commitment made by Prime Minister of India at the UN Summit for the adoption of post 2015 Development Agenda.

Pillay, Amritha (2020) stated a report by Bain & Company Google and AWE foundation on titled Can Carid-19 be the turning point to women employees in India? Further, "The report finds about 31 percent women citing personal challenges; 44 percent lack of customer order, 28 percent supply chain disruption, 24 percent limited access to workforce and 22 percent responded stated about financed crunch.

Rajivlochan, Meeta. (2020) stated the 2019 Safe City Index, prepared by the Economist Intelligence Unit, ranks Mumbai and Delhi as one of the worst cities where women's safety is concerned. The Index ranked cities on indicators of personal security, digital security and infrastructure security, among other things. All these have a multiplier effect on the position of women these can negatively affect their access to public spaces, jobs, and even how much leisure time they can spend. Indifference to concerns of women results in a difficult commute and poor childcare facilities.

DISCUSSION OF THE PAPER AND DATA ANALYSIS

Women entrepreneurs often have to work twice as hard to be taken as seriously as their male counterparts. They usually shy away from self-promotional. Women get a disproportionate share of opinions and feedback. When women set up a business, they also try to solve for the problem of gender disparity in the workforce by hiring more women. Women entrusted to go in the "Cockroach-mode" and invoke their extraordinary surviving skills. Disruptions due to Covid-19 has hit most business in the country, including those owned by women. "Mission Shakti like Women Help Desk at all 1535 police stations of the state, dedicated Women's Help desk at all 350 Tehsils to resolve revenue-related complaints of women and deployment of women personnel at these help desks". "Besides it was also decided to have 20 percent of women compulsorily in UP Police force for reaching out to women victims".

As per the Global Gender Gap report (2018) by World Economic Forum stated the rank as Western Europe (76), North America (73), Eastern Europe and Central Asia (71), "Latin America and the Caribbean (71), East Asia and the Pacific (68), Global Weighted Average (68), Sub-Saharan Africa (66), South Asia (66) and Middle East and North Africa (60)". "Further, it covers all 149 countries featured in the 2018 index". Moreover, it has been bringing out the Global Gender Gap Index since2006. "The index provides a framework for capturing the magnitude of gender-based disparities across four thematic dimensions or sub - divisions such as (a)Economic Participation and Opportunity, (b)Educational Attainment, (c) Health and Survival, and (d) Political Empowerment". Further, As can be seen, the gender gap is relatively small across countries when it comes to health but widens considerably when it comes to political empowerment or economic participation. However, India's overall score has improved, in two sub-categories-economic participation and health and survival-the gender gap has worsened.

Table 8. Stated the Gender Gaps of the leading countries in 2018-19

Country	Rank	Score
Iceland	1	0.858
Rwanda	6	0.804
South Africa	19	0.755
United States	51	0.720
Indonesia	85	0.691
Brazil	95	0.681
China	103	0.673
India	108	0.665
Saudi Arabia	141	0.590
Pakistan	148	0.550

Note: Covers all 149 countries featured in the 2018 index,
Source: The Global Gender Gap report (2018) by World Economic Forum

Table 9. Stated the Performance of India as regards to Global Gender Gap

	2006		2008		
	Rank	Score	Rank	Score	Average
Global Gender Gap score	98	0.601	108	0.665	
Economic participation and opportunity	110	0.397	142	0.385	0.586
Educational attainment	102	0.819	114	0.953	0.949
Health and survival	103	0.962	147	0.940	0.955
Political empowerment	20	0.227	19	0.382	0.223
Rank out	**115**		**149**		

Note: Covers all 149 countries featured in the 2018 index
Source: The Global Gender Gap report (2018) by World Economic Forum

Table 10. Stated the position of India in south Asia

Country	Overall rank	Overall score
Bangladesh	48	0.721
Sri Lanka	100	0.676
Nepal	105	0.671
India	108	0.665
Maldives	113	0.662
Bhutan	122	0.638
Pakistan	148	0.550

Note: Covers all 149 countries featured in the 2018 index,
Source: The Global Gender Gap report (2018) by World Economic Forum

Table 11. Stated the Rankings and Scored by each sub-Index as per Global Gender Gap Report-2018

Economic Participation and Opportunity			Educational Attainment		
Country	Rank	Score	Country	Rank	Score
Lao PDR	1	0.915	Brazil	1	1.000
China	86	0.653	South Africa	72	0992
Indonesia	96	0.629	China	111	0958
India	142	0.385	India	114	0.953
Iraq	149	0.264	Chad	149	0.575

Note: Covers all 149 countries featured in the 2018 index,
Source: The Global Gender Gap report (2018) by World Economic Forum

Table 12. Stated the Rankings and Scored by each sub-Index as per Global Gender Gap Report-2018

Health and survival					
Country	Rank	Score	Country	Rank	Score
Brazil	1	0.980	Rwanda	4	0.539
Indonesia	79	0.974	India	19	0.382
Pakistan	145	0.946	US	98	0.125
India	147	0.940	Brazil	112	0.101
China	149	0.915	Yemen	149	0.014

Note: Covers all 149 countries featured in the 2018 index,
Source: The Global Gender Gap report (2018) by World Economic Forum

Table 13. Stated the Council Ministers (women) in India

Year	Cabinet Minister	Minister of State
2014-15	23	22
2015-16	23	22
2016-17	26	49
2017-18	27	48
2018-19	25	49
2019-20	24	33

Source: NSSO and Lok Sabha Secretariat

Women entrepreneurs in India are too few in number such as the MAKERS India Report- State of Women in Tech Entrepreneurship in India, Venture Intelligence, Master card Index of Women Entrepreneurs 2019 report stated that only 7.4 percent of businesses in India are owned by women. But things are slowly starting to change. Here's a look at the scenario for women-led firms in the Indian start-up ecosystem, the investments they attract, the sectors they focus on and more. The funding in women-founder/co-founded start-ups accounted for a very small fraction of the total investments. "The total start-up investments $29.41 billion, funding in start-ups with at least one-woman founder $1.69 billion and funding in start-ups with at only one-woman founder with $480 billion". The Fin-tech tops the list followed by e-commerce in sector-wise focus of Women Tech Entrepreneurs such as (a) Fin-Tech companies (25.8 percent), (b) E-commerce firms(20.2percent) (c) Ed-Tech (18.0 percent), (d) Health-Tech (16.4 percent), Media (10.20 percent) and Food and Beverages (9.3 percent) respectively. Moreover, the few VCs, accelerators, incubators that help women entrepreneurs such as (a) She Capital, (b) Rebalance, (c) Encubay, (d) Excellerate HER, (e) WE HUB and Womennovator. The percentage of women founded/co-founded firms in top 150 funded start-ups. 2018-19(9.2 percent), 2019-20(13.7 percent) and 2020-21 as of November 2020 (17.8 percent). Notable Indian Unicorns with women as founder/co-founders such as (a) Divya Gokulnath, Co-founder, Byju's, (b) Falguni Nayar, Founder, Nykaa, (c) Radhika Aggarwal, co-founder, Shopclus, and (d) Gazal Kalra, co-founder, Rivigo. "The company Up Grad's organisational gender ratio of 30 percent women employees in 2019, has moved up to 34 percent so far in 2020". "The organisations sale force is already at gender parity". "This is higher than the combined share of women employees in 77 of the S&P BSE 100 index companies, which was at 22.51 percent for 2019" (Pillay, Amritha 2020).

CONCLUSION

The pandemic of Covid-19 has changed the workplace globally, but India's new standards are especially relevant. Millions of skilled female workers have been shut out by social norms that forced women to travel to their husband's places or remain with family in small towns or simply be available within the home to care for elders and children. Greater versatility will give those options and the chance to work from anywhere. Generally, the world over, women enter the labour force after their education. There is usually a drop in female labour force participation when women have children, whether they go back in to work and other policies.

REFERENCES

Deshpande, A. (2020, November 6). On Gender Equity, Press Reset. *The Indian Express*, p. 7.

India Report Makers. (2019). State of Women in Tech Entrepreneurship in India, Venture Intelligence, Master card Index of women entrepreneurs 2019 report. Academic Press.

Khatri, T. (2020, October 11). Despite celebration on Ground Zero let her live with her head held high. *The Free Press Journal*, p. 2.

Kochhar, K. (2020, November 7). Empowering women via work raises GDP and a company's profitability. *The Economic Times*, p. 10.

NSO Time Use Survey. (2019). *Care Work and Care Jobs for the future of decent work*. ILO.

Pande, R. (2020, November 7). Financial inclusion, peers, role models empower women. *The Economic Times*, p. 10.

Pillay, A. (2020, October 19). Housework burden Just got heavier for women entrepreneurs. *Business Standard*, p. 6.

Pillay, A. (2020, September 21). Lockdown diaries: women ride the ed-tech boom as opportunities click. *Business Standard*, p. 2.

Rai, Saritha. (2020, November 26th). Pandemic is a surprise boon for women in the world's back office, *Business Standard*, p.2.

Rajivlochan, M. (2020). Redesigning urban spaces for women. *The Hindustan Times*, p. 13.

Saurabh. (2020, November 11). Gender Sensitization with the law may prove to be good for women. *The Avenue*, p. 7.

Shah, A. (2020, September 21). Equal treatment for Women on inheritance. *Business Standard*, p. 11.

Srivastav, K.K. (2020, November 22). Women in a just society in New India. *The Pioneer*, p. 3.

The Global Gender Gap Report. (2018). World Economic Forum.

Chapter 10
A Bibliographic Analysis of E-Waste Recycling Research

Rajeev Srivastava
University of Petroleum and Energy Studies, India

Prakash Chandra Bahuguna
University of Petroleum and Energy Studies, India

ABSTRACT

The tremendous increase in the amount of e-waste and its impact on the environment and human health is a concern for the whole world. The low rate of recycling of e-waste as compared to the rate at which e-waste is increasing is a matter of concern and needs immediate action. Negative environmental consequences of e-waste have prompted the interest of both academia and industry alike. The objective of the study is to study the yearly growth pattern for the last 20 years, recognize relevant scholars, and explore collaborations among various institutes, authors, and countries over time. The study also intends to identify any shift in the field of e-waste recycling. So to better understand the development of this field in the past 20 years, its required to study the yearly growth pattern of publication and to identify the relevant collaborations among authors, institutes, and countries that contributed to this field. In line with this, this study is conducted to examine the research landscape of e-waste recycling by using comprehensive bibliometric analysis.

1. BACKGROUND

The amount of e-waste is growing rapidly due to frequent changes in technology, shortening of the life span of electronic devices, lack of recycling and disposal

DOI: 10.4018/978-1-7998-8258-9.ch010

facilities, import of e-waste in the form of second-hand goods, less focus on recycling and reuse (Srivastava, 2020). During the literature review of recycling e-waste, many issues and benefits of e-waste recycling were discussed. As per literature, e-waste contains different types of hazardous material (Halluite et al., 2005) and a large part of the e-waste is sold to informal recycling sectors (Eugster et al., 2004, Honda et al., 2016). The main location in India, for informal recycling, are New Delhi, Bangalore Chennai, Kolkata (Toxics Link, 2016). The informal sector used crude techniques (Realff, 2004) for recycling which has negative social impacts (Blevis, 2007). The recycling rate for e-Waste is low worldwide. The two reasons for that are the consumers have few recycling options and they have to pay substantial end-of-life fees (GAO, 2005). Regarding rules and regulations, many countries have regulations to ban illegal importation and informal recycling (An et al., 2015), and recycling facilities to manage e-Waste should be supported by the government (Gupta et al., 2012). The management of e-waste in developing countries is a big challenge due to lack of proper collection and recycling, less awareness among citizens about the hazardous nature of e-waste, and poor legislation in comparison to developed countries (Srivastava et al., 2020). Literature also talks about the benefits of formal recycling like it saves energy, expenses, reduce environmental pollution & fewer chances of health hazardous. (Leung et al., 2011). Recycling can help to recover precious materials such as copper, gold, and silver (Berkhout et al., 2004). With the help of recycling, one can save the environment and get better economic performance (Susan et al., 2008).

During the literature discussed in the above part related to the review of e-waste recycling, it is found that mostly the issues and benefits of e-waste recycling were discussed. Few studies have been done to understand the pattern of publication in this field, to know the relevant collaboration between various authors, Institutes, and Countries who contributed most in this field, and to understand the network between various authors, journals, and countries. So to better understand the development of this field in the past twenty years its require to study the yearly growth pattern of publication. To identify the relevant collaborations among authors, institutes, and countries that contributed to this field.

1.1 Research objectives

The objective of the study is to study the yearly growth pattern for the last twenty years; recognize relevant scholars, and explore collaborations among various institutes, authors, and countries over time. The study also intends to identify any shift in the field of e-waste recycling. The study seeks to answer the research question that how the research in the field of e-waste recycling has progressed over the last twenty years in terms of publications, thematic background, institutes, authors, and country's contributions, and finally the future direction of the research?

2. METHODOLOGY

This study is conducted to examine the research landscape of E-waste recycling using comprehensive bibliometric analysis. Bibliometrix package of R language is used to perform the bibliometric analysis of these documents. Bibliometric mapping has emerged as a popular approach to perform bibliometric analysis in different disciplines (Arici et al., 2019; Aria & Cuccurullo, 2017; Song et al., 2019). The availability of various tools to perform bibliometric analysis makes this analysis more suitable for scholars (Aria & Cuccurullo, 2017). The methodology used to perform the bibliometric analysis is divided into two parts as shown in Fig 1. The first part includes data extraction and data conversion. The second part includes the various steps of analysis. The details of the analysis are presented in this section.

2.1 Collection of Data

In the first step, the web of science database is used to extract the documents and related information based on the keywords "e-waste recycling". The analysis included the last twenty years' documents from 2000 to 2020. The keyword used for the literature search is ((e-waste or "Electronic Waste") AND Recycling). It considers various categories of documents like articles, proceedings, reviews, book chapters.

2.2 Data Extraction, Loading, and Conversion

This study includes 2,474 documents extracted from the Web of Science database based during the last 20 years. These documents were stored in the notepad file in the form of plain text. Bibliometrix package of R language is used to perform the bibliometric analysis of these documents

2.3 Bibliometric Analysis and Software Package

In this paper, a bibliometric analysis using R package bibliometrix is used to understand the literature review in the field of e-waste recycling to synthesize the findings of past research and use that existing knowledge base for further study in this field (Massimo A. and Corrado C., 2017).

R language is open-source and provides an integrated environment for statistical computing and graphics (R Core Team, 2016). This language also provides various graphical and statistical techniques along with the capacity of extension in the future (Matloff, 2011).

2.4 Data Synthesis

In the second part, detail of the analysis is presented which is comprised of descriptive analysis, document X attribute matrix, Network matrix, and data reduction, and finally mapping of these documents fields. Descriptive analysis is used to get the information related to the number and types of a document collected for analytics and Social Structure networks were identified to know the network between various fields like authors, countries. In the final part mapping between various field were presented.

Figure 1. Bibliometric analysis workflow

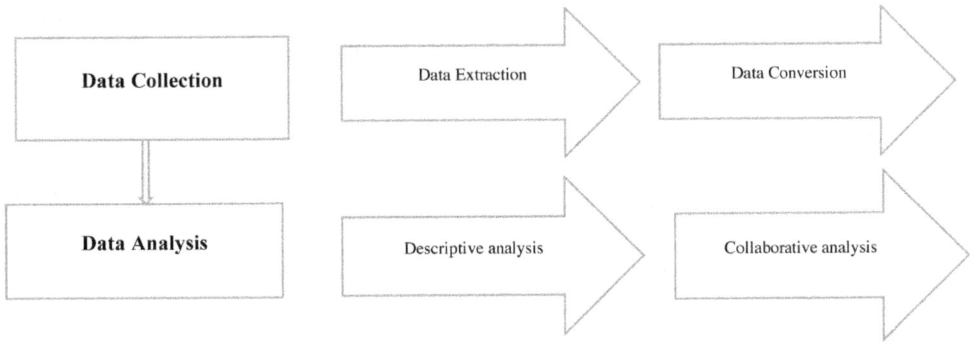

3. RESULTS AND DISCUSSIONS

The result and discussion of the analysis are presented in this section. This section is presented in three parts. In the first part, the result and discussion of descriptive analysis are presented in terms of the total number of documents, types of sources, average citations, and references related to e-waste recycling. In the second part result and discussion related to the relevant sources and documents of E-waste, recycling publications are presented. In the third and final part results and discussion in terms of a collaborative study between relevant authors, institutes, and Countries that contributed to the field of E-waste recycling are presented. The main result of the bibliometric analysis from the bibliometric data frame is presented in different tables and figures.

3.1 Descriptive Analysis

This analysis provides some relevant information which includes types of documents included in the study, details of authors contributed in this field. It also includes the total number of documents, types of sources, average citations, and references of e-waste recycling. The purpose of descriptive analysis is to get the information related to the number and types of a document collected for analytics. It also involves the analysis of relevant sources and authors who contributed to the field of E-Waste recycling.

The data related to the keyword "e-waste recycling" is extracted from the Web of Science database. Publication details of a total of 2,474 documents are presented in Table 1. The main information shows that it includes documents from the year 2000 to the current year. This extracted data include a total of 749 types of sources, and with average citations per document is 23.76. The different types of documents used in analysis consist of 1751 articles, 324 proceedings, and more than 250 book chapters and reviews. Total 5912 authors contributed in this field among which 164 documents were single-authored and 5748 have multiple-authored.

Table 1. Main Information about Data

MAIN INFORMATION ABOUT DATA	
Timespan	2000 to 2021
Sources (Journals, Books, etc)	749
Documents	2474
Average citations per document	23.76
Average citations per year per doc	3.176
References	61717
DOCUMENT TYPES	
Article	1751
Book chapter	53
Proceedings paper	324
Review	206
AUTHORS	
Authors	5912
Author Appearances	11240
Authors of single-authored documents	164
Authors of multi-authored documents	5748

The year-wise publication for the last twenty years is shown in Table 2. This indicates that the number of publications is increasing at an annual growth rate of 7.97%. The number of publications is continuously increasing in the last twenty years. The growing publication trend of these articles is shown in Fig 3. The trend shows that from 2014 onwards there is a huge jump in the number of publications. The number of publications has increased from 153 publications in 2014 to 299 publications in 2019, which is almost double. This indicates that the field of e-waste recycling is still emerging and the number of publications will keep on increasing in the coming years too.

Table 2. Year-wise publication

Year	Articles
2019	299
2018	265
2017	245
2016	230
2015	201
2014	153
2012	138
2013	135
2011	115
2010	92

3.2 Collaboration Between Authors, Institutes, and Countries in the Field of E-Waste Recycling

In this section, the result of bibliometric analysis based on c*ollaboration between authors, institutes, and countries* in the field of E-waste recycling has been presented. Which is based on the collaborative analysis. Collaboration Network is used to create a collection of bibliographic networks following the approach proposed by Batagelj & Cerinsek (2013) and Aria & Cuccurullo (2017). It is used to identify the collaborations between various authors, institutions, and countries.

3.2.1 Network Analysis of Authors in the Field of E-Waste Recycling

Six clusters that emerge in the collaboration network between various authors are represented by different colors in figure 2. Each cluster present that these authors published most of the articles together. Similarly, the other clusters are shown in different colors shows that they published most of the publications together in this field. The second thing to be noticed is that the font size of authors is also varying in different clusters. The big size font indicates that this particular author contributed more papers in this field. The purple color cluster showing that the author "Mai B. X." and "Luo X. Z." have published most of the articles together. Similarly, the blue color cluster showing that the author "Huo X." and "Xu X. J." have published most of the articles together as co-authors." The detail of all the eight clusters is shown in Table 3. Cluster 4 has the maximum number of authors

Figure 2. Network Analysis of Authors

Table 3. Clusters identified during network analysis of authors

Cluster 1	Cluster 2	Cluster 3	Cluster 4	Cluster 5	Cluster 6
Song QB	Li Y	Xu ZM	Luo X J	Zeng EY	Wong MH
Yuan WY	Xu XJ	Zhang W	Sun Z	Asante KA	Li GY
Duan HB	Huo X	Lin KF	Zhang Y	Tue NM	An TC
Li JH	Zhang B	Tang XJ	Liu Y	Takahashi S	Sheng GY
Liu Ll	Zhang Yl	Li J	Zeng YH	Tanabe S	Fu JM
Zeng Xl	Chen AM	Luo Cl	Mai BX	Viet PH	
	Liu JX	Wang Y	Zheng J		
	Wu KS	Zhang G	Chen SJ		
		Chen L	Jiang GB		
		Shen CF	Zheng XG		
			Wang T		
			Wu JP		
			Mo L		
			Yang ZY		

3.2.2 Network Analysis of Institutes in the Field of E-Waste Recycling

Six clusters that emerge in the collaboration network between various institutes/ Universities are represented by different colors in figure 3. Each cluster present that these institutes/Universities published most of the articles together. The second thing to be noticed is that the font size of authors is also varying in different clusters. The big size font indicates that this particular author contributed more papers in this field. The green color cluster showing that the "Guangzhou Inst Geochem" has published most of the articles. The green color cluster also has a maximum number of institutes/Universities that have published most of the articles together and believe in more collaborative studies between institutes of different countries. The detail of all the six clusters is shown in table 4.

Figure 3. Network Analysis of Institutes

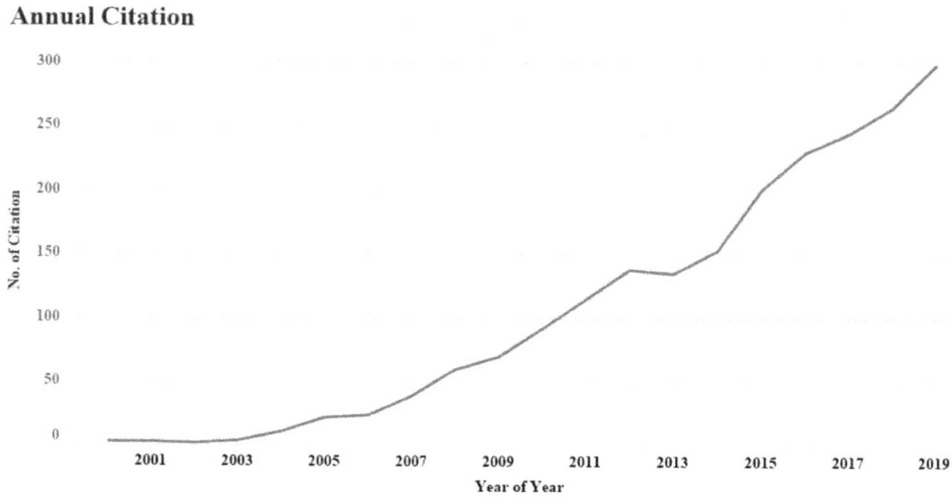

Table 4. Clusters identified during network analysis of institutes

Cluster 1	Cluster 2	Cluster 3	Cluster 4	Cluster 5	Cluster 6
Hong Kong Polytech Univ	Macau Univ Sci And Technol	Jinan Univ	Univ Birmingham	Hong Kong Baptist Univ	Shanghai Jiao Tong Univ
South China Inst Environm Sci	Shenzhen Univ	Shantou Univ	Natl Inst Environm Studies	Educ Univ Hong Kong	Chinese Res Inst Environm Sci
Guangzhou Inst Geochem	Tsinghua Univ	Univ Groningen	Univ Queensland	Zhejiang Univ	Univ Calif Irvine
Sun Yat Sen Univ	Inst Proc Engn	Univ Cincinnati	Csir Water Res Inst	Chinese Acad Sci	Peking Univ
Guangdong Univ Technol	Delft Univ Technol		Univ Alberta	Univ Hong Kong	Sch Publ Hlth
South China Agr Univ	Univ Sci And Technol Beijing		Univ Republica	Nanjing Univ	E China Univ Sci And Technol
Univ Chinese Acad Sci			Ehime Univ		
Dalian Univ Technol			Kyoto Univ		
Nankai Univ			Icahn Sch Med Mt Sinai		
Shanghai Univ			Hanoi Univ Sci		
Univ Lancaster					
Univ Ibadan					
Grad Univ					
Grad Sch					

3.2.3 Network Analysis of Countries in the Field of E-Waste Recycling

Five clusters that emerge in the collaboration network between various countries are represented by different colors in figure 4. Each cluster present that these countries published most of the articles together. Similarly, the other clusters are shown in different colors shows that they published most of the publications together in this field. The second thing to be noticed is that the font size of authors is also varying in different clusters. The red color cluster showing that China has published most of the articles together with the USA. Similarly, the pink color cluster showing that France, China, Canada, and Italy. The detail of the five clusters identified through network analysis is shown in Table 5.

Figure 4. Network Analysis of Countries

Table 5. Clusters identified during network analysis of institutes

Cluster 1	Cluster 2	Cluster 3	Cluster 4	Cluster 5
China	India	Vietnam	Switzerland	United Kingdom
Canada	U Arab Emirates	Poland	France	Romania
USA	Brazil	Indonesia	Finland	Greece
Netherlands	Australia	Japan	Germany	South Africa
Iran	Spain	Malaysia	Ghana	Egypt
Ireland	Turkey	Bangladesh	Sweden	Italy
Israel	Iraq	Philippines	Thailand	Nigeria
Russia			Mexico	Norway
Pakistan			Uruguay	Serbia
Korea				Belgium
Saudi Arabia				Austria
Czech Republic				Portugal
				Denmark

The collaboration among various countries is shown in Fig 5. This figure shows that China has a maximum number of collaborations with other country's authors. The details of the top five countries which have done maximum collaborative studies with other countries are shown in Table 6.

Table 6. Number of collaboration of top 5 countries

Country	Collaboration with other countries
China	380
USA	144
Canada	95
India	89
Germany	79

The detail of most relevant collaboration between various countries is shown in Table 7. This shows that China is doing most of the collaborative studies with countries like USA, Australia, Netherlands, Canada, UK, Japan, Korea.

Figure 5. Collaborative Analysis of Countries

Table 7. Detail of relevant collaboration among countries

Canada	USA (23), Ghana (10)
China	USA (105), Australia (43), Netherlands (36), Canada (25), UK (23), Japan (13), Korea (11)
Germany	Ghana (11), UK (11)
India	Australia (13), USA (11)
USA	Ghana (11), Sweden (11), Japan (10), UK (10)

4. CONCLUSION

Past studies show that many authors have done literature reviews in the field of e-waste recycling. These studies mainly focus on many issues and benefits of e-waste recycling. The various issues related to e-waste recycling discussed in the literature are types of hazardous material, informal recycling, crude techniques, negative social impacts, low recycling rate, and illegal import. The benefits of recycling discussed in the literature are like it helps to save the environment and get better economic performance, saves energy, expenses, reduces environmental pollution & fewer chances of health hazards and it helps to recover precious materials. Few studies have been done to understand how the research in the field of e-waste recycling progress over the last twenty years in terms of publications, thematic background, institutes, authors, and country's contributions, and finally the future direction of the research? This study includes 2,474 documents related to the keyword "e-waste recycling" is selected from the Web of Science database published during the last 20 years. The R-language package Bibliometrix is used to perform the statistical analysis of these documents. This extracted data include a total of 749 types of sources, and with average citations per document is 23.76. The different types of documents used in analysis consist of 1751 articles, 324 proceedings, and more than 250 book chapters and reviews. Total 5912 authors contributed their documents in this field among which 164 were single-authored and 5748 have multiple authors.

The year-wise publication for the last twenty years indicates that the number of publications is increasing at an annual growth rate of 7.97%. The trend shows that from 2014 to 2019 number of publications become almost double. Total 5912 authors contributed to this field. From 2014 onwards there is a huge jump in the number of publications. During network analysis, it is found that the two authors "Iuo, X. J." and "Mai, B. X. have published the maximum number of articles together. China and the USA are the countries having a maximum number of collaborations among them and China has a maximum number of collaborations with other countries. The result of bibliometric analysis based on collaboration between authors, institutes, and countries in the field of E-waste recycling has been presented in the second part. In this section, the scholar has tried to find the clusters of authors, institutes, and countries that are working in collaboration with each other. It has been found that the author "Mai B. X." and "Luo X. Z." have published most of the articles together. The "Guangzhou Inst Geochem" institute is involved in collaboration with other institutes. China is doing most of the collaborative studies with countries like USA, Australia, Netherlands, Canada, UK, Japan, Korea.

5. STUDY LIMITATIONS

The study has certain limitations. The sample was collected from the Web of Science database, which may have resulted in missing out on some relevant data. Collecting samples from multiple databases would improve the study in a significant way. The keywords used could be improvised to consist of more relevant keywords in querying the database. These limitations should encourage future researchers to explore new ways of collecting data from multiple databases with expanded keywords for in-depth analysis. The findings of the study may provide insight to scholars researching in the field of customer retention regarding research landscape and research hotspots. The findings of the study provide an overview of the output in the area of retention over years and a relevant pointer to the direction for future research in the area of E-waste recycling.

REFERENCES

An, D., Yang, Y., Chai, X., Xi, B., Dong, L., & Ren, J. (2015). Mitigating pollution of hazardous materials from WEEE of China: Portfolio selection for a sustainable future based on multi-criteria decision making. Resour. *Conserv Recycl, 105*, 198–210. doi:10.1016/j.resconrec.2015.10.025

Berkhout, F., & Hertin, J. (2004). De-materialising and re-materialising: Digital technologies and the environment. *Futures, 36*(8), 903–920. doi:10.1016/j.futures.2004.01.003

Blevis, E. (2007). Sustainable Interaction Design: Invention & Disposal, Renewal & Reuse. CHI 2007 Proceedings, 503-512.

Callon, M., Courtial, J.-P., Turner, W. A., & Bauin, S. (1983). From translations to problematic networks: An introduction to co-word analysis. *Social Sciences Information. Information Sur les Sciences Sociales, 22*(2), 191–235. doi:10.1177/053901883022002003

Dakare, A., & Thakare, A. P. (2012). Recycling and reusing the e-waste. *IJMIE, 2*(6).

Eugster, M. (2004). Knowledge partnership with developing and transition countries in E-Waste recycling. Presented at the *International Conference on Electric Waste and Producer's Environmental Responsibilities in China*, Beijing, China.

Fu, J., Zhou, Q., Liu, J., Liu, W., Wang, T., Zhang, Q., & Jiang, G. (2008). High levels of heavy metals in rice (Oryza sativa L.) from a typical e-Waste recycling area in southeast China and its potential risk to human health. *Chemosphere*, *71*(7), 1269–1275. doi:10.1016/j.chemosphere.2007.11.065 PMID:18289635

Gupta, P. (2012). The Hazardous and Problems of E-Waste Management in India and its Strategies for Better Tomorrow. *RJEBS*, *1*(5).

Halluite, J, Linton, J.D., Yeomans, J.S., & Yoogalingam, R. (2005). The challenge of hazardous waste management in a sustainable environment: insights from electronic recovery laws. *Corporate Social Responsibility and Environmental Management*, *12*, 31 37.

Honda, S., Khetriwal, D. S., & Kuehr, R. (2016). *Regional E-waste Monitor: East and Southeast Asia*. United Nations University.

Hosoda, E. (2007). International aspects of recycling of electrical and electronic equipment: Material circulation in the East Asian region. *J Mater Cycles Waste*, *9*(2), 140–150. doi:10.100710163-007-0179-8

Leung, A. O. W., Jinshu, Z., Chik, K. Y., Wing, K. L., Wong, K. C., Zongwei, C., & Wong, M. H. (2011, July 1). Polybrominated Diphenyl Ethers, and Polychlorinated Dibenzo-p-dioxins and Dibenzofurans in Surface Dust at an E-Waste Processing Site in Southeast China. *Environmental Science & Technology*, *45*(13), 5775–5782. doi:10.1021/es103915w PMID:21639085

Link, T. (2016). *What India Knows ABOUT E-WASTE. Report on Awareness Levels of E-waste amongst common citizens in India*. Toxics Link. http://toxicslink.org/docs/What-India-knows-about-e-waste.pdf

Massimo, A., & Corrado, C. (2017). bibliometrix: An R-tool for comprehensive science mapping analysis. *Journal of Informetrics*, *11*(4), 959–975. doi:10.1016/j.joi.2017.08.007

Matloff, N. (2011). *The art of R programming: A tour of statistical software design*. No Starch Press.

R Core Team. (2016). *R: A language and environment for statistical computing*. Vienna, Austria: R Foundation for Statistical Computing. https://www.R-project.org

Realff, M. J., Ammons, J. C., & Newton, D. J. (2004). Robust reverse production system design for carpet recycling. *IIE Transactions*, *36*(8), 767–776. doi:10.1080/07408170490458580

Srivastava, R. (2020). A Literature Review and Classification of e-Waste Management Research. *Journal of Solid Waste Technology Management*, *46*(2), 258–273. doi:10.5276/JSWTM/2020.258

Srivastava, R., & Dhingra, T. (2020). Towards a Model for Effective e-Waste Management: A Study of Software Industry in India. *International Journal of Environment and Waste Management*, *27*(1), 61–73. doi:10.1504/IJEWM.2021.111905

Susan, A. F., Jeremy, R. G., & Randolph, E. K. (2008). Characterizing architectural options for electronic waste recycling systems. *IEEE International Symposium on Electronics and the Environment*, 1-6.

Tienhua, W. T., & Yenming, J. C. (2008). Understanding population dynamics of WEEE recycling system in the developing countries: A SIR model. *IEEE International Symposium on Electronics and the Environment*, 1-6.

Zhiduan, X., & Guo, Y. G. (2005). Study and Design on Third-party Take-back Mode Management Information System. In Latest China Information System Study and Application. Tsinghai University.

Chapter 11
On Humanizing Work in the Digital Age

Andriyana Andreeva
University of Economics, Varna, Bulgaria

Galina Yolova
University of Economics, Varna, Bulgaria

ABSTRACT

The chapter addresses the problem of humanization of labour in the digital age. With technological advancement worldwide, notwithstanding economic and political differences among individual states, digitalisation has invariably put its mark on human relationships. And it is about to transform both individual and social relations also in the labour law. The purpose of the present study is to examine the acts and documents at European level and offer an up-to-date analysis on applicable aspects of introducing AI in the labour process, its role in facilitating employees work alongside potential threats and negatives. Based on said analysis, the authors offer their views on the challenges to be faced and outline ongoing trends in the doctrine, the European community and legislation, to put in place a regulatory framework towards humanization of work in the digital age.

INTRODUCTION

Humanization is a category that is inherent to the development of human society. In this sense, it can be presented as a continual process that has its clear purpose and content. During different periods of social history, humanization has been dependent on the individual's moral principles and community culture. Society has treated the

DOI: 10.4018/978-1-7998-8258-9.ch011

process of humanization in different ways and this has had a correlative effect on the result – humanizing relations in the respective community or industry sector. Seen as phenomenology by labour sociology and management sciences, humanization of labour concerns some basic principles and rules which are to ensure congenial micro-ecology of labour, healthy and safe work and living conditions, good work-life balance, in other words, a humanely orientated approach to the workforce in general. In the focus of study are placed the principles of humanization being established over the years, in particular the principle of safety, the principle of justice, the principle of developed personality and the principle of democracy in its aspects of shared workload and responsibility between the administrative apparatus and staff self-government. Considered from the point of view of human resources management, humanization of labour translates into a toolkit of organizational, technical and socio-economic measures which aim to improve working conditions and the work environment, broaden the meaning and content of labour and forms and methods of management devised to achieve maximum correspondence between the individual and the workforce.

Humanization of labour is recognized by the International Labour Organization (ILO) as a leading trend in the development of social and labour relations from which its legal and moral aspects can be defined.

The topic of humanization of labour in the digital age is important as it is seen as an integral part of law alongside specific industry sectors but it is also related to some basic notions running like a red thread through different groups of social relations. Humanization of society is not a task performed by a separate branch of law. It is in fact, the driver regulating relations within a national law system but also seen as a guarantor of this value internationally. Modern society has entered a new dimension in its development. The fourth industrial revolution and the aggressive digitalisation of labour relations present a qualitatively different stage in the development of the economy and the right to work, posing serious challenges to the labour market and the development of labour relations. As a natural continuation of digitalization and automation of production, it is associated with the interaction of autonomous cyber-physical systems capable of operating independently, processing and analyzing large data arrays and making decisions using artificial intelligence (AI), robotics, digital modelling and smart automation. On the one hand, this leads to a radical change in the labour markets which increasingly leave out large groups of workers with low or no digital competence, and associated social policies, related to long-term or permanent unemployment and the need to adapt these policies to the demands for social inclusion of vulnerable groups of society. There are persistent trends in the digitalisation of a large number of jobs and creation of legal relationships with atypical entities being associated with permanent unemployment in some sectors and displacement of the typical holder of the right to work. Labour law does not explicitly state the principle of humanization of labour and yet humanization of labour is its driving force as it underlines legal principles and institutions, becoming the main reason to place man in the foreground. Indeed, this characteristic of the legal branch arising from the inseparability of work force from the individual, makes labour law the 'humane' branch in the whole set of norms, which are aimed at regulating the relations between the parties so as to balance the interests of both parties.

Today, the digital environment is the scene of typical labour law relationships and entry of AI at different levels of employment now poses new challenges for the regulatory mechanism in terms of protection of the right to work, fair and equal treatment, safeguarding against new means for monitoring and control of the work process, protecting personal space of the individual and accountability in using artificial intelligence.

In the above aspects, the study examines the impact of AI on labour relations and subsequent demand to rethink established concepts and institutes of labour law. In retrospect, the change in labour legislation is presented with a focus on development of social relations over different historical periods, as well as current trends reflecting common European policies on digitalization of labour and related Acts of various regulatory bodies aimed at creating an adaptive, adequate and common regulatory framework.

The focus of the authors' interest is placed on the principles of labour law which are seen as the driving force for the development of the industry sector, humanizing work and ensuring protection of workers and employees respectively. A normative analysis is also performed on individual labour institutes, which are most affected by the process of digitalization and the need to update the regulatory framework at international and national level is articulated in order to balance the interests of the parties in the labour law relationship. The labour law is relevant to the private law branches in view of the dispositive method used in this branch which takes into account the specifics in the existing employment relationship. In this respect, the relationships of equality between employer and employee and the extent of employer power in the work environment are the subject of examination and analysis. The study reveals their true nature and substance, as well as their new forms of development, in terms of transformation of the typical subjects of the employment relationships, transformation of the legal relations worker – employer, the forms of work seen through the prism of specific negotiations and nature of work – remote or using digital platforms (Банов, 2020), replacing classical work force with artificial intelligence and all related challenges to the legal doctrine and rule of law. Undoubtedly, this comes as a response to the urgent need for a timely yet adequate to the dynamics of legal relations regulatory framework. Emergence of digitalization processes is closely related to the right to work in a more dynamic economic and information environment on the one hand, and on the other – the right to work in an environment of vulnerability and displacement of the subject of labour /where human labour is replaced by robotic systems and digital technologies. The same holds true when a legally sound framework is in place, to outline the scope of usage of robotic systems under conditions of full or limited autonomy as well as the protection of the personal rights of those exercising their right to work as a basic right of modern constitutionalism. It is essential to justify the need for additional guarantees in the form of legal principles which are to set clear limits in several basic directions – man – robot; personal – professional life; freedom of labour – work discipline.

At this stage, all acts and documents are examined at European level, and applicability of AI to the work process is also discussed, eliciting the degree to which AI can facilitate the work of employees and staff. Possible risks and disadvantages are being considered too. It is also essential to analyse typical European policies on labour protection mechanisms in the context of digitalization, preserving the status quo to protect the basic right to work, coordinating and making social security systems more meaningful for those who are made permanently redundant on the job market and envisaging protective measures against displacement of human labour by AI.

In terms of subject matter, the authors have set a number of restrictions, giving a priority treatment to the substantive side of liability and avoiding procedural issues. At the same time, the research aims to identify emerging trends and tackle current issues not being yet addressed or covered by a specific legislation or issues that are still debated by European institutions.

BACKGROUND

The topicality of the researched topic is indisputable as it addresses the problem of humanity in the labour law in answer to emerging trends driven by the introduction of AI in the labour process, and it is likely to provoke debates both on a scientific level and internationally at Community institutions. On the one side, the relevance of the researched issues can be attributed to the rapid pace of the digital revolution which radically transformed patterns of work, but as a whole it concerns the relationships between the parties involved in the specific labour relation in general. This poses the need for a doctrinal examination of the above interrelations to ensure adoption of an adequate regulatory mechanism and legal guarantees for a humane, just and honourable labour. Maintaining the leading role of man and placing him at the centre of labour relations are issues that need urgent consideration at various levels. In addition, the topicality is associated with the need to bridge present and future to the benefit of man. In this sense further support is needed so that workers are able to adapt to new labour realities starting from professional improvement –

knowledge, skills and competences that not only will make them eligible on the labour market but will also enhance their career opportunities.

The purpose of the present study is to examine current trends in humanizing work considered from the point of view of digital reality, the process of digitalization and their impact on the very nature of labour relations and worker – employer relationship. To this end, certain acts and documents are discussed at European level and AI is discussed in terms of its applicability to the work process and its impact on facilitating workers and employees together with potential hazards and downsides. In this line, typical European policies are discussed, with a focus on labour protection mechanisms in the context of digitalization, preservation of the status quo to protect the basic right to work, coordinating and making social security systems more meaningful for those who are made permanently redundant on the job market as well as the need for protective measures against displacement of human labour by AI.

Given the above analysis, challenges and trends are outlined in relation to the doctrine, the European community and legislature needed to put a regulatory framework into place towards humanizing work in the present digital age. Similarly, summaries and proposals are put forward arguing specific normative hypotheses about how to defend traditional principles of labour law, freedom to exercise one's right to work and equal opportunities to exercise that right in the new conditions of social development.

The methodological basis of this research is related to the cumulative use of traditional methods for legal research such as: comparative law, formal logic law and general cognitive methods of induction, deduction, analysis and synthesis. The study is in accordance with national legislation and leading European sources as of March 30th, 2021.

ON HUMANIZING WORK IN THE DIGITAL AGE – REGULATORY FRAMEWORK AND PRINCIPLES

The origins of labour law and the history of its development are associated with the struggle to establish the rights of the worker and employee. The legal branch boasts a long history by first bringing its protective function into effect over the economically weaker side in the employment relationship (Банов, 2020). Each historic period has put the doctrine and the law enforcer to the test. The 21st century is no exception marked by the digital age, the fourth industrial revolution, the onset of artificial intelligence (AI) – the many faceted phenomenon which has driven changes in all walks of social and private life, posing some of the greatest challenges unknown to law so far (Андреева, А., Йолова, Г, 2020).

Labour is at the very core of the employment relationship whereas legislation is largely aimed at satisfying the interests of both sides for the respective historical period. The employer's interest is to generate economic benefits, and benefits for the worker respectively, alongside the material benefits in the form of wages paid to the worker, where the protection of labour is deemed really essential.

Humanization of labour concerns both sides of the legal relationship and depending on their specific role, the manifestation is different. From the employer's point of view, labour law translates into employer power which gives him the authority to run the work process. It is in this capacity, that he should create such working conditions which will help the worker make quality products in a safe and healthy work environment. Throughout separate stages of its development, labour legislation has laid down different principles and introduced legal institutions as a whole, embracing the idea of humanizing work. But the norms only create the legal framework while the parties are the ones who are called to implement them, with regulatory bodies having the task to ensure their compliance to norms of the existing labour legislation.

Humanization of labour suggests optimal interrelation between the worker and working conditions. The worker must be provided not only with basic conditions to be able to exercise his right to work but these should be such as to help him preserve his work potential, his good health and at the same time stimulate the development of his personality and creative abilities.

Seen in a broader context, humanization of labour should be seen through the prism of worker's motivation to enter into a labour relation on the one hand, and on the other –maintain the acquired level of knowledge and skills, adding new competences, new methods of work, etc. Technical progress facilitates the job of workers and employees but it also places on them new demands for improvement, honing their abilities to work with new technologies, make them aspire to new work culture and innovations in the work process.

The entry of AI into the labour process calls for transformation of humanity and its reinvention on a different level.

For one thing, it is necessary to actualize the traditional content of humanity and update the regulatory basis with new aspects of labour humanization, placing man once more in the focus as the subject of labour but this time taking into account man's interaction with robotic systems.

On the other hand, if we look at the concept of humanity in a broader sense, we must also assume that we need guarantees for its observance. We believe that one of the forms will fall within the different types of legal liability. In this line of reasoning, we think that we should dwell on the problem of responsibility in using AI, including damages inflicted by robots substituting for traditional workforce whilst making the good old jobs redundant, and the need to urgently adopt a common regulatory framework at European and international level (Andreeva, A., Yolova, G., 2021) .

Scientific and technological advances are at the very heart of the change in labour content. This process is not new, but with the ongoing fourth industrial revolution, the pace of AI entry into the labour process is so dramatic that urgent regulations are needed to set the limits and scope of man-robot interaction. The latter is of key importance and a prerequisite for humanization of labour.

Digitalization and robotics enhance the ergonomics of the workplaces and lead to their humanization accordingly (Walwei, 2016). When robots perform heavy-duty operations or dangerous work, they actually help lessen the number of accidents and illnesses at the workplace. On the other hand, the authors fear that in the future, regardless of skyrocketing profits and high productivity, in certain industry sectors demand for real workers will be steadily falling away (Ford, 2015) and human labour will be replaced by digital algorithms (Brynjolfsson & McAfee, 2011).

It is clear that the interrelations between AI, workforce and the individual worker are affecting the very nature and content of labour and composition of workforce. But in this symbiosis, the role of the employer and his economic gain shall not be overlooked. The employer is still the one responsible for the organization of labour. Moreover, the efficiency of the work process largely depends on the optimal combination of man-AI which is articulated in the humanization of labour.

Improvement of business processes and digitalization entering in every work process should run parallel to the development of human potential. The workforce needs conditions in which to develop and improve their skills to achieve the right balance between worker and AI systems.

The rapid pace of digitalisation processes and the intensity with which they influence social relationships are factors to which the legal framework is by far unable to respond adequately (Александров, 2019) (Александров, 2020). This trend has a somewhat disconcerting effect on the concepts of the legal doctrine, ethical and legal philosophy and last but not least on the regulatory mechanism.

To recap, the topic related to humanization of labour in the digital age focuses on **several basic aspects, namely:**

- Where is the boundary between the use of traditional labour force and AI?
- Should extended employer power, and responsibility for the use of AI in the work process be regulated;
- Should the meaning of the term 'humanization' be broadened?

The above three questions do not exhaust in full all the problems associated with artificial intelligence (AI) and its introduction into the work process. At the same time, they cut off the main moral and social aspects which are already a reality and yet to become the subject of debate in the legal doctrine and subsequently in the area of legislation activity.

Still, we must not forget one more aspect of the problem which is concerned with **social responsibility when displacement of traditional workforce is in the focus of debate.**

A NEED TO ARRANGE FOR HUMAN-AI INTERACTION TOWARDS A MORE HUMANE FUTURE OF LABOUR

In terms of prevention of work hazards in the labour process, the future regulatory framework needs to put forward requirements to be observed by the parties in the labour relation. In the first place, they should focus on the employer who in his capacity as leader of the organization is deemed responsible for the logistics of the entire working process. The employer also bears responsibility for the effective management of the organization and provision of safe and healthy conditions of work for the organization employees (Blagoycheva, H., Andreeva, A. & Yolova, G, 2019).

The digital revolution witnessed in the social/public relations, and in particular - the labour market and associated with it labour relations, pose some real challenges to the national and Community legislation. Rapid AI integration into the work process and displacement of man in the classical labour relationship formula, outline trends for displacement of the classical labour law and legal institutes, revising the basic concept of legal personality and transforming the content of subject of the right to work in general. The latter in turn, hinders the doctrinal and normative development of principles for labour protection and labour law, while imposing urgent regulatory mechanisms to stabilize relationships when automation is increasingly used to substitute or displace physical labour. Undoubtedly, robotics creates new opportunities for employees by automating repetitive and monotonous tasks and replacing these with operational systems becomes an important part in the process of work humanization. But the issue of the new digital environment is already giving rise to more pros and cons in the debate for the real benefits and harms of AI use.

At European level, the digitalisation of labor and the use of AI is a component of the Digital Europe program, which aims to achieve a digital transformation in the EU in the period 2021-2027 with maximum benefits for businesses, public administrations and society. The policies of the Digital Europe program focus on five main areas: high-performance computing; AI; cybersecurity and trust; advanced digital skills; interoperability and digital transformation.

In this sense, several characteristic trends are emerging, which can be outlined at the following levels, directly concerning the new social and economic realities arising from the digitalization of labor:

1. the need for protection of the classical labor force in the replacement and/or use of AI in the realization of the labor function,
2. specific trends in the transformation of the typical employment relationship and the need for a regulatory framework stipulating the liability and legal principles in the use of cyber physical systems and artificial intelligence,
3. the need to build a new level of digital competencies as a typical characteristic and prerequisite for exercising the right to work.

The replacement of the classical labor force that happens with the use of AI in the realization of the labor function is a typical manifestation of the processes of dehumanization of labor. The permanent displacement of the subject of the right to work is the result of many aspects of the EU policies aimed at creating legal balances between the ethics and dignity of the individual and the use of robots in the labor relations. Principles concerning robotics are set out in a basic form in a report of the Committee on Legal Affairs, 27.1.2017, containing recommendations to the Commission on civil law on robotics (2015/2103 (INL)).

The Opinion of the Committee on Employment and Social Affairs (9.11.2016) addressed to the attention of the Committee on Legal Affairs containing recommendations to the Commission on "Civil law for robotics" (2015/2103 (INL)) emphasizing the importance of ethical and social principles, calls on the Commission to make a comprehensive assessment of the impact of robotics on the number and types of jobs and, in particular, whether the proliferation of robotics in itself leads to prosperity and progress, whether it makes human labor unnecessary within the traditional structure of production and services and, if so, what conditions - apart from financial security - are needed to ensure that people are healthy (in terms of both mental and physical well-being), happy and active citizens and whether the theoretical benefits of human-machine symbiosis really contribute to prosperity and development. On the other hand, emphasis is placed on the need to assess whether, in a changing labor market, Member States' law and practices can guarantee a socially just, inclusive and sustainable approach to reducing inequalities, poverty and social exclusion, as well as an environment, in which all human beings have equal opportunities to develop their talent, their skills and their self-awareness as people. In this context, it is considered particularly important that robots should be designed using procedures that ensure human control and reversibility of the robot actions, as well as the understanding that it is essential for the Union to define legislation that reflects the complex nature of robotics and its many social consequences, notably by studying the effects of digitalisation, robotics and artificial intelligence on mental stress. (Андреева, А., Йолова, Г.., 2018).

Recognizing that artificial intelligence may exceed human intellectual capacity in the long term, the European Parliament's Motion for a Resolution containing recommendations to the Commission on civil law for robotics (2015/2103 (INL)) emphasizes the urgent need to develop ethical principles, in accordance with the principles and values enshrined in Article 2 of the Treaty on European Union and the Charter of Fundamental Rights, such as human dignity, equality, justice and fairness, non-discrimination, informed consent, protection of private and family life and data, as well as other fundamental principles and values of Union law, such as non-stigmatization, transparency, autonomy, individual responsibility and social responsibility, and existing ethical practices and codes under these basic guidelines. Along these lines, the so-called user license has been created as a guiding legal framework, providing for the establishment of several fundamental principles, namely: use of robots without risk or fear of physical or mental harm, while fully respecting human vulnerability - physical, as well as mental and the emotional needs of people, fully respecting the privacy rights of individuals, in a manner consistent with ethical and legal principles and standards.

It is obvious that enduring policy trends pointing to an enhanced protective function of the humanization of labor are aimed at protecting basic human rights and freedoms in a non-discriminatory, fair and sustainable way, balancing the new industrial revolution with a mechanism: both legal and ethical, preserving human dignity in working in the aggressive conditions of increasing digitalization.

Specific trends in the transformation of the typical employment relationship and the need for a regulatory framework for accountability and principles in the use of cyber physical systems is a trend concerning the development of humanistic guidelines in an ethically justified and legally regulated aspect. These current trends are mainly set out in the White Paper on Artificial Intelligence - Europe in Search of Excellence and an Atmosphere of Confidence, Brussels, 19.02.2020 COM (2020), based on the AI strategy developed by the Commission (25 April 2018) tailored to socio-economic aspects, research, innovation and AI capacity across the EU. The published guidelines on reliable AI include the published Communication of the European Commission, COM (2019) 168, which, in addition to an enhanced anthropocentric approach, sets out the seven key requirements for the use of AI in labor relations, namely **the human factor and supervision, technical stability and security, data management and privacy, transparency, diversity, non-discrimination and fairness, public and environmental well-being, accountability**. They should be further developed into an adequate and sustainable framework for reliable artificial intelligence based on excellence and trust, which aims, through a partnership between the private and public sectors, to mobilize resources throughout the value chain and create the right incentives for the accelerated deployment of AI, including in small and medium-sized enterprises.[1]

The report on the impact of artificial intelligence, the Internet of objects and robotics on safety and responsibilities is the report accompanying the White Paper, analyzing the relevant legal framework of the levels of responsibility and risks in the use of AI in labor relations. Emphasizing the uncertain aspects of the application of this framework with respect to the specific risks posed by AI systems, the issue of the direct threat of the characteristics of digital technologies, such as AI, Internet of Things and robotics putting to the test the framework of rules, concerning liability and reducing its effectiveness, is justifiably analyzed. In this sense, the AI White Paper also recognizes that some of these characteristics may make it difficult to trace the damage to a person, which would be necessary in the event of a claim based on culpable liability in accordance with most national rules. This calls for a reform of the safety concept and, in particular, to extend it to risks that are not currently explicitly mentioned in EU legislation: cyber threats, personal safety risks (related to new AI applications, e.g. in household appliances), risks arising from loss of internet connection, etc. In this sense, the understanding is reaffirmed that the EU should make full use of the tools at its disposal to enrich the evidence gained so far on the potential risks associated with the use of AI, including the experience of the EU Cyber Security Agency (ENISA) in assessing the variety of possible risks.

Assuming that the future regulatory framework should give priority to the participant or participants - the developers of AI systems, the implementer or the direct employer, who are best able to respond to all potential risks, the understanding is confirmed that the new regulatory framework for AI - principles of use and liability should be effective and achieve its objectives without being overly prescriptive, disproportionate or over-regulatory. Along these lines are the adopted indicators for high-risk technologies, namely - violating safety, consumer rights and fundamental rights, which should be taken cumulatively and include two elements: the application of AI is in a sector where the predominant activities and their characteristics suggest the presence of significant risks or is applied in the sector in question in such a way that significant risks are likely to arise. [2]

At the same time, it is considered that there may be exceptional cases where, due to possible risks, the use of AI applications for certain purposes should **always be considered as high-risk** in itself, and in all cases where its importance for individuals and **the acquis of employment equality, the use of AI applications in the recruitment process, as well as in situations affecting workers' rights and freedoms, the use of AI applications for the purposes of remote biometric identification and surveillance technologies that violate privacy**. In view of the high-risk applications are also the proposed procedures for preliminary conformity assessment, including testing, inspection or certification.

In view of the above, the principle is rightly accepted that in order to ensure the reliability and security of AI systems in compliance with European values and rules, the applicable legal requirements must be observed in practice and effectively applied by both the competent national and European authorities and by the parties concerned, and the competent authorities should be able to investigate individual cases but also assess the impact on the society as a whole. The planned "ecosystem of trust" has been devised as a basis for the future regulatory framework for AI in Europe, aimed at ensuring compliance with EU rules, including those for the protection of fundamental rights, by providing the necessary legal certainty for innovation using AI.

The need to build a new level of digital competencies is the trend that is increasingly emerging as a typical feature and prerequisite for exercising the right to work. On the one hand, it is related to the trend typical for the humanization of labor, towards innovation and mastery of technology and production, insofar as it is understood that humanization directly affects the attitude of workers to the means of labor, the level of knowledge and skills and their creative use in search of new methods of work.

Typical European policies in this direction are developed in the campaign "Electronic Skills for Jobs" from 2015 to 2016 and the related documents: "Manifesto for Electronic Skills", 2016, European Qualifications Framework, the Coalition for Skills and Jobs in the field of digital technologies, the Europass framework, the Detailed Action Plan for Sectoral Skills Cooperation, the Recommendation on Monitoring the Performance of Graduates, and the mechanisms for implementing the Directive on the recognition of professional qualifications. A number of EESC opinions have also been developed, in particular on the digital single market and SMEs, the new skills agenda, digital literacy, e - skills and e - inclusion, the fourth industrial revolution and the digital transformation, and the information report on the mid - term evaluation of the Erasmus + program.

The tendency for the recognition of digital literacy as a key element of modern concepts of literacy in general is obvious, and its establishment as a trend and process of imposing the requirements for the realization of the right to work is permanently enshrined in all leading policies of modern labor market strategies. Moreover, the synchronization of human society with the new conditions on the path to global prosperity is impossible without putting knowledge at the center of attention. (Blagoycheva, 2020, p. 56).

Based on the understanding that "the workers of the future will need skills to enable them to create economic value in a world in which automation, software and robots will enter more and more sectors of the labor market", the Manifesto of Electronic skills is key in justifying the need to develop and achieve a new level of digital competences and high digital literacy in jobs in various fields. Along these lines are also the recommendations included in the Manifesto, which should be further developed in the common European policies and strategic documents, namely:

- Promoting the European framework for e-competences and ICT work profiles in order to standardize competences, role profiles and education.
- Improving IT education for non-specialists.
- Building close links between industry and educational institutions.
- Improving the relationships and understanding between IT functions and executive teams
- Promoting IT among young people and developing IT professions
- Encouraging the establishment of national e-leadership working groups

It is obvious that requirements for employees involved in the work process with AI should include mandatory initial and ongoing training to work with AI systems, as well as compliance with safety rules and instructions for working with AI systems, including ethical aspects of use.

The current Bulgarian legislation still lacks detailed regulations concerning the inclusion of AI in the labor process, respectively the commitments of the parties to the employment relationship and regulation of specifics in liability for violations, although a number of normative acts have been created and are applicable in the field of information and communication technologies (ICT) in Bulgaria. The most significant of them are the Personal Data Protection Act (Promulgated in the State Gazette, issue 1 of January 4, 2002, amended and supplemented, SG No. 17 of February 26, 2019), the Electronic Communications Act (Promulgated in the State Gazette, SG No. 41 of 22 May 2007, amended and supplemented, SG No. 17 of 26 February 2019), Law on Electronic Government (Promulgated, SG No. 46 of 12 June 2007, amended and supplemented SG No. 94 of 13 November 2018), Law on the Electronic Document and Electronic Certification Services (Promulgated SG No. 34 of 6 April 2001, amended, SG No. 1 of 3 January 2019), Law on Provision of Distance Financial Services (Promulgated SG No. 105 of December 22, 2006, amended SG No. 20 of March 6, 2018), Cyber Security Act (Promulgated SG No. 94 of November 13, 2018).

At the same time, the development and application of information technologies is the subject of many strategic documents, in particular the National Program "Digital Bulgaria 2025" and the Roadmap for the period 2018 - 2025 of the Ministry of Transport, Information Technology and Communications, Concept for digital transformation of Bulgarian industry (Industry 4.0), National Cyber Security Strategy, Cyber-Sustainable Bulgaria 2020, Innovation Strategy for Intelligent Specialization of the Republic of Bulgaria 2014 - 2020, etc.

It is evident from European and national policies that digital literacy is increasingly emerging as a leading priority in recruitment and sustainable integration of jobs. However, its use in the practice of employers leads to both positive and negative trends. In this sense, it is clear that people with low or absent digital skills permanently drop out of the labor market, and their inclusion in forms of training outside the training within the labor process as a commitment of the employer is impossible to implement and in practice worsens the circle of absence from work - low digital literacy (Банов, 2020) (Банов, 2020) (Банов, 2020).

We believe that the steps that should be taken are at several levels:

- introducing basic requirements in the general source of the Labor Code, which should supplement the content of the employment relationship with rights and obligations when using AI in the labor process;
- strategies for training of unemployed persons, applying developed mechanisms for adaptability to the new labor relations and adequate inclusion in the labor market with a basic level of acquired digital skills;
- permanent and continuous improvement of digital skills in the course of realization of labor relations;
- involvement of employers and especially of the bodies of the tripartite cooperation in upholding legally guaranteed mechanisms for lifelong learning.

It is obvious that the current study cannot cover all possible nuances of the transformation of humanization in labor law with the inclusion of AI in the labor process. It aims to raise the main issues that arise at this stage and to seek logic in thinking at the doctrinal level, in order to support the future legal framework in this direction.

FUTURE RESEARCH DIRECTIONS

National legislations follow guidelines and are in no position to introduce independent regulatory solutions, both given the scale of the problems to be solved, the pace of development and the global nature of the processes. Labor law is the legal sector with the highest degree of protection of the interests of individuals in relation to their workforce, and in this sense the issue of its adaptation and evolution towards its humanization also in the digital age is of particular importance, both internationally and for each specific country. Adjustments in labor law are needed, but they must be made after careful scrutiny of the problem and in a timely manner. This combination is especially difficult given the dynamics of the modern world, when processes and changes do not happen over years, but within days and hours. It is clear that basic and stable legal institutes should undoubtedly be revised, legal principles should be rethought, new guarantees should be introduced, but everything should be subordinated to the general idea that man and his work should be placed at the center of protection. In this difficult process, the economic interests of employers should be skillfully combined with those of workers, the necessary balance should be found in order to preserve the equality of the parties and not to violate the freedom of labor of the individual at the expense of the unregulated use of AI in the labor process.

CONCLUSION

Humanization in labor law is a global process that has a centuries-old history and traditions, corresponding to the development of society; it is characterized by specifics, reflecting the democracy and values in the respective country. The present study raises issues from the most recent stage of development, namely the fourth industrial revolution and its impact on the evolution of the concept of humanization in the context of labor law.

National legislation should not lag behind the trends to which the introduction of new subjective rights and obligations of the parties point, given the need for them to be the basis of a guaranteed labor process with the use of AI systems.

1. Legislative adjustment of basic principles and concepts related to the humanization of labor and their adaptive expansion in the direction of protection of the right to work and its dignified exercise in a fair and non-discriminatory manner.
2. In accordance with the European Community framework, outlining national legal provisions setting out additional guarantees and mechanisms for protection in the exercise of the right to work at the level of responsibility when replacing the classic workforce with AI.
3. Introduction of specific norms concerning the rules and mechanisms for liability for damages caused by AI, both direct and indirect, including: affecting basic human rights such as equality, non-discrimination, personal inviolability and dignity of the individual.
4. Introduction of imperative norms setting limits to the employers' legal capacity in a digital environment.
5. Legal guarantees for maintaining the balance between personal and professional life.
6. At the national level, introduction of the right to detach from the working environment in hypotheses that lead to continuous connectivity, overtime work and violation of the right to rest and leave of absence.
7. Commitments to the creation and validation of digital skills throughout life in compliance with the principles of non-discrimination and equal access to learning.

Traditional labor law is still not at the stage to regulate all aspects of the impact associated with AI in the labor process. The dynamics of change in public relations is at a stage where traditional labor legislation not only fails anticipate, but it can not even catch up with. This is a serious challenge to the law, hitherto uncharacteristic in all its stages of development. The question here is not how to uphold traditional labor rights in general and the most basic of them - the right to work, in particular, but how to protect them in a humane and fair way from aggressive digitalisation, which affects too often and too abruptly the most sensitive human rights.

In the present study, a number of questions have been raised on the border between law and morality, which obviously have yet to find their solutions. The challenge for modern society is to respond to them with its familiar mechanisms so as to preserve the humanity and dignity of man in the most just and ethical way.

REFERENCES

Aleksandrov, A. (2019). Mitove i fakti v trudovoto i osiguritelnoto pravo: za digitaliziraneto na trudovopravnite dokumenti. *Trud i pravo, 12*, 13-19.

Aleksandrov, A. (2020). Za nesluchiloto se digitalizirane na trudovopravnata dokumentatsia i pravorazdavaneto po trudovi sporove i vredite, koito ponasya obshtestvoto ot tova. In *Pravoto i biznesat v savremennoto obshtestvo. Sbornik s dokladi ot 3-ta Natsionalna nauchna konferentsia*. Nauka i ikonomika.

Andreeva, A., & Yolova, G. (2018). Za subekta na pravoto na trud i predizvikatelstvata na tehnologichnoto obshtestvo. In *Tsifrova ikonomika i blokcheyn tehnologii: Edinadeseta mezhdunarodna nauchno-prilozhna konferentsia*. Largo siti.

Andreeva, A., & Yolova, G. (2020). Pravni aspekti na balansa mezhdu lichen i profesionalen zhivot. In *Pravoto i biznesat v savremennoto obshtestvo: Sbornik s dokladi ot 3-ta Natsionalna nauchna konferentsia*. Nauka i ikonomika.

Andreeva, A., & Yolova, G. (2021). Liability in Labor Legislation: New Challenges Related to theUse of Artificial Intelligence. In Responsible AI and Ethical Issues for Businesses and Governments. IGI Global.

Banov, H. (2020). Prekratyavane na trudovoto pravootnoshenie ot rabotnika ili sluzhitelya sreshtu plashtane po chl. 232, al. 3 ot Kodeksa na truda. *De Jure*, *2*, 110–120.

Banov, H., (2020). Prekratyavane na trudovoto pravootnoshenie pri obuchenie po vreme na rabota na osnovaniyata po chl. 232, al. 2 i 3 ot Kodeksa na truda. *Norma, 10*, 80–108.

Banov, H., (2020). Trudovopravni problemi pri obyavyavaneto na izvanredno polozhenie (chast II). *Obshtestvo i pravo, 5*, 70–86.

Banov, H. (2020). *Trudovoto vaznagrazhdenie pri trudovia dogovor za obuchenie po vreme na rabota. Aktualni problemi na trudovoto i osiguritelnoto pravo. T. XIII. Individualen trudov dogovor.* Kliment Ohridski.

Blagoycheva, H. (2020). The digitalisation as a stimulus for corporate social responsibility. In CSR and Socially Responsible Investing Strategies in Transitioning and Emerging Economies. IGI Global.

Blagoycheva, H., Andreeva, A., & Yolova, G. (2019). Obligation and Responsibility of Employers to Provide Health and Safety at Work – Principles, Current Regulation and Prospects. *Economic Studies*, *28*(2), 115–137.

Brynjolfsson, E., & Mcafee, A. (2011). *Race against the machine: how the digital revolution is accelerating innovation, driving productivity, and irreversibly transforming employment and the economy*. Digital Frontier Press.

Ford, M. (2015). *Rise of the robots: Technology and the threat of a jobless future*. Basic Books.

Walwei, U. (2016). *Digitalization and structural labour market problems: The case of Germany*. ILO Research Paper No. 17. Retrieved May 12, 2019, from: https://www.ilo.org/wcmsp5/groups/public/--- dgreports/---inst/documents/publication/wcms_522355.pdf

ADDITIONAL READING

Mrachkov, V. (2010). *Trudovo pravo*. Sibi.

Mrachkov, V., Sredkova, K., & Vasilev, A. (2009). *Komentar na Kodeksa na truda*. Sibi.

Radoilski, L. (1957). Trudovo pravo na Narodna Republika Bulgaria. Sofia: Nauka i izkustvo

Sredkova, K. (2011). *Trudovo pravo*. Sv. Kliment Ohridski.

KEY TERMS AND DEFINITIONS

Employer's Legal Capacity: Is a component derived from the legal definition of the term employer (Andreeva & Yolova, 2020). It can also be considered as a legal construction given the inclusion of elements that define the essence of the concept. In this sense, it is the legal opportunity provided by law to establish, manage, and terminate employment.

Employer's Power: It incorporates the rights that an employer (natural person or a legal entity) exercises when hiring and managing employees under an employment contract. In the Bulgarian labor law doctrine, they are defined as a triad of basic rights of the employer, including the components: managerial powers, rule-making powers, disciplinary powers.

EU Legal Acts: Sources of norms for the Community legal order. They are mainly divided into primary legislation, including the Treaty on European Union, the Treaty on the Functioning of the European Union and the protocols thereto, the Charter of Fundamental Rights of the European Union, the Treaty establishing the European Atomic Energy Community (Euratom), international agreements and general principles of EU law. The secondary legislation includes regulations, directives, decisions, recommendations, and opinions which the institutions of the Union may adopt only if express competence has been conferred on them by the provisions of the Treaties.

Freedom of Labor: A principle that penetrates at different levels in relations between the parties. It is fundamental to the development of relations between the parties, thus corresponding to democratic values and free economic initiative. Freedom of labor is enshrined at the highest level in our national legislation in the norm of Article 48, paragraphs 3 and 4 of the Constitution. This principle is applied in the field of labor law and according to the content criterion it refers to the general basic principles. The term freedom, included as the basis of the principle refracted through the prism of labor, aims to emphasize the wider choices provided to the person who is the provider of labor. The application of the constitutional norm in the sphere of the individual employment relationship is realized through and within the framework of an employment contract.

Humanization of Labor: Recognized by the ILO as a leading trend in the development of social and labor relations. Considered from the aspects of human resource management, the humanization of labor is closely linked to a toolkit of organizational, technical, and socio-economic measures to improve working conditions and the working environment, to enrich the content of labor, as well as the forms and methods of management in order to achieve an optimal match between the person and the provided workforce.

Principles of Labor Law: Basic guidelines of the industry, embodied in explicit legal norms or derived in an interpretative way from the norms of the sources.

Protective Function of Labor Law: Historically the earliest emerging function of the industry. It is enshrined in Bulgarian labor law at constitutional level in Article 16 of the Constitution and Article 1, paragraph 3 of the Labor Code. This function is also performed through a number of legal institutes, such as: working hours, vacations, holidays, safe and healthy working conditions, limited property liability, etc.

ENDNOTES

1. COM(2019) 168 final: Building trust in human-oriented artificial intelligence, 08.04.2019,https://eur-lex.europa.eu/legal-ontent/BG/TXT/PDF/?uri=CELEX:52019DC0168&from=en
2. The assessment of the level of risk for an application may be based on the consequences for the parties concerned. For example, AI applications that have legal or other similar material consequences for the rights of an individual or company; such that pose a risk of injury, death or significant material or non-material damage; such that give rise to consequences which natural or legal persons cannot avoid except through extraordinary efforts.

Chapter 12
Integrating Spirituality at the Workplace for Well-Being:
A Study on Academia in Higher Education

Tilottama Singh
https://orcid.org/0000-0001-6152-4658
Amity University, Noida, India

Sukanta Kumar Baral
https://orcid.org/0000-0003-2061-714X
Indira Gandhi National Tribal University, India

ABSTRACT

The notion of spirituality is a divisive area when it moves to its applicability in organizations. In today's scenario with so much of chaos and volatility in organization especially after the pandemic, one cannot ignore the significance of spiritual practices. With changing time, the significance of spirituality becomes more pertinent for employee wellbeing. With numerous studies being conducted in this field, however the research gap provides enough space for authors to work on understanding and deciding the substantial factors affecting spirituality among academicians. This study employs a positivist research approach, comprising of a quantitative basis of enquiry, and assembled data via survey questionnaires. A total of 358 questionnaires were allocated, and finally, 240 usable cases were selected for study. The factor structure was proved by using SEM. This study raises awareness on the significance of spirituality in the university wellbeing which will ultimately contribute to improving academic delivery and bringing more satisfaction. Further factor loading helps in assessment.

DOI: 10.4018/978-1-7998-8258-9.ch012

INTRODUCTION

The growing interest of people in the journey of life and death is an important catalyst in promoting the research in area of life meaning, understanding oneself and leading a calm clear and joyful life. The concept of spirituality has been a controversial topic, moving around the themes of religion or self-understanding. A lot of studies in this domain have demonstrated the glancing effect of this concept which has proved to be vital for individual development. The paths and definitions may be contradictory, but the results have been productive. The studies have shown a strong inclination towards spirituality during the uncertain times. The knocking of Covid across nations was alarming . It instigated a lot of people and organization to take step towards finding and implanting spiritual practices. The spiritual loss leads to insecurity amongst people (Obregon et al 2021). The question today is not to do with defining or supporting spirituality in form of religion rather it is to imbibe spiritual practices. There are varied professions and organizations taking small steps towards building spiritual and sustainable organizations (Shamsevi et al., 2021). Academics is one such field where spirituality flows from institution to teachers and further to the coming generations. Most of the researchers adjusted spirituality to reason for individual life which gives meaning, inward mindfulness, and information with feeling of presence. Uttami, et al, 2021 depicted otherworldliness like "attempting to grasp water", a few researchers like Claxton (2002) have strikingly recorded profound characteristics that can be educated to understudies, including aliveness, having a place, a proclivity with the obscure, and true serenity. Fenwick and Lange (1998) investigated how otherworldliness might be cognizant with learning and work through substitute methodologies that are more comprehensive, environmental, ecumenical, and moral. The studies highlight the relevance of spirituality in academics and routine of teacher. The success of an efficient teacher lies in the effectiveness of teaching with the amount of impression that teacher holds in life of students. This could only be achieved with talent accompanied by spiritual phenomena in a true academician role.

The progression in business education had been overwhelming in past twenty years but the last few years have witnessed the dropping of trends. The output generated through talent production has seen a fall (Chapman et al., 2021) which has been added after Covid scenario. Illes and Zsolnai (2017) contended that there is a solid lopsidedness in business schooling between giving freedoms and dynamic, objective ideas for self-awareness. To get ready understudies for the intricacies and difficulties of the working environment, it appears to be attractive for guides to send advantages of otherworldliness. Self-disclosure and investing energy getting to know their "actual self" are a pivotal piece of the improvement of future business experts. Rahman et al. (2015) led a review on Malaysian higher learning foundation, wherein they intended to increase the value of the momentum research on information sharing, examined the precursors of information sharing conduct by inserting work environment otherworldliness and trust variable. The otherworldliness of individuals and instructors creates after some time and is impacted by critical associations with others through lived encounters (Ambrose, 2005). Studies have substantiated that spirituality in academics tend to shape effective learning environment and enhancing teaching skills. World class universities are practicing training for building spiritual organizations. Few of them have even started with spirituality courses. The shift towards spirituality is phenomenal and has glaring results, academics promising the same through the country builders, the teachers.

However the exact examinations have accentuated on significance, challenges, conversations on benefits, yet the writing needs creating extensive investigation on the variables affecting otherworldliness in the academicians (Madero, 2021). The researchers point in defeating these gaps by examining the variables, unveiling their insight regarding explicit industry. Meager examination has driven us to embrace exploratory element investigation and clarify the most ruling difficulties through this methodology. The current study aims to examine the impact of spirituality on the performance of teachers in university during COVID times, where the immense transition of movement to online teaching was challenging but imperative for excellence as the teaching profession carries a lot of efforts in shaping the future through effective teaching, mentoring and guidance by the teachers. For the study, a sample of 358 teachers working in Delhi NCR during lockdown time has been taken. Further the factor structure was validated by using partial least square structure equation modeling. The study reveals the importance of spirituality as a measure to overcome various hindrances in effective teaching.

The education industry has been evolving with competitiveness and the need to keep in pace with economic transition is still relying on the soundness, principles and ethnicity grace. In the globalized world the essence of instructive framework is changing from solid images of social greatness to dynamic and adapting ivory pinnacles of information the board. The otherworldliness of individuals and instructors creates after some time and is affected by critical associations with others through lived encounters (Ambrose, 2005). When the idea of otherworldliness is examined, there are various ways to decipher it, on an individual level, and on a gathering focused, religious level, trailed by mainstream worries in the schools. Consequently, Watson (2000) asks how far we can install otherworldliness into common school conditions while bringing up the secularization of religion on one hand, and the religionization of skepticism in the schools and recommend that the two finishes should compromise. These gatherings are assisting with building individual relationship and social abundance in the society (Hedges and Schneider, 2005). Instructing is an honorable calling with commitments. Educators' working environment circumstances are deciding the instructors' accomplishment in this calling. Educating as work is a "call out" for most instructors. The mental self portrait of instructor consistently stays at focus with solid perspectives about the work (Gillespie, 2021).

METHODOLOGY

The study initiated a pilot study which comprised of fifty-two teachers from universities in Delhi NCR. During this stage, the factor assessment was performed for questionnaire designing. Hence the variables having communalities less than 0.40 and once with cross loading were eliminated. Thereby the final variable taken were 12 (Table 1). For the study 358 questionnaires were distributed out of which 262 were received and finally after scrutiny 240 questionnaires were taken for the study. Out of the total respondents, 90 were males and 172 were females. The value of Cronbach`s α for variables in the measurement scale was 0.79. The item V8 (I feel connected to my workplace) presented highest mean value of 4.16. While the item V4 (I feel stable in handling stress situations) presented lowest mean value of 2.72.

Table 1.

Item	Variable
Items in questionnaire	
V1	I feel independent in my job
V2	I feel motivated for the classes I take
V3	I am willing to take additional responsibility apart from teaching
V4	I feel stable in handling stress situations
V5	I can influence my peer group positively
V6	My workplace encourages more of experiential sharing during teaching
V7	I have a non-bias workplace
V8	I feel connected to my workplace
V9	I get growth opportunities at my workplace
V10	My work trains me for leadership roles in academics
V11	I feel contended with my teaching style and routine
V12	I have a flexible working scenario

Exploratory Factor Analysis (EFA)

The exploratory component investigation was applied to separate the variables by utilizing SPSS 18. In this examination the proportion of test size to variable is almost 20:1. The Bartlett's Test of Sphericity was performed to recognize the examples in crude information. The outcomes appear to connote the examples in dataset ($\chi 2 = 626.46$, df = 65, $p < .001$). To check the inspecting ampleness Kaiser-Meyer-Olkin measure was utilized with a test worth of 0.69. In the exploratory variable investigation head part examination extraction strategy was utilized. The Varimax with Kaiser Normalization was utilized as turn technique. The investigated model clarified 63.96 percent of absolute change with 4 dormant elements having Eigen esteems ≥ 1. The factors are showing communalities from 0.48 to 0.71. The aftereffects of EFA are given beneath (see Table 3).

Table 2.

Results of Factor Analysis (N = 240)				
Rotated Component Matrix				
Factors				
Item	**Output based work**	**Worthful Life**	**Good relations**	**Positive work environment**
V1	0.624			
V2	0.656			
V3	0.746			
V4	0.789			
V5		0.75		
V6		0.662		
V7		0.722		
V8			0.721	
V9			0.65	
V10			0.552	
V11				0.788
V12				0.678

The four extracted factors were (1) Output Based Work (2) Worthful Life(3) Good relations (4) Positive work environment.

- Output Based Work: 21.23% of variance with Eigen value of 2.54 was explained by the factor output based work. The variable refers to the understanding of work profile with reference to output and clarity in process, which brings satisfaction. The variables loadings were from 0.62 to 0.71.
- Worthful life: 14.40 percent of variance is depicted by the factor Worthful life and had Eigen value of1.74. The stability in emotions and understanding of people around instigate in leading a life of value. The loadings were from 0.650 to 0.70.
- Good relations: This factor explained the 14.17 percent of variance with Eigen value of 1.67. It emphasizes on relevance of cordial interpersonal relation which is a predicament for well being. The factor loadings were 0.55 to 0.73.
- Positive work environment: This explained the 12.13 percent of variance with loading of 0.62 and 0.81. It refers to the effect of others behavior on your well being and working in organization.
- The EFA signifies the underlying factor structure of perceived workplace spirituality the hypothesis H1 accepted.

A set of four latent variables representing work, life, relationship and working environment were explored and used for structure validation.

Model Validation

The underlying model was approved by utilizing PLS-SEM 2.0. The component loadings, T-esteem, inactive factors file worth and way still up in the air for second request underlying model of workplace spirituality. The legitimacy and dependability of model were tried as far as normal change extricated (AVE); composite unwavering quality (CR) and commonness esteems (see Table 3). The factual upsides of AVE and CR for all elements addressed a substantial and dependable calculate structure the underlying model.

Table 3.

Factors Reliability & Validity Statistics			
Factors	**AVE/ Average Variance extracted**	**CR/ Composite Reliability**	**Communality**
Output based work	0.596	0.753	0.587
Worthful life	0.543	0.853	0.593
Good relations	0.533	0.689	0.459
Positive work environment	0.589	0.722	0.599

The bootstrapping was performed to analyze the significance of factor loadings of formative constructs. The T Value is given in Table 5. PLS algorithm was used to calculate the path coefficients and latent variables index value for structural model. The factor output based work represented highest path coefficient with a factor loading of 0.622. While positive work environment represented lowest value of path coefficient with a factor loading of 0.189 (see Table 4).

Table 4.

Path Coefficient, Factor Loadings and T-Value of Workplace Spirituality Model (PLS-SEM)				
Factors	**Factor Loading**	**T-Value**	**Factor Index Value**	**Path Coefficient**
Output based work	0.622	10.46	3.778	0.677
Worthful life	0.245	3.413	3.388	0.268
Good relations	0.344	5.587	3.199	0.287
Positive work environment	0.189	2.897	3.543	0.159

The outcomes from Figure 1 are plainly showing yield-based work as a fundamental part of spirituality among academicians, upheld by relational great relations with associates. The teachers perceived spirituality at work environment by acquiring importance out of their work jobs in study halls by self-acknowledgment by means of showing understudies and afterward by collaborating with individual educators to create thought of shared liability at work. The initiative, soundness, and security in work jobs of instructors are creating significant life at work environment. The positive work space was the most un-contributing element in the concentrate however showing a critical effect on the working environment otherworldliness of educators. The outcomes from Table 4 and Table 5 plainly demonstrated that the conjectured model fitted the information. The variables contributed essentially toward the otherworldliness among academicians in advanced education. The instructors recognized their work and which means drawn from their work as a fundamental power contributing toward work workplace spirituality.

DISCUSSION

The effective application of spirituality at work is promising the reinvention of charm and values in the classrooms. This will not only help the professors to overcome challenges and task they are facing but also help the whole learning system. Implementation and transfer of transcendent values to classrooms will help to create teachers' conduct full of human values, helping the behavior and rewarding the outcome. Spirituality at work though meaningful work and healthy work environment. The future researchers can check the relationship at outcomes level. Also the spirituality here is not in context to following any religion or faith, rather its much beyond and deals with intrinsic awareness and self-morale.

CONCLUSION

The review gives a scientific system to the decision makers in the education sector. The examination focused on investigating the elements affecting the spirituality among academicians. The current scenario has increased the relevance of spirituality across every organization. With massive transformation in academics its become imperative to understand the factors effecting spiritual quotient of teachers as they are the catalyst towards building a sustainable and poised future leaders, entrepreneurs and workforce. The motivation behind the present study is to equip the Indian education sector to understand the benefits of spiritual organizations and overcome the hurdles in its implementation.

The study adopts methodology based on EFA to understand the factor relationship among the factors contributing to spirituality in teachers. The aim of the paper was to identify the factors and to establish the relationship for further studies. The relevancy of the factors is checked through factor loading followed by model fit. As per our research all the factors are highly important for influencing spirituality amongst teachers in higher education. The result stated that the most relevant factor is out based work, and the least is positive work environment as for an academician who is high on spirituality, external environment does not matter. It can also be concluded that cause from any factor very much affects the other factor.

The future scope and research include assessment of the research on the primary data and use of other methodologies.

REFERENCES

Obregon, S. L., Lopes, L. F. D., Kaczam, F., da Veiga, C. P., & da Silva, W. V. (2021). Religiosity, Spirituality and Work: A Systematic Literature Review and Research Directions. *Journal of Business Ethics*, 1–23. doi:10.100710551-021-04856-7

Utami, N. M. S., Sapta, I., Verawati, Y., & Astakoni, I. (2021). Relationship between workplace spirituality, organizational commitment and organizational citizenship behavior. *The Journal of Asian Finance, Economics, and Business*, *8*(1), 507–517.

Shamsiev, J. M. U., Rashidova, R. R., & Tajibaev, M. A. (2021). The role of teachers in building the future of the nation. *Science Progress*, *1*(5).

Chapman, A. L., Foley, L., Halliday, J., & Miller, L. (2021). Relational spirituality in K-12 education: A multi-case study. *International Journal of Children's Spirituality*, •••, 1–25.

Zsolnai, L., & Illes, K. (2017). Spiritually inspired creativity in business. *International Journal of Social Economics*.

Rahman, M. S., Osmangani, A. M., Daud, N. M., Chowdhury, A. H., & Hassan, H. (2015). Trust and work place spirituality on knowledge sharing behaviour: Perspective from non-academic staff of higher learning institutions. *The Learning Organization*.

Claxton, G. (2002). *Building learning power*. TLO Limited Bristol.

Fenwick, T., & Lange, E. (1998). Spirituality in the workplace: The new frontier of HRD. *Canadian Journal for the Study of Adult Education*, *12*(1), 63–87.

Madero, C. (2021). Because I Am called: How a calling to teach emerges and develops in teachers working in catholic high schools. *Teaching and Teacher Education*, *101*, 103319. doi:10.1016/j.tate.2021.103319

Gillespie, A. (2021). Teachers' Spirituality or Spiritualities? In *Spirituality in Education: Professional Accounts of the Impact of Spirituality on Education*. Emerald Publishing Limited. doi:10.1108/978-1-83909-894-920211003

Hedges, L. V., & Schneider, B. (Eds.). (2005). *The social organization of schooling*. Russell Sage Foundation.

Watson, J. (2000). Whose model of spirituality should be used in the spiritual development of school children? *International Journal of Children's Spirituality*, *5*(1), 91–101. doi:10.1080/713670894

Ambrose, R. (2005). Relational spirituality and the lived experiences of classroom community. *Journal of Curriculum and Pedagogy*, *2*(2), 93–96. doi:10.1080/15505170.2005.10411554

Chapter 13
Distribution of Wealth for Sustainable Happiness

Sheakh Reyad Muhammad Noor
Dhaka University, Bangladesh

Zobaida Afroz
Siddheswari Girls' College, Bangladesh

Ayesha Akter Mousumi
Arctech, Bangladesh

ABSTRACT

The richest one percent of the entire population of the world now owns more than half of the global wealth which shows global wealth is unequally distributed. Moreover, this is assumed that sustainable growth is impossible based on impossibility theorem. Considering the above, the study has been conducted and critically overviewed the wealth distribution of an ancient period based on Islamic rules and practice. Upon study, it has been found that people are very much self-centered and unaware of the broader perspective like searching happiness instead of immediate wealth maximization. The finding has also shown that right of inheritances, relatives, neighbors, society, and state should be defined clearly and need distribution of wealth based on definition. If we become more self-centered, we will find ourselves helpless. Here, wealth means knowledge and physical assets.

INTRODUCTION

Every rich people are not happy as all like every poor are not unhappy. A news published in ABC news on March 18, 2021 where they mentioned that survey of

DOI: 10.4018/978-1-7998-8258-9.ch013

"Joys and Dilemma of Wealth" done by Boston College. In the survey it is found that we assumed poor is very miserable but it turns out money doesn't buy as much happiness as people think it would buy. Elizebeth Dunn, researcher said that money might not provide as much happiness as people want because people might not spend the money rightly. They also found that people get more happiness by spending money on others.

In the research, they are yet to provide any specific way for distribution of wealth for inclusive and sustainable development which has justified to write this chapter.

Objective of the Study

Study has been conducted for the following objectives:

i. Finding the appropriate ways of wealth distributions and reason of which.
ii. Finding the appropriate ways of wealth expenditure for happiness.

LITERATURE REVIEW

Stephen Polasky (2015) Inclusive wealth is well-defined as the collective value of all capital assets. Rises in inclusive wealth indicate an enhanced industrious base capable of supportive a higher standard of living in the upcoming days. Despite the pragmatic challenges, inclusive wealth gives a clear, comprehensible, and systematic framework for speaking sustainable development.

Glenn-Marie Lange (29 October 2012) Considering the growth in economy, several studies attempted to measure total national wealth or changes in wealth but have been hampered by a insufficient data, especially for natural and human capital. Considering newly accessible accounts for natural capital in Namibia, total state wealth accounts are made and used to assess its development indicators, comparing it to its neighbor, Botswana. In Namibia's before 1990 (pre-independence period), there was noteworthy liquidation of capital, natural and produced. With new policies and a new investment environment since independence, Namibia has slowly started to rebuild its national wealth although per capita wealth has not recovered to the level of 1980

Eli P. Fenichel (2016) The study implies that sustainable development considering climate change requires a coherent approach that assimilates biophysical and social measurement. Inclusive wealth offers a measure that indicates sustainability and added an organizational framework for integrating the many disciplines studying global change.

Rintaro Yamaguchi (2016) The study construct a regional inclusive wealth as an indicator of sustainability in Miyagi Prefecture, Japan. Findings of the study show, regional wealth index already in declining during the 2000s due to stagnant investment into capital assets, oil capital loss, and budget deficit.

R. Costanza (2002) This chapter has studied with the relationship among wealth, resources, distribution, and quality of life. Policy goals for improving or maintaining quality of life can seek to create the objective conditions associated with a superior quality of life or attempt to change people's subjective assessment of conditions in a way that improves quality of life.

JUSTIFICATION OF THE STUDY

People are searching happiness and pursuing that money making will make them happy but the research shows if they don't know the right expenditure ways the rich people cannot be happy at all. In the earlier research the researchers are yet to show right path of wealth distribution and expenditure which has justified for further study.

METHODOLOGY OF THE STUDY

In the study, in depth interview of 20 number of rich people have been taken based on open ended questions, law and practice of ancient period has been revalued of ancient period, story of some poor have been observed in depth and finally concluded that wealth distribution and expenditure guidelines given in holy books can be acceptable for all human considering the human welfare. Bulletin, Articles in Newspaper and journal have also reviewed, blogs and journals have been reviewed for the purpose of findings.

WEALTH DISTRIBUTION BASED ON HOLY QURAN

Material Wealth

How Inheritance is Distributed

As per guidelines of Holy Quran, Inheritance has been distributed to the primary beneficiaries, and contingent beneficiaries.

The spouse, children, and parents are the primary beneficiaries. A range of people, upstream, downstream and sideways are the contingent beneficiaries. They are the grandparents, siblings, grandchildren, uncles and aunts and so forth. The relationship is matters.

Inheritance Fixed and Variable

The shares of the primary heirs have two types, i.e. fixed and variable. Spouse and Parent are taking based of fixed shares like, husband's share is either ¼ or ½, depending on children. It is either 1/8 or 1/4, for wife depending on children again. But 1/6 for the father, and 1/6 for the mother. The remaining part goes to the children, where two shares for the son for every share of the daughter.

Example of Inheritance Distribution

Example: At her death, Salma was married to Kalam and had two sons, Jobbar and Bimol, and one daughter, Bithi. Her parents, Afroza and Iqbal also survive her. She also has two brothers, Ishaq and Yacoob, and a sister, Sarah. Inheritance from Salma would be distributed as follows:

- Kamal: gets ¼
- Jobbar and Bimol get 1/6 each
- Bithi gets 1/12
- Afroza and Iqbal get 1/6 each
- Her brothers and sister do not inherit at all.

If we change the facts a little though, Say Salma is not survived by her father but all other survived as mentioned above. In that case, the brothers and sister still do not inherit, the husband Kamal and mother Bithi get the same amount as before, but all the children will get more. So, the universe of heirs is not increased. The daughter then gets 7/60 and the sons get 7/30. The husband remains at ¼ and the mother at 1/6. This is the simple example only.

Sharing Prosperity for Happiness

Doing expenditure for others are making us happy. For happiness we can follow the guidelines of Zakath as follows:

Payment made annually under Quran on certain kinds of property is called Zakath. The general practice is that the amount of zakat paid on monetary assets i.e. 2.5% (1/40) on unused (within one year) assets.

Zakath is payable favoring the following based on holy Quran:

1. Those are poor
2. Those cannot meet their basic needs
3. Those who collectors of zakath.
4. To persuade to come in the line of Quran.
5. To free from their master who have purchased them for slavery.
6. Those have incurred overwhelming debts for attempting their basic needs.
7. Those fighting for Quran.
8. Wayfarers, stranded travelers.

Parents, grandparents, children, grandchildren, spouses of zakath payers are not eligible to receive zakath.

Distribution of Wealth of Attitude

Attitude makes us success and happiness. Example of some good attitudes are given below which might be make us happy:

1. *Steps to take good work*: Business without hampering the environment and human health can be considered as good work. Good work is also considered as prayer, so every steps of good work make us happy.
2. *Enjoying good to others:* Giving sincere and good advice to others; saying a good word to others; encouraging others on the right path, all of these can make you happy.
3. *Smiling:* Only few can smile in hard time who can truly depend of creature. So, keep smiling for happiness.
4. *Sharing Knowledge:* If you know something good, teach it to others, it will make you happy. Sharing knowledge, you can increase your knowledge.

All are the wealth of attitude that can make us happy, which cannot buy through money but needs good heart.

FINDINGS OF THE STUDY

Findings of the study shows that wealth is not for own consumptions and consumption of wealth by himself no one can be happy but create unhappiness.

In the short time we can be happy by purchasing materials goods and services. Then we will require more and more buying for short time happiness. We can move the buying for ourselves to buying for others like orphan, poor, needy and less wealthy person. We should have distributed our material wealth to the successors and neighbors for their happiness which will ultimately revert our happiness. If we don't provide the wealth to the successors they may go to court and some of them may do unlawful activities. If neighbors are in very much needy and cannot arrange their basic needs they may create safety and security problem of rich. Moreover, poor are labor of rich house/factory as well as consumer of their business goods. So, if the poor has money they will buy the goods of rich business men and earnings of rich will also increase.

As such, a standard rate based on Quran is very much acceptable for sharing prosperity and distribution of wealth to the successors and neighbors. We also find that the guidelines Quran is making happy to every human not mandatory to be a Muslim.

CONCLUSION

The study provides how to share the assets among several stakeholders like distribution of wealth among inheritance based of Quran, donating poor neighbors and relatives, providing zakath to the identified eight sectors at distinct rate like 2.50% on unutilized assets, and also doing good deeds through good attitude can make us happy. Through this way all the rich can be happy like enlighten human irrespective of poor and rich.

RECOMMENDED FOR FURTHER STUDY

Finding happiness of require specific index and primary data of several social representatives. Considering the fact, we also recommend further study upon obtaining primary data considering the guidelines of holy books and also guidelines of social leaders/ philosopher.

REFERENCES

Aid, M. (2020). *5 Acts of Sadaqah Jaariyah in Islam*. Retrieved from https://www.muslimaid.org/media-centre/blog/5-acts-of-sadaqah-jaariyah-in-islam/

Brown. (2018). *Why Over-Consumption Is Making Us Unhappy*. Academic Press.

Fenichel. (2016). Wealth reallocation and sustainability under climate change. *Nature Climate Change*.

Ikeda. (2017). *Inclusive wealth of regions: the case of Japan*. Springer.

Jingyu. (2020, June 15). Measuring inclusive wealth of China: Advances in sustainable use of resources. *Journal of Environmental Management, 264*.

Kurniawan. (2018). Economic Growth and Sustainable Development in Indonesia. Bulletin of Indonesian Economic Studies, 54.

Lange. (2012). *Natural Capital, Total Wealth and Sustainable Development in Namibia*. Springer.

Polasky. (2015). *Annual Review of Environment and Resources, Inclusive Wealth as a Metric of Sustainable Development*. Academic Press.

Shams, Z. A. (2018). *10 ways to give Sadaqah other than giving money*. Retrieved from https://sarahmuzaffar.wordpress.com/2018/02/09/10-ways-to-give-sadaqah-other-than-giving-money/

Steblyanskaya. (2021). Changes in sustainable growth dynamics: The case of China and Russia gas industries. *Energy Strategy Reviews, 33*.

Yamaguchi. (2016). *Measuring Regional Wealth and Assessing Sustainable Development: An Application to a Disaster-Torn Region in Japan*. Springer.

Zakat. (n.d.). In *Wikipedia*. Retrieved from https://en.wikipedia.org/wiki/Zakat

Compilation of References

Abi-Habib. (2020). Millions Had Risen Out of Poverty. *New York Times.*

Afşar, M. (2007). *The Causality Relationship between Economic Growth & Foreign Direct Investment in Turkey.* Conference Paper, "Business & Economics Society International 2007 (B&ESI), Antibes, France.

Ahmed, S. (2018). *Bike makers ride into booming market.* Available at: https://www.theindependentbd.com/printversion/details/155994

Ahmed, J. U., Gazi, M. A., Iqbal, R., Islam, Q. T., & Talukder, N. (2020). Value co-creation through social innovation in healthcare: A case of WE CARE Solar. *World Journal of Entrepreneurship, Management and Sustainable Development, 16*(4), 341–357. doi:10.1108/WJEMSD-03-2020-0024

Aid, M. (2020). *5 Acts of Sadaqah Jaariyah in Islam.* Retrieved from https://www.muslimaid.org/media-centre/blog/5-acts-of-sadaqah-jaariyah-in-islam/

Aida, J., Kondo, K., Kondo, N., Watt, R. G., Sheiham, A., & Tsakos, G. (2011). Income inequality, social capital and self-rated health and dental status in older Japanese. *Social Science & Medicine, 73*(10), 1561–1568. doi:10.1016/j.socscimed.2011.09.005 PMID:21982631

Airbnb, Inc. (2019). *Airbnb Newsroom.* Available at: https://news.airbnb.com/fast-facts/

Alagöz, M., Erdoğan, S., & Topallı, N. (2008). Foreign Direct Investment and Economic Growth: Evidence from Turkey 1992-2007. *Gaziantep University Journal of Social Sciences, 7*(1), 79–89.

Aleksandrov, A. (2019). Mitove i fakti v trudovoto i osiguritelnoto pravo: za digitaliziraneto na trudovopravnite dokumenti. *Trud i pravo, 12*, 13-19.

Aleksandrov, A. (2020). Za nesluchiloto se digitalizirane na trudovopravnata dokumentatsia i pravorazdavaneto po trudovi sporove i vredite, koito ponasya obshtestvoto ot tova. In *Pravoto i biznesat v savremennoto obshtestvo. Sbornik s dokladi ot 3-ta Natsionalna nauchna konferentsia.* Nauka i ikonomika.

Alpert, M. I., & Peterson, R. A. (1972). On the Interpretation of Canonical Analysis. *JMR, Journal of Marketing Research, 9*(2), 187–192. doi:10.1177/002224377200900211

Alverado, F., & Cjancel, L. (2018). *World Inequality Report*. World Inequality Lab. Press. doi:10.4159/9780674984769

Ambrose, R. (2005). Relational spirituality and the lived experiences of classroom community. *Journal of Curriculum and Pedagogy*, *2*(2), 93–96. doi:10.1080/15505170.2005.10411554

An, D., Yang, Y., Chai, X., Xi, B., Dong, L., & Ren, J. (2015). Mitigating pollution of hazardous materials from WEEE of China: Portfolio selection for a sustainable future based on multi-criteria decision making. Resour. *Conserv Recycl*, *105*, 198–210. doi:10.1016/j.resconrec.2015.10.025

Andreeva, A. (2020). Digitalization as a Factor for the Development of the Modern Labour Legislation. In *Digital Economy: Azerbaijan at the New Stage of Economic Development: Conference Proceedings of the International Scientific-Practical Conference*. Baku Business University.

Andreeva, A., & Yolova, G. (2017). Tendentsii i predizvikatelstva pred trudovoto i osiguritelnoto zakonodatelstvo - deset godini sled chlenstvoto na R. Bulgaria v ES. *Nauchni trudove na Instituta za darzhavata i pravoto, 16*, 251 - 261.

Andreeva, A., & Yolova, G. (2018). Za subekta na pravoto na trud i predizvikatelstvata na tehnologichnoto obshtestvo. In *Tsifrova ikonomika i blokcheyn tehnologii: Edinadeseta mezhdunarodna nauchno-prilozhna konferentsia*. Largo siti.

Andreeva, A., & Yolova, G. (2019). The Right to Work in a Digital Society: Evolution and Trends. Mezhdunarodni klasterni politiki: Balgaro-kitayski forum: Sbornik s dokladi ot mezhdunarodna konferentsia. Varna: Nauka i ikonomika.

Andreeva, A., & Yolova, G. (2020). Liability in Labour Legislation: New Challenges Related to the Use of Artificial Intelligence. In Responsible AI and Ethical Issues for Businesses and Governments (pp. 214-232). IGI Global.

Andreeva, A., & Yolova, G. (2020). Pravni aspekti na balansa mezhdu lichen i profesionalen zhivot. In *Pravoto i biznesat v savremennoto obshtestvo: Sbornik s dokladi ot 3-ta Natsionalna nauchna konferentsia*. Nauka i ikonomika.

Andreeva, A., & Yolova, G. (2020). *Trudovo i osiguritelno pravo*. Nauka i ikonomika.

Andreeva, A., & Yolova, G. (2021). Liability in Labor Legislation: New Challenges Related to theUse of Artificial Intelligence. In Responsible AI and Ethical Issues for Businesses and Governments. IGI Global.

Andreeva, A., & Dimitrova, D. (2019). *Spetsifiki na kontrola na izpalnitelna agentsia glavna inspektsia po truda, v konteksta na garantsiite za izplashtane na trudovoto vaznagrazhdenie*. Burgaski svoboden universitet.

Aouhassi, S., & Hanoune, M. (2019). Specific Qualification for Information System Components from Managers and Technical Staff Perspective. In Y. Farhaoui & L. Moussaid (Eds.), *Big Data and Smart Digital Environment. ICBDSDE 2018. Studies in Big Data* (Vol. 53). Springer. doi:10.1007/978-3-030-12048-1_6

Arısoy, İ. (2012). The Impact of Foreign Direct Investment on Total Factor Productivity & Economic Growth in Turkey. *Journal of Developing Areas*, *46*(1), 17–29. doi:10.1353/jda.2012.0013

Aslaksen, E. W. (2020). Political and Economic Factors. In *The Stability of Society. Lecture Notes in Networks and Systems* (Vol. 113). Springer. doi:10.1007/978-3-030-40226-6_7

Audette. (2019). *Gender report policy*. https://genderpolicyreport.umn.edu/gender-equality-supports-happiness/

Awan, U., Kanwal, N., & Bhutta, M. (2020). A Literature Analysis of Definitions for a Circular Economy. *Ecoproduction*, 19-34. doi:10.1007/978-3-642-33857-1_2

Babones, S. J. (2008). Income inequality and population health: Correlation and causality. *Social Science & Medicine*, *66*(7), 1614–1626. doi:10.1016/j.socscimed.2007.12.012 PMID:18222588

Baker, S. R., Bloom, N., Davis, S. J., Kost, K., Sammon, M., & Viratyosin, T. (2020). *The unprecedented stock market reaction to COVID-19*. National Bureau of Economic Research Working Paper, 26945. https://www.nber.org/papers/w26945

Banov, H., (2020). Prekratyavane na trudovoto pravootnoshenie pri obuchenie po vreme na rabota na osnovaniyata po chl. 232, al. 2 i 3 ot Kodeksa na truda. *Norma, 10*, 80–108.

Banov, H., (2020). Trudovopravni problemi pri obyavyavaneto na izvanredno polozhenie (chast II). *Obshtestvo i pravo, 5*, 70–86.

Banov, H. (2020). Prekratyavane na trudovoto pravootnoshenie ot rabotnika ili sluzhitelya sreshtu plashtane po chl. 232, al. 3 ot Kodeksa na truda. *De Jure*, *2*, 110–120.

Banov, H. (2020). *Trudovoto vaznagrazhdenie pri trudovia dogovor za obuchenie po vreme na rabota. Aktualni problemi na trudovoto i osiguritelnoto pravo. T. XIII. Individualen trudov dogovor.* Kliment Ohridski.

Bardhi, F., & Eckhardt, G. M. (2012). Access-Based Consumption: The Case of Car Sharing. *The Journal of Consumer Research*, *39*(4), 881–898. doi:10.1086/666376

Battacharya, M. (2010). Causal Nexus Trade, FDI and Economic Growth -Evidence from India. *Paradigm*, *14*(1), 12–23. doi:10.1177/0971890720100104

Batten, J., & Vo, X. V. (2009). An analysis of the relationship between foreign direct investment and economic growth. *Applied Economics*, *41*(13), 1621–1641. doi:10.1080/00036840701493758

Belek, İ. (2001). *Sosyal Devletin Çöküşü ve Sağlığın Ekonomi Politiği*. Sorun Yayınları.

Belk, R. (2014). You are what you can access: Sharing and collaborative consumption online. *Journal of Business Research*, *67*(8), 1595–1600. doi:10.1016/j.jbusres.2013.10.001

Benoit, S., Baker, T. L., Bolton, R. N., Gruber, T., & Kandampully, J. (2017). A triadic framework for collaborative consumption (CC): Motives, activities and resources & capabilities of actors. *Journal of Business Research*, *79*, 219–227. doi:10.1016/j.jbusres.2017.05.004

Berkhout, F., & Hertin, J. (2004). De-materialising and re-materialising: Digital technologies and the environment. *Futures*, *36*(8), 903–920. doi:10.1016/j.futures.2004.01.003

Bilgili, F., Tülüce, N. S. H., & Doğan, İ. (2012). The determinants of FDI in Turkey: A Markov Regime-Switching approach. *Economic Modelling*, *29*(4), 1161–1169. doi:10.1016/j.econmod.2012.04.009

Blagoycheva, H. (2016). Employment and the "Working Poor" Phenomenon in the EU. *International Journal of Economics and Business Administration, 4*(3), 3 - 18.

Blagoycheva, H. (2020). The digitalisation as a stimulus for corporate social responsibility. In CSR and Socially Responsible Investing Strategies in Transitioning and Emerging Economies. IGI Global.

Blagoycheva, H., Andreeva, A., & Yolova, G. (2018). Legal Framework of Occupational Health Servicesin the EU and in Bulgaria. Izvestiya Journal of Varna University of Economics, 62(3-4), 250 - 264.

Blagoycheva, H., Andreeva, A., & Yolova, G. (2019). Obligation and Responsibility of Employers to Provide Health and Safety at Work – Principles, Current Regulation and Prospects. *Economic Studies*, *28*(2), 115–137.

Blevis, E. (2007). Sustainable Interaction Design: Invention & Disposal, Renewal & Reuse. CHI 2007 Proceedings, 503-512.

BLI. (2021, March 15). *Better life index*. http://www.oecdbetterlifeindex.org/#/11111111111

Block, J. H., Fisch, C. O., & Praag, M. (2016). The Schumpeterian entrepreneur: A review of the empirical evidence on the antecedents, behaviour and consequences of innovative entrepreneurship. *Industry and Innovation*, *24*(1), 61–95. doi:10.1080/13662716.2016.1216397

Bloom, D. E., Canning, D., & Jamison, D. T. (2004). *Health, Wealth and Welfare, Health and Development*. IMF Publishing.

Botsman, R., & Rogers, R. (2010). *What's Mine Is Yours: The Rise of Collaborative Consumption*. Harper Collins.

Bozma, G., Eren, M., & Başar, S. (2018). Income distribution inequality and life expectancy relationships: Wilkinson hypothesis. *Atatürk Üniversitesi İktisadi ve İdari Bilimler Dergisi*, *32*(3), 793–805.

Brinkman, R. L., & Brinkman, J. E. (2011). GDP as a measure of progress and human development: A process of conceptual evolution. *Journal of Economic Issues*, *45*(2), 447–456. doi:10.2753/JEI0021-3624450222

Brown. (2018). *Why Over-Consumption Is Making Us Unhappy*. Academic Press.

Brundtland, G. H., Khalid, M., Agnelli, S., Al-Athel, S., & Chidzero, B. J. N. Y. (1987). Our common future. Academic Press.

Brynjolfsson, E., & Mcafee, A. (2011). *Race against the machine: how the digital revolution is accelerating innovation, driving productivity, and irreversibly transforming employment and the economy*. Digital Frontier Press.

Bryson, L. (1992). *Welfare and the state: Who benefits?* Macmillan/British Sociological Association. doi:10.1007/978-1-349-22282-7

Büyükakın, F., Bozkurt, H., & Cengiz, V. (2015). The Analysis of the Interest Channel of the Monetary Flows in Turkey with the Granger Causality and Toda-Yamamoto Methods. İİBF Journal of the Erciyes University, 33, 101-118.

Çalışkan, Ş., Karabacak, M., & Meçik, O. (2017). The Education Expenses in the Turkish Economy and its Correlation to Economic Growth. The Bootstrap Toda-Yamamoto Causality Test Approach. *KOSBED*, *33*(1), 45–56.

Callon, M., Courtial, J.-P., Turner, W. A., & Bauin, S. (1983). From translations to problematic networks: An introduction to co-word analysis. *Social Sciences Information. Information Sur les Sciences Sociales*, *22*(2), 191–235. doi:10.1177/053901883022002003

Çankaya, S. (2005). *Kanonik Korelasyon Analizi ve Hayvancılıkta Kullanımı* (Unpublished doctoral dissertation). Çukurova Üniversitesi Fen Bilimleri Enstitüsü, Adana, Turkey.

Chancel, L. (2019). *Ten facts about inequality in advanced economies*. WID Working Paper.

Chandrasekhar, C. P., & Ghosh, J. (2002). *The Market that Failed*. Leftword Books.

Chapman, A. L., Foley, L., Halliday, J., & Miller, L. (2021). Relational spirituality in K-12 education: A multi-case study. *International Journal of Children's Spirituality*, •••, 1–25.

Cheng, M. (2016). Sharing economy: A review and agenda for future research. *International Journal of Hospitality Management*, *57*, 60–70. doi:10.1016/j.ijhm.2016.06.003

Choudhari, R. (2020). COVID 19 pandemic: Mental health challenges of internal migrant workers of India. *Asian Journal of Psychiatry*, *54*, 102254. doi:10.1016/j.ajp.2020.102254 PMID:32593122

Chowdhury, A., & Mavrotas, G. (2006). FDI & Growth: What Causes What? *World Economy*, *29*(1), 9–19. doi:10.1111/j.1467-9701.2006.00755.x

Cipollina, M., Giovannetti, G., Pietrovito, F., & Pozzolo, A. (2012). FDI and Growth: What Cross-country Industry Data Say. *World Economy*, *35*(11), 1599–1629. doi:10.1111/j.1467-9701.2012.01478.x

Clark, G. (2013). *Fukaralığa Veda Dünyanın Kısa İktisadi Tarihi* (Vol. 1). Baskı, Bilgi Üniversitesi Yayınları.

Claxton, G. (2002). *Building learning power*. TLO Limited Bristol.

Cobb, C., Halstead, T., & Rowe, J. (1995). If the GDP is up, why is America down? *Atlantic Monthly*, *276*, 59–78.

Corak, M. (2020). COVID-19 is not the great leveller, it's the great revealer. *Economics for Public Policy, 13*. https://milescorak.com/2020/04/13/covid-19-is-not-the-great-leveller-its-the-great-revealer/

Corona, B., Shen, L., Reike, D., Carreón, J. R., & Worrell, E. (2019). Towards sustainable development through the circular economy—A review and critical assessment on current circularity metrics. *Resources, Conservation and Recycling, 151*, 104498. doi:10.1016/j.resconrec.2019.104498

Costanza, R., Hart, M., Posner, S., & Talberth, J. (2009). *Beyond GDP: The need for new measures of progress. The Pardee Papers, No. 4*. Boston University.

Couchsurfing International, Inc. (2017). *About Couchsurfing*. Available at: https://www.couchsurfing.com/about/about-us/

Çukur, A., & Bekmez, S. (2011). The Relationship between Income, Income Inequality and Health in Turkey: Evidence from Panel Data Analysis. *Gaziantep Üniversitesi Sosyal Bilimler Dergisi, 10*(1), 21–40.

Dakare, A., & Thakare, A. P. (2012). Recycling and reusing the e-waste. *IJMIE, 2*(6).

Davidson, A., Habibi, M. R., & Laroche, M. (2017). Materialism and the sharing economy: A cross-cultural study of American and Indian consumers. *Journal of Business Research, 82*, 364–372. doi:10.1016/j.jbusres.2015.07.045

Deaton, A. (2003). Health, Inequality, and Economic Development. *Journal of Economic Literature, 41*(1), 113–158. doi:10.1257/jel.41.1.113

Delhey, J., & Kroll, C. (2012). "Happiness Test" for the new measures of national well- being: how much better than gdp are they? *Wissenschaftszentrum Berlin für Sozialforsclung (WZB) Discussion Paper*, (201), 1-33.

Deshpande, A. (2020, November 6). On Gender Equity, Press Reset. *The Indian Express*, p. 7.

Detollenaerea, J., Desmarest, A. S., Boeckxstaens, P., & Willems, W. (2018). The link between income inequality and health in Europe, adding strength dimensions of primary care to the equation. *Social Science & Medicine, 201*, 103–110. doi:10.1016/j.socscimed.2018.01.041 PMID:29471179

Dicky, D., & Fuller, W. (1981). Likelihood Ratio Statistics for Autoregressive Time Series with A Unit Root. *Econometrica, 49*(4), 1057–1072. doi:10.2307/1912517

Dimelis, S., & Papaioannou, S. (2010). FDI and ICT Effects on Productivity Growth: A Comparative Analysis of Developing and Developed Countries. *European Journal of Development Research, 22*(1), 79–96. doi:10.1057/ejdr.2009.45

Dimitrova, D. (2019). Savremenni tendentsii v administrativnoto zakonodatelstvo na Bulgaria. In Pravoto i biznesat v savremennoto obshtestvo: Sbornik s dokladi ot 2-ra Natsionalna nauchna konferentsia. Nauka i ikonomika.

Dimitrova, D. (2020). Po nyakoi vaprosi na administrativnopravnata zashtita na pravoto na trud. In Pravoto i biznesat v savremennoto obshtestvo: Sbornik s dokladi ot 3-ta Natsionalna nauchna konferentsia. Nauka i ikonomika.

EF. (2021, March 15). *Ecological footprint.* https://www.footprintnetwork.org/our-work/ecological-footprint/

Elkington, J. (2004). Enter the triple bottom line. *The triple bottom line: Does it all add up, 11*(12), 1-16.

Elliot, G., Rothenberg, T., & Stock, J. (1996). Efficient Tests for An Autoregressive Unit Root. *Econometrica, 64*(4), 813–836. doi:10.2307/2171846

England, R. W. (1998). Measurement of social well-being: Alternatives to gross domestic product. *Ecological Economics, 25*(1), 89–103. doi:10.1016/S0921-8009(97)00098-0

Eugster, M. (2004). Knowledge partnership with developing and transition countries in E-Waste recycling. Presented at the *International Conference on Electric Waste and Producer's Environmental Responsibilities in China*, Beijing, China.

European Commission. (n.d.). Retrieved from https://ec.europa.eu/international-partnerships/sdg/peace-justice-and-strong-institutions_en

Eurostat. (2017). *Sustainable Development in the European Union 2017.* European Union Publishing.

Fenichel. (2016). Wealth reallocation and sustainability under climate change. *Nature Climate Change.*

Fenwick, T., & Lange, E. (1998). Spirituality in the workplace: The new frontier of HRD. *Canadian Journal for the Study of Adult Education, 12*(1), 63–87.

Filho, A. D. P. C., Kawachi, I., Wang, Y. P., Viana, M. C., & Andrade, L. H. S. G. (2013). Does income inequality get under the skin? A multilevel analysis of depression, anxiety and mental disorders in Sao Paulo, Brazil. *Journal of Epidemiology and Community Health, 67*(11), 966–972. doi:10.1136/jech-2013-202626 PMID:23908459

Fisch, C., & Block, J. (2018). Six tips for your (systematic) literature review in business and management research. *Management Review Quarterly, 68*(2), 103–106. doi:10.100711301-018-0142-x

Ford, M. (2015). *Rise of the robots: Technology and the threat of a jobless future*. Basic Books.

Forti, V., Baldé, C. P., Kuehr, R., & Bel, G. (2020). *The Global E-waste Monitor 2020. United Nations University (UNU), International Telecommunication Union (ITU) & International Solid Waste Association.* ISWA.

Frenken, K., & Schor, J. (2017). Putting the sharing economy into perspective. *Environmental Innovation and Societal Transitions, 23*, 3–10. doi:10.1016/j.eist.2017.01.003

Fu, J., Zhou, Q., Liu, J., Liu, W., Wang, T., Zhang, Q., & Jiang, G. (2008). High levels of heavy metals in rice (Oryza sativa L.) from a typical e-Waste recycling area in southeast China and its potential risk to human health. *Chemosphere*, *71*(7), 1269–1275. doi:10.1016/j.chemosphere.2007.11.065 PMID:18289635

Ganguly, D., Misra, S., & Goli, S. (2020). *India's COVID-19 episode: resilience, response, impact and lessons*. https://www.nytimes.com/2020/05/30/opinion/sunday/india-coronavirus-lockdown-inequality.html

Gillespie, A. (2021). Teachers' Spirituality or Spiritualities? In *Spirituality in Education: Professional Accounts of the Impact of Spirituality on Education*. Emerald Publishing Limited. doi:10.1108/978-1-83909-894-920211003

Global Goals for Sustainable Development. (n.d.). *No Poverty*. Retrieved from https://www.globalgoals.org/1-no-poverty

Good Deeds Day. (2021). *What You Can Do to End Poverty and Hunger*. https://www.good-deeds-day.org/sdg-1/

Goossens, Y., Schepelmann, P., & Kuhndtand, M. (2007). *Alternative progress indicators to Gross Domestic Product (GDP) as a means towards sustainable development*. European Parliament, Policy Department A: Economic and Scientific Policy.

Granger, C. W. J. (1969). Investigating Causal Relations by Econometric Models and Cross Spectral Methods. *Econometrica*, *37*(3), 424–438. doi:10.2307/1912791

Grasso, M., & Canova, L. (2008). An assessment of the quality of life in the european union based on the social ındicators approach. *Social Indicators Research: An International and Interdisciplinary Journal for Quality-of-Life Measurement, Springer*, *87*(1), 1–25. doi:10.100711205-007-9158-7

Gujarati, D. (2003). *Basic Econometrics* (4th ed.). McGraw-Hill.

Gupta, P. (2012). The Hazardous and Problems of E-Waste Management in India and its Strategies for Better Tomorrow. *RJEBS*, *1*(5).

Habibi, M. R., Davidson, A., & Laroche, M. L. (2016). What managers should know about the sharing economy. *Business Horizons. Journal of the Association for Information Science and Technology*, *60*(1), 113–121.

Halisçelik, E., Acaravcı, A., & Güzel, A. S. (2019). Income Distribution, Health Expenditure and Life Expectancy Nexus in Turkey: ARDL Bounds Testing Analysis. *International Journal of Economics and Innovation*, *5*(2), 263–275.

Halluite, J, Linton, J.D., Yeomans, J.S., & Yoogalingam, R. (2005). The challenge of hazardous waste management in a sustainable environment: insights from electronic recovery laws. *Corporate Social Responsibility and Environmental Management, 12*, 31 37.

Hamari, J., Sjöklint, M., & Ukkonen, A. (2015). The Sharing Economy. *Why People Participate in Collaborative Consumption.*, *67*(9), 2047–2059.

Hausman, D., & McPherson, M. (2009). Preference satisfaction and welfare economics. *Economics and Philosophy*, *25*(1), 1–25. doi:10.1017/S0266267108002253

Hawlitschek, F., Teubner, T., & Gimpel, H. (2016). *Understanding the Sharing Economy—Drivers and Impediments for Participation in Peer-to-Peer Rental. 49th Hawaii International Conference on System Sciences.*

HCI. (2021, March 15). *Human capital index.* https://datacatalog.worldbank.org/dataset/human-capital-index

Hedges, L. V., & Schneider, B. (Eds.). (2005). *The social organization of schooling*. Russell Sage Foundation.

Herzer, D., & Nunnenkamp, P. (2014). *Income Inequality and health: evidence from developed and developing countries*. Helmut Schmidt Universität Hamburg, Working Paper No. 141.

Hicks, D. A. (1997). The inequality-adjusted human development ındex: A constructive proposal. *World Development*, *25*(2), 1283–1298. doi:10.1016/S0305-750X(97)00034-X

Hoang, T. T., Wiboonchutikula, P., & Tubtimtong, B. (2010). Does Foreign Direct Investment Promote Economic Growth in Vietnam? *ASEAN Economic Bulletin*, *27*(3), 295–303. doi:10.1355/ae27-3d

Holcombe, R. (2009). A reformulation of the foundations of welfare economics. The Review of Austrian Economics, *Springer. Society for the Development of Austrian Economics*, *22*(3), 209–224. doi:10.100711138-009-0089-1

Honda, S., Khetriwal, D. S., & Kuehr, R. (2016). *Regional E-waste Monitor: East and Southeast Asia*. United Nations University.

Hopkinson, P., Zils, M., Hawkins, P., & Roper, S. (2018). Managing a Complex Global Circular Economy Business Model: Opportunities and Challenges. *California Management Review*, *60*(3), 71–94. doi:10.1177/0008125618764692

Hosoda, E. (2007). International aspects of recycling of electrical and electronic equipment: Material circulation in the East Asian region. *J Mater Cycles Waste*, *9*(2), 140–150. doi:10.100710163-007-0179-8

Hotelling, H. (1935). The most predictable criterion. *Journal of Educational Psychology*, *26*(2), 139–142. doi:10.1037/h0058165

Hotelling, H. (1936). Relations between two sets of variates. *Biometrika*, *28*(3-4), 321–377. doi:10.1093/biomet/28.3-4.321

HPI. (2021, March 15). *Happy planet index.* https://happyplanetindex.org/

Ikeda. (2017). *Inclusive wealth of regions: the case of Japan*. Springer.

India Report Makers. (2019). State of Women in Tech Entrepreneurship in India, Venture Intelligence, Master card Index of women entrepreneurs 2019 report. Academic Press.

India Today. (2021). *Covid derails economy: 5 sectors that have been hit hard.* https://www.indiatoday.in/business/story/5-sectors-hit-hard-as-covid-19-derails-economic-recovery-1796662-2021-04-30

Islam, Z. (2019, July 6). Where is Pathao headed? *Star Weekend.*

Islam, S. M., & Clarke, M. (2001). The relationship between economic development and social welfare: A new adjusted gdp measure of welfare. *Social Indicators Research*, *57*(2), 201–228. doi:10.1023/A:1014481414637

Jeffrey, K., Wheatley, H., & Abdallah, S. (2016). *The happy planet index: 2016. A global index of sustainable well-being*. New Economics Foundation.

Jingyu. (2020, June 15). Measuring inclusive wealth of China: Advances in sustainable use of resources. *Journal of Environmental Management*, *264*.

Jude, C. (2019). Does FDI crowd out domestic investment in transition countries? *Economics of Transition and Institutional Change*, *27*(1), 163–200. doi:10.1111/ecot.12184

Kader, R. (2018). *The Fascinating Story Of Shohoz: An Interview With Maliha M Quadir, Founder and MD, Shohoz.* Available at: https://futurestartup.com/2018/12/17/shohoz-story-maliha-m-quadir/

Kader, R. (2019). *Intelligence Brief: The Ride-hailing Market Updates.* Available at: https://futurestartup.com/2019/01/27/the-ride-hailing-market-updates-2019/

Kamal, S. M., & Ahsan, N. A. (2018). *'Uber-Pathao' ride-share's impact on Dhaka.* Available at: https://thefinancialexpress.com.bd/views/uber-pathao-ride-shares-impact-on-dhaka-1524842540

Kanitkar, T. (2020). The COVID-19 lockdown in India: Impacts on the economy and the power sector. *Global Transitions*, *2*, 150–156. doi:10.1016/j.glt.2020.07.005

Kapur, I. (2020). COVID 19 and Migration: A Case of Indian Unorganized Laborers. *COVID 19 and Migrant Health, 35.*

Kasparian, J., & Rolland, A. (2012). OECD's better life index: Can any country be well ranked? *Journal of Applied Statistics*, *39*(10), 2223–2230. doi:10.1080/02664763.2012.706265

Katırcıoğlu, S. (2009). Foreign Direct Investment & Economic Growth in Turkey: An Empirical Investigation by the Bounds Test for Co-Integration & Causality Tests. *Economic Research Journal*, *22*(3), 1–9.

Kaza, S., Yao, L., Bhada-Tata, P., & Van Woerden, F. (2018). *What a waste 2.0: a global snapshot of solid waste management to 2050.* World Bank Publications. doi:10.1596/978-1-4648-1329-0

Kerenyi, A. (2011). The better life ındex of the organisation for economic co-operationand development. *Public Finance Quarterly*, *56*(4), 518–538.

Khan, A., & Ahmad, H. (2019). Prosperity and instability: an evaluation of legatum prosperity index. *Papers and Proceedings*, 407-431.

Khatri, T. (2020, October 11). Despite celebration on Ground Zero let her live with her head held high. *The Free Press Journal*, p. 2.

Kim & Mueller. (1978). Factor Analysis: Statistical Methods and Practical Issues (Quantitative Applications in the Social Sciences). SAGE Publications.

Kim, D., Wang, F., & Arcan, C. (2018). Geographic Association Between Income Inequality and Obesity Among Adults in New York State. *Preventing Chronic Disease*, *15*, 180–217. doi:10.5888/pcd15.180217 PMID:30316306

Kirchherr, J., Reike, D., & Hekkert, M. (2017). Conceptualizing the circular economy: An analysis of 114 definitions. *Resources, Conservation and Recycling*, *127*, 221–232. doi:10.1016/j.resconrec.2017.09.005

Kochhar, K. (2020, November 7). Empowering women via work raises GDP and a company's profitability. *The Economic Times*, p. 10.

Kothe, E. (2013). Social Factors. In M. D. Gellman & J. R. Turner (Eds.), *Encyclopedia of Behavioral Medicine*. Springer. doi:10.1007/978-1-4419-1005-9_1179

Kraay, A. C. (2018). Methodology for a world bank human capital index. *Political Economy - Development: International Development Efforts & Strategies.*

Krishnan, C., Baba, M. M., Singh, G., & Srivastava, A. (2021). COVID-19 and the Marginal People of India. Handbook of Research on the Impact of COVID-19 on Marginalized Populations and Support for the Future, 255.

Kurniawan. (2018). Economic Growth and Sustainable Development in Indonesia. Bulletin of Indonesian Economic Studies, 54.

Kwiatkowski, D., Phillips, P., Schmidt, P., & Shin, Y. (1992). Testing the Null Hypothesis of Stationarity Against the Alternative of A Unit Root: How Sure Are We That The Economic Time Series Have A Unit Root? *Journal of Econometrics*, *54*(1), 159–178. doi:10.1016/0304-4076(92)90104-Y

Lamberton, C. P., & Rose, R. L. (2012). When Is Ours Better Than Mine? A Framework for Understanding and Altering Participation in Commercial Sharing Systems. *Journal of Marketing*, *76*(4), 109–125. doi:10.1509/jm.10.0368

Lange. (2012). *Natural Capital, Total Wealth and Sustainable Development in Namibia*. Springer.

Larionova. (2020). Saving the SDGs? Strengthening Partnership for Achieving SDGs in the Post-Covid-19 Digital World. Academic Press.

Lawn, P. A. (2003). A theoretical foundation to support the index of sustainable economic welfare (ISEW), genuine progress indicator (GPI), and other related indexes. *Ecological Economics*, *44*(1), 105–119. doi:10.1016/S0921-8009(02)00258-6

Lawn, P. A. (2005). An assessment of the valuation methods used to calculate the index of sustainable economic welfare (ISEW), genuine progress indicator (GPI), and sustainable net benefit index (SNB). *Environment, Development and Sustainability*, *7*(2), 185–208. doi:10.100710668-005-7312-4

Leung, A. O. W., Jinshu, Z., Chik, K. Y., Wing, K. L., Wong, K. C., Zongwei, C., & Wong, M. H. (2011, July 1). Polybrominated Diphenyl Ethers, and Polychlorinated Dibenzo-p-dioxins and Dibenzofurans in Surface Dust at an E-Waste Processing Site in Southeast China. *Environmental Science & Technology*, *45*(13), 5775–5782. doi:10.1021/es103915w PMID:21639085

Link, T. (2016). *What India Knows ABOUT E-WASTE. Report on Awareness Levels of E-waste amongst common citizens in India*. Toxics Link. http://toxicslink.org/docs/What-India-knows-about-e-waste.pdf

LPI. (2021, March 15). *Legatum prosperity index*. https://www.prosperity.com/rankings

Madero, C. (2021). Because I Am called: How a calling to teach emerges and develops in teachers working in catholic high schools. *Teaching and Teacher Education*, *101*, 103319. doi:10.1016/j.tate.2021.103319

Massimo, A., & Corrado, C. (2017). bibliometrix: An R-tool for comprehensive science mapping analysis. *Journal of Informetrics*, *11*(4), 959–975. doi:10.1016/j.joi.2017.08.007

Matloff, N. (2011). *The art of R programming: A tour of statistical software design*. No Starch Press.

Maye-Foulkes, D., & Nunenkamp, P. (2009). Do Multinational Enterprises Contribute to Convergence or Divergence? A Disaggregated Analysis of US FDI. *Review of Development Economics*, *13*(2), 304–318. doi:10.1111/j.1467-9361.2009.00510.x

McCulla, S. H., & Smith, S. (2007). *Measuring the economy: A primer on gdp and the national income and product accounts*. Bureau of Economic Analysis: US Department of Commerce.

Mellor, J. M., & Milyo, J. (2002). Income Inequality and health status in the United States, evidence from the current population survey. *The Journal of Human Resources*, *37*(3), 510–539. doi:10.2307/3069680

Moeller, S., & Wittkowski, K. (2010). The burdens of ownership: Reasons for preferring renting. *Managing Service Quality*, *20*(2), 176–191. doi:10.1108/09604521011027598

Möhlmann, M. (2015). Collaborative consumption: Determinants of satisfaction and the likelihood of using a sharing economy option again. *Journal of Consumer Behaviour*, *14*(3), 193–207. doi:10.1002/cb.1512

Monica, P. R. L. (2019). *Uber and Lyft both hit all-time lows and continue to struggle since their IPOs*. Available at: https://edition.cnn.com/2019/09/04/investing/uber-lyft-ipo-market/index.html

Montañez. (2017). The Persistent Problem of Gender Inequality. *Scientific American*.

Moore, S. (2006). Peripherality, income inequality, and life expectancy: Revisiting the income inequality hypothesis. *International Journal of Epidemiology*, *35*(3), 623–632. doi:10.1093/ije/dyl026 PMID:16507644

Nedyalkova, P. (2019). Government Supervision – A Factor for Business Development. Journal of Management Policy and Practice, 20(2), 114 – 120.

Nedyalkova, P. (2019). Quality of Internal Auditing in the Public Sector. Perspectives from the Bulgarian and International Context. *Springer International Publishing*.

Ng, S., & Perron, P. (2001). Lag Length Selection and The Construction of Unit Root Tests with Good Size and Power. *Econometrica*, *69*(6), 1519–1554. doi:10.1111/1468-0262.00256

Nicole, M., Alsafi, Z., Sohrabi, C., Kerwan, A., Al-Jabir, A., Losifidis, C., ... Agha, R. (2020). The socio-economic implications of the coronavirus and covid-19 pandemic: A review. *International Journal of Surgery*, *78*, 185–193. doi:10.1016/j.ijsu.2020.04.018 PMID:32305533

Nilsson, T., & Bergh, A. (2012). *Income Inequality and Individual Health: Exploring the Association in a Developing Country*. IFN Working Paper No. 899.

NSO Time Use Survey. (2019). *Care Work and Care Jobs for the future of decent work*. ILO.

Obregon, S. L., Lopes, L. F. D., Kaczam, F., da Veiga, C. P., & da Silva, W. V. (2021). Religiosity, Spirituality and Work: A Systematic Literature Review and Research Directions. *Journal of Business Ethics*, 1–23. doi:10.100710551-021-04856-7

Orr, J., Smith, M., Burchill, C., Katz, A., & Fransoo, R. (2016). Outcomes of an investment in administrative data infrastructure: An example of capacity building at the Manitoba Centre for Health Policy. *Canadian Journal of Public Health*, *107*(4-5), e480–e481. doi:10.17269/CJPH.107.5659 PMID:28026717

Oxfam. (2016). *210 Oxfam Briefing Paper*. Oxfam.

Oxfam. (2020). *Why majority of the world's poor are woman*. https://www.oxfam.org/en/why-majority-worlds-poor-are-women

Özdamar, K. (2004). *Paket programlar ile istatistiksel veri analizi* (Vol. 5). Baskı, Kaan Kitabevi.

Öztürk, İ., & Acaravcı, A. (2010). FDI, Trade and Growth in Turkey: Evidence from ARDL Bounds Testing Approach. *Argumenta Oeconomica*, *25*(2), 95–115.

Pamuk, Ş. (2017). *Türkiye'nin 200 Yıllık İktisadi Tarihi* (Vol. 8). Baskı, Kültür Yayınları.

Pande, R. (2020, November 7). Financial inclusion, peers, role models empower women. *The Economic Times*, p. 10.

Pasquini, A., & Rosati, F. (2020). *A human capital index for the Italian provinces*. Discussion Paper Series. IZA Institute of Labor Economics.

Phillips, P., & Peron, P. (1988). Testing for A Unit Root in Time Series Regression. *Biometrika*, *75*(2), 335–346. doi:10.1093/biomet/75.2.335

Pickett, K. E., James, O., & Wilkinson, R. G. (2006). Income inequality and the prevalence of mental illness: A preliminary international analysis. *Journal of Epidemiology and Community Health*, *60*(7), 646–647. doi:10.1136/jech.2006.046631 PMID:16790839

Pickett, K. E., & Wilkinson, R. (2007). Child wellbeing and income inequality in rich societies: Ecological cross sectional study. *British Medical Journal*, *335*(7629), 1080–1087. doi:10.1136/bmj.39377.580162.55 PMID:18024483

Pigou, A. C. (1962). *The economics of welfare*. Macmillian.

Pillay, A. (2020, October 19). Housework burden Just got heavier for women entrepreneurs. *Business Standard*, p. 6.

Pillay, A. (2020, September 21). Lockdown diaries: women ride the ed-tech boom as opportunities click. *Business Standard*, p. 2.

Polasky. (2015). *Annual Review of Environment and Resources, Inclusive Wealth as a Metric of Sustainable Development*. Academic Press.

Popova, Zh. (2011). *Pravo na Evropeyskia sayuz*. Siela.

PricewaterhouseCoopers LLP. (2015). *The Sharing Economy*. Author.

R Core Team. (2016). *R: A language and environment for statistical computing*. Vienna, Austria: R Foundation for Statistical Computing. https://www.R-project.org

Rahman, R. (2019). *Motorbike ride-sharing alleviates Dhaka traffic chaos*. Available at: https://www.reuters.com/article/us-bangladesh-ridesharing/motorbike-ride-sharing-a-panacea-for-dhaka-traffic-chaos-idUSKBN1WC098

Rahman, M. S., Osmangani, A. M., Daud, N. M., Chowdhury, A. H., & Hassan, H. (2015). Trust and work place spirituality on knowledge sharing behaviour: Perspective from non-academic staff of higher learning institutions. *The Learning Organization*.

Rai, Saritha. (2020, November 26th). Pandemic is a surprise boon for women in the world's back office, *Business Standard*, p.2.

Rajivlochan, M. (2020). Redesigning urban spaces for women. *The Hindustan Times*, p. 13.

Ram, R. (2005). Income inequality, poverty, and population health: Evidence from recent data for the United States. *Social Science & Medicine*, *61*(12), 2568–2576. doi:10.1016/j.socscimed.2005.04.038 PMID:15963618

Ray, D., & Linden, M. (2018). Health, inequality and income: A global study using simultaneous model. *Journal of Economic Structures*, *7*(22), 1–28. doi:10.118640008-018-0121-3

Realff, M. J., Ammons, J. C., & Newton, D. J. (2004). Robust reverse production system design for carpet recycling. *IIE Transactions*, *36*(8), 767–776. doi:10.1080/07408170490458580

Rodgers, G. B. (1979). Income and inequality as determinants of mortality: An international cross-section analysis. *Population Studies*, *33*(2), 343–351. doi:10.1080/00324728.1979.10410449

Rostila, M., Kölegård, M. L., & Fritzell, J. (2012). Income inequality and self-rated health in Stockholm, Sweden: A test of the 'income inequality hypothesis' on two levels of aggregation. *Social Science & Medicine*, *74*(7), 1091–1098. doi:10.1016/j.socscimed.2011.11.027 PMID:22336734

Sahoo, P., & Ashwani. (2020). COVID-19 and Indian Economy: Impact on Growth, Manufacturing, Trade and MSME Sector. *Global Business Review*, *21*(5), 1159–1183. doi:10.1177/0972150920945687

Salinas-Jiménez, M. M., & Salinas-Jiménez, J. (2011). Corruption and total factor productivity: Level or growth effects? *Portuguese Economic Journal*, *10*(2), 109–128. doi:10.100710258-010-0059-3

Saurabh. (2020, November 11). Gender Sensitization with the law may prove to be good for women. *The Avenue*, p. 7.

Scheiber, N., Schwartz, N., & Hsu, T. (2020). White-collar quarantine' over virus spotlights class divide. *The New York Times*. https://nyti.ms/2Jm2SVa

Schultz, T. P. (2009). *Population and Health Policies*. IZA Disccussion Paper Series, No: 4340.

Sen, A. (1999). *Development as freedom*. Alfred A. Knopf.

Şener, O. (2006). *Teoride ve Uygulamada Kamu Ekonomisi*. Beta Yayınevi.

Shah, A. (2020, September 21). Equal treatment for Women on inheritance. *Business Standard*, p. 11.

Shams, Z. A. (2018). *10 ways to give Sadaqah other than giving money*. Retrieved from https://sarahmuzaffar.wordpress.com/2018/02/09/10-ways-to-give-sadaqah-other-than-giving-money/

Shamsiev, J. M. U., Rashidova, R. R., & Tajibaev, M. A. (2021). The role of teachers in building the future of the nation. *Science Progress*, *1*(5).

Sharma, R. (2020, May 30). The rich love India's lockdown. For the poor it's another story. *The New York Times*.

Sharma, S. (1996). *Applied Multivariate Techniques*. John Wiley & Sons, Inc.

Short, J. (2009). The Art of Writing a Review Article. *Journal of Management*, *35*(6), 1312–1317. doi:10.1177/0149206309337489

Şimşek; M. & Behdioğlu, S. (2006). The Impact of FDI on Economic Growth in Turkey: An Empirical Study. *İİBF Journal of the Atatürk University*, *20*(2), 47-65.

Singh, B. P. (n.d.). Impact of COVID-19 on Rural Economy in India. *SSRN Electronic Journal*. doi:10.2139/ssrn.3609973

Sohini & Jha. (2020). Social Policy COVID 19 and impoverished migrants: Challenges and prospects in Locked Down India. *The International Journal of Community and Social Development, 2*(2).

So, K. K. F., Oh, H., & Min, S. (2018). Motivations and constraints of Airbnb consumers: Findings from a mixed-methods approach. *Tourism Management, 67*, 224–236. doi:10.1016/j.tourman.2018.01.009

Somers, M. R., & Block, F. (2005). From Poverty to perversity: Ideas, markets, and ınstitutions over 200 years of welfare debate. *American Sociological Review, 70*(2), 260–287. doi:10.1177/000312240507000204

SPI. (2021, March 15). *Social progress imperative*. https://www.socialprogress.org/

Srivastav, K.K. (2020, November 22). Women in a just society in New India. *The Pioneer*, p. 3.

Srivastava, R. (2020). A Literature Review and Classification of e-Waste Management Research. *Journal of Solid Waste Technology Management, 46*(2), 258–273. doi:10.5276/JSWTM/2020.258

Srivastava, R., & Dhingra, T. (2020). Towards a Model for Effective e-Waste Management: A Study of Software Industry in India. *International Journal of Environment and Waste Management, 27*(1), 61–73. doi:10.1504/IJEWM.2021.111905

Steblyanskaya. (2021). Changes in sustainable growth dynamics: The case of China and Russia gas industries. *Energy Strategy Reviews, 33*.

Stiglitz, J. E. (2015). *Eşitsizliğin Bedeli. Bugünün Bölünmüş Toplumu Geleceğimizi Nasıl Tehlikeye Atıyor?* İletişim Yayınları.

Stiglitz, J., Sen, A., & Fitoussi, J. P. (2009). *The measurement of economic performance and social progress revisited: Reflections and Overview*. Commission on the Measurement of Economic Performance and Social Progress.

Sun, P., Unger, J. B., Palmer, P., Ma, H., Xie, B., Sussman, S., & Johnson, C. A. (2012). Relative income inequality and selected health outcomes in urban Chinese youth. *Social Science & Medicine, 74*(1), 84–91. doi:10.1016/j.socscimed.2011.10.010 PMID:22137733

Susan, A. F., Jeremy, R. G., & Randolph, E. K. (2008). Characterizing architectural options for electronic waste recycling systems. *IEEE International Symposium on Electronics and the Environment*, 1-6.

Sutherland, W., & Jarrahi, M. H. (2018). The sharing economy and digital platforms: A review and research agenda. *International Journal of Information Management, 43*, 328–341. doi:10.1016/j.ijinfomgt.2018.07.004

Täuscher, K., & Kietzmann, J. (2017). Learning from Failures in the Sharing Economy. *Management Information Systems Quarterly Executive, 16*(4), 253–263.

Terzi, H., & Yurtkuran, S. (2016). The correlation between education and economic growth in Turkey: Sims and Toda-Yamamoto Analysis. *Eskişehir Osmangazi University İİBF Journal, 11*(2), 7–24.

The Global Gender Gap Report. (2018). World Economic Forum.

The World Bank. (2016). *India's Poverty Profile.* https://www.worldbank.org/en/news/infographic/2016/05/27/india-s-poverty-profile

Tienhua, W. T., & Yenming, J. C. (2008). Understanding population dynamics of WEEE recycling system in the developing countries: A SIR model. *IEEE International Symposium on Electronics and the Environment*, 1-6.

Toda, H., & Yamamoto, T. (1995). Statistical inference in vector autoregressions with possibly integrated processes. *Journal of Econometrics, 66*(1-2), 225–250. doi:10.1016/0304-4076(94)01616-8

Tussyadiah, I. P., & Pesonen, J. (2018). Drivers and barriers of peer-to-peer accommodation stay – an exploratory study with American and Finnish travellers. *Current Issues in Tourism, 21*(6), 703–720. doi:10.1080/13683500.2016.1141180

Tweed, E. J., Allardic, G. M., McLoone, P., & Morrison, D. S. (2018). Socio-economic inequalities in the incidence of four common cancers: A population-based registry study. *Public Health, 154*, 1–10. doi:10.1016/j.puhe.2017.10.005 PMID:29128730

Uber Technologies Inc. (2019). *Uber Newsroom.* Available at: https://www.uber.com/newsroom/company-info/

UNDP. (2010). Human Development Report 2010. United Nations Development Programme (UNDP).

UNDP. (2021a, March 15). *United Nations Development Programme.* http://hdr.undp.org/en/content/human-development-index-hdi

UNDP. (2021b, March 15). *United Nations Development Programme.* http://hdr.undp.org/en/data

UNDR. (1990). Human development report: overview. United Nations Development Programme.

Utami, N. M. S., Sapta, I., Verawati, Y., & Astakoni, I. (2021). Relationship between workplace spirituality, organizational commitment and organizational citizenship behavior. *The Journal of Asian Finance, Economics, and Business, 8*(1), 507–517.

Utting, P. (2018). *Achieving the Sustainable Development Goals through Social and Solidarity Economy: Incremental Versus Transformative Change.* UNRISD.

Veenhoven, R. (2002). Why social policy needs subjective indicators. *Social Indicators Research, 11*(1/3), 33–45. doi:10.1023/A:1015723614574

Veenhoven, R. (2009). Well-being in nations and well-being of nations Is there a conflict between individual and society. *Social Indicators Research, 91*(1), 5–21. doi:10.100711205-008-9323-7

Venetoulis, J., & Talberth, J. (2006). Refining the ecological footprint. *Environment, Development and Sustainability, 10*(4), 441–469. doi:10.100710668-006-9074-z

Vergin, J. (2019). *Psychology: A happy partner is the elixir of longer life*. DW News. Retrieved from https://www.dw.com/en/psychology-a-happy-partner-is-the-elixir-of-longer-life/a-48762543

Wagstaff, A., & Doorslaer, E. (2000). Income inequality and health: What does the literature tell us? *Annual Review of Public Health, 21*(1), 543–567. doi:10.1146/annurev.publhealth.21.1.543 PMID:10884964

Walwei, U. (2016). *Digitalization and structural labour market problems: The case of Germany*. ILO Research Paper No. 17. Retrieved May 12, 2019, from: https://www.ilo.org/wcmsp5/groups/public/--- dgreports/---inst/documents/publication/wcms_522355.pdf

Watson, J. (2000). Whose model of spirituality should be used in the spiritual development of school children? *International Journal of Children's Spirituality, 5*(1), 91–101. doi:10.1080/713670894

Webster, J., & Watson, R. T. (2002). Analyzing the Past to Prepare for the Future: Writing a Literature Review. *Management Information Systems Quarterly, 26*(2), xiii–xxiii.

WHO. (2004). *Investing in Health for Economic Development*. WHO Publishing.

Wilkinson, R. G. (1997). Socioeconomic determinants of health Health inequalities: Relative or absolute material standards? *BMJ (Clinical Research Ed.), 314*(7080), 591–599. doi:10.1136/bmj.314.7080.591 PMID:9055723

Yadav, S. (2020). Precarity as a coping strategy of the Gonds: A study of insecure and long-distance seasonal migration in Central India. *Indian Journal of Human Development, 14*(1), 7–22. doi:10.1177/0973703020909328

Yamaguchi. (2016). *Measuring Regional Wealth and Assessing Sustainable Development: An Application to a Disaster-Torn Region in Japan*. Springer.

Zakat. (n.d.). In *Wikipedia*. Retrieved from https://en.wikipedia.org/wiki/Zakat

Zhao, C., & Du, J. (2007). Causality Between FDI and Economic Growth in China. *Chinese Economy, 40*(6), 68–82. doi:10.2753/CES1097-1475400604

Zhiduan, X., & Guo, Y. G. (2005). Study and Design on Third-party Take-back Mode Management Information System. In Latest China Information System Study and Application. Tsinghai University.

Zsolnai, L., & Illes, K. (2017). Spiritually inspired creativity in business. *International Journal of Social Economics*.

Related References

To continue our tradition of advancing information science and technology research, we have compiled a list of recommended IGI Global readings. These references will provide additional information and guidance to further enrich your knowledge and assist you with your own research and future publications.

Abtahi, M. S., Behboudi, L., & Hasanabad, H. M. (2017). Factors Affecting Internet Advertising Adoption in Ad Agencies. *International Journal of Innovation in the Digital Economy*, *8*(4), 18–29. doi:10.4018/IJIDE.2017100102

Agrawal, S. (2017). The Impact of Emerging Technologies and Social Media on Different Business(es): Marketing and Management. In O. Rishi & A. Sharma (Eds.), *Maximizing Business Performance and Efficiency Through Intelligent Systems* (pp. 37–49). Hershey, PA: IGI Global. doi:10.4018/978-1-5225-2234-8.ch002

Alnoukari, M., Razouk, R., & Hanano, A. (2016). BSC-SI: A Framework for Integrating Strategic Intelligence in Corporate Strategic Management. *International Journal of Social and Organizational Dynamics in IT*, *5*(2), 1–14. doi:10.4018/IJSODIT.2016070101

Alnoukari, M., Razouk, R., & Hanano, A. (2016). BSC-SI, A Framework for Integrating Strategic Intelligence in Corporate Strategic Management. *International Journal of Strategic Information Technology and Applications*, *7*(1), 32–44. doi:10.4018/IJSITA.2016010103

Altındağ, E. (2016). Current Approaches in Change Management. In A. Goksoy (Ed.), *Organizational Change Management Strategies in Modern Business* (pp. 24–51). Hershey, PA: IGI Global. doi:10.4018/978-1-4666-9533-7.ch002

Alvarez-Dionisi, L. E., Turner, R., & Mittra, M. (2016). Global Project Management Trends. *International Journal of Information Technology Project Management*, *7*(3), 54–73. doi:10.4018/IJITPM.2016070104

Anantharaman, R. N., Rajeswari, K. S., Angusamy, A., & Kuppusamy, J. (2017). Role of Self-Efficacy and Collective Efficacy as Moderators of Occupational Stress Among Software Development Professionals. *International Journal of Human Capital and Information Technology Professionals*, *8*(2), 45–58. doi:10.4018/IJHCITP.2017040103

Aninze, F., El-Gohary, H., & Hussain, J. (2018). The Role of Microfinance to Empower Women: The Case of Developing Countries. *International Journal of Customer Relationship Marketing and Management*, *9*(1), 54–78. doi:10.4018/IJCRMM.2018010104

Arsenijević, O. M., Orčić, D., & Kastratović, E. (2017). Development of an Optimization Tool for Intangibles in SMEs: A Case Study from Serbia with a Pilot Research in the Prestige by Milka Company. In M. Vemić (Ed.), *Optimal Management Strategies in Small and Medium Enterprises* (pp. 320–347). Hershey, PA: IGI Global. doi:10.4018/978-1-5225-1949-2.ch015

Aryanto, V. D., Wismantoro, Y., & Widyatmoko, K. (2018). Implementing Eco-Innovation by Utilizing the Internet to Enhance Firm's Marketing Performance: Study of Green Batik Small and Medium Enterprises in Indonesia. *International Journal of E-Business Research*, *14*(1), 21–36. doi:10.4018/IJEBR.2018010102

Atiku, S. O., & Fields, Z. (2017). Multicultural Orientations for 21st Century Global Leadership. In N. Baporikar (Ed.), *Management Education for Global Leadership* (pp. 28–51). Hershey, PA: IGI Global. doi:10.4018/978-1-5225-1013-0.ch002

Atiku, S. O., & Fields, Z. (2018). Organisational Learning Dimensions and Talent Retention Strategies for the Service Industries. In N. Baporikar (Ed.), *Global Practices in Knowledge Management for Societal and Organizational Development* (pp. 358–381). Hershey, PA: IGI Global. doi:10.4018/978-1-5225-3009-1.ch017

Ávila, L., & Teixeira, L. (2018). The Main Concepts Behind the Dematerialization of Business Processes. In M. Khosrow-Pour, D.B.A. (Ed.), Encyclopedia of Information Science and Technology, Fourth Edition (pp. 888-898). Hershey, PA: IGI Global. doi:10.4018/978-1-5225-2255-3.ch076

Bartens, Y., Chunpir, H. I., Schulte, F., & Voß, S. (2017). Business/IT Alignment in Two-Sided Markets: A COBIT 5 Analysis for Media Streaming Business Models. In S. De Haes & W. Van Grembergen (Eds.), *Strategic IT Governance and Alignment in Business Settings* (pp. 82–111). Hershey, PA: IGI Global. doi:10.4018/978-1-5225-0861-8.ch004

Bashayreh, A. M. (2018). Organizational Culture and Organizational Performance. In W. Lee & F. Sabetzadeh (Eds.), *Contemporary Knowledge and Systems Science* (pp. 50–69). Hershey, PA: IGI Global. doi:10.4018/978-1-5225-5655-8.ch003

Bedford, D. A. (2018). Sustainable Knowledge Management Strategies: Aligning Business Capabilities and Knowledge Management Goals. In N. Baporikar (Ed.), *Global Practices in Knowledge Management for Societal and Organizational Development* (pp. 46–73). Hershey, PA: IGI Global. doi:10.4018/978-1-5225-3009-1.ch003

Benmoussa, F., Nakara, W. A., & Jaouen, A. (2016). The Use of Social Media by SMEs in the Tourism Industry. In I. Lee (Ed.), *Encyclopedia of E-Commerce Development, Implementation, and Management* (pp. 2159–2170). Hershey, PA: IGI Global. doi:10.4018/978-1-4666-9787-4.ch155

Berger, R. (2016). Indigenous Management and Bottom of Pyramid Countries: The Role of National Institutions. In U. Aung & P. Ordoñez de Pablos (Eds.), *Managerial Strategies and Practice in the Asian Business Sector* (pp. 107–123). Hershey, PA: IGI Global. doi:10.4018/978-1-4666-9758-4.ch007

Bharwani, S., & Musunuri, D. (2018). Reflection as a Process From Theory to Practice. In M. Khosrow-Pour, D.B.A. (Ed.), Encyclopedia of Information Science and Technology, Fourth Edition (pp. 1529-1539). Hershey, PA: IGI Global. doi:10.4018/978-1-5225-2255-3.ch132

Bhatt, G. D., Wang, Z., & Rodger, J. A. (2017). Information Systems Capabilities and Their Effects on Competitive Advantages: A Study of Chinese Companies. *Information Resources Management Journal*, *30*(3), 41–57. doi:10.4018/IRMJ.2017070103

Bhushan, M., & Yadav, A. (2017). Concept of Cloud Computing in ESB. In R. Bhadoria, N. Chaudhari, G. Tomar, & S. Singh (Eds.), *Exploring Enterprise Service Bus in the Service-Oriented Architecture Paradigm* (pp. 116–127). Hershey, PA: IGI Global. doi:10.4018/978-1-5225-2157-0.ch008

Bhushan, S. (2017). System Dynamics Base-Model of Humanitarian Supply Chain (HSCM) in Disaster Prone Eco-Communities of India: A Discussion on Simulation and Scenario Results. *International Journal of System Dynamics Applications*, *6*(3), 20–37. doi:10.4018/IJSDA.2017070102

Biswas, A., & De, A. K. (2017). On Development of a Fuzzy Stochastic Programming Model with Its Application to Business Management. In S. Trivedi, S. Dey, A. Kumar, & T. Panda (Eds.), *Handbook of Research on Advanced Data Mining Techniques and Applications for Business Intelligence* (pp. 353–378). Hershey, PA: IGI Global. doi:10.4018/978-1-5225-2031-3.ch021

Bücker, J., & Ernste, K. (2018). Use of Brand Heroes in Strategic Reputation Management: The Case of Bacardi, Adidas, and Daimler. In A. Erdemir (Ed.), *Reputation Management Techniques in Public Relations* (pp. 126–150). Hershey, PA: IGI Global. doi:10.4018/978-1-5225-3619-2.ch007

Bureš, V. (2018). Industry 4.0 From the Systems Engineering Perspective: Alternative Holistic Framework Development. In R. Brunet-Thornton & F. Martinez (Eds.), *Analyzing the Impacts of Industry 4.0 in Modern Business Environments* (pp. 199–223). Hershey, PA: IGI Global. doi:10.4018/978-1-5225-3468-6.ch011

Buzady, Z. (2017). Resolving the Magic Cube of Effective Case Teaching: Benchmarking Case Teaching Practices in Emerging Markets – Insights from the Central European University Business School, Hungary. In D. Latusek (Ed.), *Case Studies as a Teaching Tool in Management Education* (pp. 79–103). Hershey, PA: IGI Global. doi:10.4018/978-1-5225-0770-3.ch005

Campatelli, G., Richter, A., & Stocker, A. (2016). Participative Knowledge Management to Empower Manufacturing Workers. *International Journal of Knowledge Management, 12*(4), 37–50. doi:10.4018/IJKM.2016100103

Căpusneanu, S., & Topor, D. I. (2018). Business Ethics and Cost Management in SMEs: Theories of Business Ethics and Cost Management Ethos. In I. Oncioiu (Ed.), *Ethics and Decision-Making for Sustainable Business Practices* (pp. 109–127). Hershey, PA: IGI Global. doi:10.4018/978-1-5225-3773-1.ch007

Carneiro, A. (2016). Maturity in Health Organization Information Systems: Metrics and Privacy Perspectives. *International Journal of Privacy and Health Information Management, 4*(2), 1–18. doi:10.4018/IJPHIM.2016070101

Chan, R. L., Mo, P. L., & Moon, K. K. (2018). Strategic and Tactical Measures in Managing Enterprise Risks: A Study of the Textile and Apparel Industry. In K. Strang, M. Korstanje, & N. Vajjhala (Eds.), *Research, Practices, and Innovations in Global Risk and Contingency Management* (pp. 1–19). Hershey, PA: IGI Global. doi:10.4018/978-1-5225-4754-9.ch001

Chandan, H. C. (2016). Motivations and Challenges of Female Entrepreneurship in Developed and Developing Economies. In N. Baporikar (Ed.), *Handbook of Research on Entrepreneurship in the Contemporary Knowledge-Based Global Economy* (pp. 260–286). Hershey, PA: IGI Global. doi:10.4018/978-1-4666-8798-1.ch012

Charlier, S. D., Burke-Smalley, L. A., & Fisher, S. L. (2018). Undergraduate Programs in the U.S: A Contextual and Content-Based Analysis. In J. Mendy (Ed.), *Teaching Human Resources and Organizational Behavior at the College Level* (pp. 26–57). Hershey, PA: IGI Global. doi:10.4018/978-1-5225-2820-3.ch002

Chaudhuri, S. (2016). Application of Web-Based Geographical Information System (GIS) in E-Business. In U. Panwar, R. Kumar, & N. Ray (Eds.), *Handbook of Research on Promotional Strategies and Consumer Influence in the Service Sector* (pp. 389–405). Hershey, PA: IGI Global. doi:10.4018/978-1-5225-0143-5.ch023

Choudhuri, P. S. (2016). An Empirical Study on the Quality of Services Offered by the Private Life Insurers in Burdwan. In U. Panwar, R. Kumar, & N. Ray (Eds.), *Handbook of Research on Promotional Strategies and Consumer Influence in the Service Sector* (pp. 31–55). Hershey, PA: IGI Global. doi:10.4018/978-1-5225-0143-5.ch002

Dahlberg, T., Kivijärvi, H., & Saarinen, T. (2017). IT Investment Consistency and Other Factors Influencing the Success of IT Performance. In S. De Haes & W. Van Grembergen (Eds.), *Strategic IT Governance and Alignment in Business Settings* (pp. 176–208). Hershey, PA: IGI Global. doi:10.4018/978-1-5225-0861-8.ch007

Damnjanović, A. M. (2017). Knowledge Management Optimization through IT and E-Business Utilization: A Qualitative Study on Serbian SMEs. In M. Vemić (Ed.), *Optimal Management Strategies in Small and Medium Enterprises* (pp. 249–267). Hershey, PA: IGI Global. doi:10.4018/978-1-5225-1949-2.ch012

Daneshpour, H. (2017). Integrating Sustainable Development into Project Portfolio Management through Application of Open Innovation. In M. Vemić (Ed.), *Optimal Management Strategies in Small and Medium Enterprises* (pp. 370–387). Hershey, PA: IGI Global. doi:10.4018/978-1-5225-1949-2.ch017

Daniel, A. D., & Reis de Castro, V. (2018). Entrepreneurship Education: How to Measure the Impact on Nascent Entrepreneurs. In A. Carrizo Moreira, J. Guilherme Leitão Dantas, & F. Manuel Valente (Eds.), *Nascent Entrepreneurship and Successful New Venture Creation* (pp. 85–110). Hershey, PA: IGI Global. doi:10.4018/978-1-5225-2936-1.ch004

David, F., van der Sijde, P., & van den Besselaar, P. (2016). Enterpreneurial Incentives, Obstacles, and Management in University-Business Co-Operation: The Case of Indonesia. In J. Saiz-Álvarez (Ed.), *Handbook of Research on Social Entrepreneurship and Solidarity Economics* (pp. 499–518). Hershey, PA: IGI Global. doi:10.4018/978-1-5225-0097-1.ch024

David, R., Swami, B. N., & Tangirala, S. (2018). Ethics Impact on Knowledge Management in Organizational Development: A Case Study. In N. Baporikar (Ed.), *Global Practices in Knowledge Management for Societal and Organizational Development* (pp. 19–45). Hershey, PA: IGI Global. doi:10.4018/978-1-5225-3009-1.ch002

Delias, P., & Lakiotaki, K. (2018). Discovering Process Horizontal Boundaries to Facilitate Process Comprehension. *International Journal of Operations Research and Information Systems*, *9*(2), 1–31. doi:10.4018/IJORIS.2018040101

Denholm, J., & Lee-Davies, L. (2018). Success Factors for Games in Business and Project Management. In *Enhancing Education and Training Initiatives Through Serious Games* (pp. 34–68). Hershey, PA: IGI Global. doi:10.4018/978-1-5225-3689-5.ch002

Deshpande, M. (2017). Best Practices in Management Institutions for Global Leadership: Policy Aspects. In N. Baporikar (Ed.), *Management Education for Global Leadership* (pp. 1–27). Hershey, PA: IGI Global. doi:10.4018/978-1-5225-1013-0.ch001

Deshpande, M. (2018). Policy Perspectives for SMEs Knowledge Management. In N. Baporikar (Ed.), *Knowledge Integration Strategies for Entrepreneurship and Sustainability* (pp. 23–46). Hershey, PA: IGI Global. doi:10.4018/978-1-5225-5115-7.ch002

Dezdar, S. (2017). ERP Implementation Projects in Asian Countries: A Comparative Study on Iran and China. *International Journal of Information Technology Project Management*, *8*(3), 52–68. doi:10.4018/IJITPM.2017070104

Domingos, D., Martinho, R., & Varajão, J. (2016). Controlled Flexibility in Healthcare Processes: A BPMN-Extension Approach. In M. Cruz-Cunha, I. Miranda, R. Martinho, & R. Rijo (Eds.), *Encyclopedia of E-Health and Telemedicine* (pp. 521–535). Hershey, PA: IGI Global. doi:10.4018/978-1-4666-9978-6.ch040

Domingos, D., Respício, A., & Martinho, R. (2017). Reliability of IoT-Aware BPMN Healthcare Processes. In C. Reis & M. Maximiano (Eds.), *Internet of Things and Advanced Application in Healthcare* (pp. 214–248). Hershey, PA: IGI Global. doi:10.4018/978-1-5225-1820-4.ch008

Dosumu, O., Hussain, J., & El-Gohary, H. (2017). An Exploratory Study of the Impact of Government Policies on the Development of Small and Medium Enterprises in Developing Countries: The Case of Nigeria. *International Journal of Customer Relationship Marketing and Management*, *8*(4), 51–62. doi:10.4018/IJCRMM.2017100104

Durst, S., Bruns, G., & Edvardsson, I. R. (2017). Retaining Knowledge in Smaller Building and Construction Firms. *International Journal of Knowledge and Systems Science*, *8*(3), 1–12. doi:10.4018/IJKSS.2017070101

Edvardsson, I. R., & Durst, S. (2017). Outsourcing, Knowledge, and Learning: A Critical Review. *International Journal of Knowledge-Based Organizations*, *7*(2), 13–26. doi:10.4018/IJKBO.2017040102

Edwards, J. S. (2018). Integrating Knowledge Management and Business Processes. In M. Khosrow-Pour, D.B.A. (Ed.), Encyclopedia of Information Science and Technology, Fourth Edition (pp. 5046-5055). Hershey, PA: IGI Global. doi:10.4018/978-1-5225-2255-3.ch437

Ejiogu, A. O. (2018). Economics of Farm Management. In *Agricultural Finance and Opportunities for Investment and Expansion* (pp. 56–72). Hershey, PA: IGI Global. doi:10.4018/978-1-5225-3059-6.ch003

Ekanem, I., & Abiade, G. E. (2018). Factors Influencing the Use of E-Commerce by Small Enterprises in Nigeria. *International Journal of ICT Research in Africa and the Middle East*, *7*(1), 37–53. doi:10.4018/IJICTRAME.2018010103

Ekanem, I., & Alrossais, L. A. (2017). Succession Challenges Facing Family Businesses in Saudi Arabia. In P. Zgheib (Ed.), *Entrepreneurship and Business Innovation in the Middle East* (pp. 122–146). Hershey, PA: IGI Global. doi:10.4018/978-1-5225-2066-5.ch007

El Faquih, L., & Fredj, M. (2017). Ontology-Based Framework for Quality in Configurable Process Models. *Journal of Electronic Commerce in Organizations*, *15*(2), 48–60. doi:10.4018/JECO.2017040104

El-Gohary, H., & El-Gohary, Z. (2016). An Attempt to Explore Electronic Marketing Adoption and Implementation Aspects in Developing Countries: The Case of Egypt. *International Journal of Customer Relationship Marketing and Management*, *7*(4), 1–26. doi:10.4018/IJCRMM.2016100101

Entico, G. J. (2016). Knowledge Management and the Medical Health Librarians: A Perception Study. In J. Yap, M. Perez, M. Ayson, & G. Entico (Eds.), *Special Library Administration, Standardization and Technological Integration* (pp. 52–77). Hershey, PA: IGI Global. doi:10.4018/978-1-4666-9542-9.ch003

Faisal, M. N., & Talib, F. (2017). Building Ambidextrous Supply Chains in SMEs: How to Tackle the Barriers? *International Journal of Information Systems and Supply Chain Management*, *10*(4), 80–100. doi:10.4018/IJISSCM.2017100105

Fernandes, T. M., Gomes, J., & Romão, M. (2017). Investments in E-Government: A Benefit Management Case Study. *International Journal of Electronic Government Research*, *13*(3), 1–17. doi:10.4018/IJEGR.2017070101

Fouda, F. A. (2016). A Suggested Curriculum in Career Education to Develop Business Secondary Schools Students' Career Knowledge Management Domains and Professional Thinking. *International Journal of Technology Diffusion*, *7*(2), 42–62. doi:10.4018/IJTD.2016040103

Gallardo-Vázquez, D., & Pajuelo-Moreno, M. L. (2016). How Spanish Universities are Promoting Entrepreneurship through Your Own Lines of Teaching and Research? In L. Carvalho (Ed.), *Handbook of Research on Entrepreneurial Success and its Impact on Regional Development* (pp. 431–454). Hershey, PA: IGI Global. doi:10.4018/978-1-4666-9567-2.ch019

Gao, S. S., Oreal, S., & Zhang, J. (2018). Contemporary Financial Risk Management Perceptions and Practices of Small-Sized Chinese Businesses. In I. Management Association (Ed.), Global Business Expansion: Concepts, Methodologies, Tools, and Applications (pp. 917-931). Hershey, PA: IGI Global. doi:10.4018/978-1-5225-5481-3.ch041

Garg, R., & Berning, S. C. (2017). Indigenous Chinese Management Philosophies: Key Concepts and Relevance for Modern Chinese Firms. In B. Christiansen & G. Koc (Eds.), *Transcontinental Strategies for Industrial Development and Economic Growth* (pp. 43–57). Hershey, PA: IGI Global. doi:10.4018/978-1-5225-2160-0.ch003

Gencer, Y. G. (2017). Supply Chain Management in Retailing Business. In U. Akkucuk (Ed.), *Ethics and Sustainability in Global Supply Chain Management* (pp. 197–210). Hershey, PA: IGI Global. doi:10.4018/978-1-5225-2036-8.ch011

Giacosa, E. (2016). Innovation in Luxury Fashion Businesses as a Means for the Regional Development. In L. Carvalho (Ed.), *Handbook of Research on Entrepreneurial Success and its Impact on Regional Development* (pp. 206–222). Hershey, PA: IGI Global. doi:10.4018/978-1-4666-9567-2.ch010

Giacosa, E. (2018). The Increasing of the Regional Development Thanks to the Luxury Business Innovation. In L. Carvalho (Ed.), *Handbook of Research on Entrepreneurial Ecosystems and Social Dynamics in a Globalized World* (pp. 260–273). Hershey, PA: IGI Global. doi:10.4018/978-1-5225-3525-6.ch011

Gianni, M., & Gotzamani, K. (2016). Integrated Management Systems and Information Management Systems: Common Threads. In P. Papajorgji, F. Pinet, A. Guimarães, & J. Papathanasiou (Eds.), *Automated Enterprise Systems for Maximizing Business Performance* (pp. 195–214). Hershey, PA: IGI Global. doi:10.4018/978-1-4666-8841-4.ch011

Gianni, M., Gotzamani, K., & Linden, I. (2016). How a BI-wise Responsible Integrated Management System May Support Food Traceability. *International Journal of Decision Support System Technology*, *8*(2), 1–17. doi:10.4018/IJDSST.2016040101

Glykas, M., & George, J. (2017). Quality and Process Management Systems in the UAE Maritime Industry. *International Journal of Productivity Management and Assessment Technologies*, *5*(1), 20–39. doi:10.4018/IJPMAT.2017010102

Glykas, M., Valiris, G., Kokkinaki, A., & Koutsoukou, Z. (2018). Banking Business Process Management Implementation. *International Journal of Productivity Management and Assessment Technologies*, *6*(1), 50–69. doi:10.4018/IJPMAT.2018010104

Gomes, J., & Romão, M. (2017). The Balanced Scorecard: Keeping Updated and Aligned with Today's Business Trends. *International Journal of Productivity Management and Assessment Technologies*, *5*(2), 1–15. doi:10.4018/IJPMAT.2017070101

Gomes, J., & Romão, M. (2017). Aligning Information Systems and Technology with Benefit Management and Balanced Scorecard. In S. De Haes & W. Van Grembergen (Eds.), *Strategic IT Governance and Alignment in Business Settings* (pp. 112–131). Hershey, PA: IGI Global. doi:10.4018/978-1-5225-0861-8.ch005

Grefen, P., & Turetken, O. (2017). Advanced Business Process Management in Networked E-Business Scenarios. *International Journal of E-Business Research*, *13*(4), 70–104. doi:10.4018/IJEBR.2017100105

Haider, A., & Saetang, S. (2017). Strategic IT Alignment in Service Sector. In S. Rozenes & Y. Cohen (Eds.), *Handbook of Research on Strategic Alliances and Value Co-Creation in the Service Industry* (pp. 231–258). Hershey, PA: IGI Global. doi:10.4018/978-1-5225-2084-9.ch012

Haider, A., & Tang, S. S. (2016). Maximising Value Through IT and Business Alignment: A Case of IT Governance Institutionalisation at a Thai Bank. *International Journal of Technology Diffusion*, *7*(3), 33–58. doi:10.4018/IJTD.2016070104

Hajilari, A. B., Ghadaksaz, M., & Fasghandis, G. S. (2017). Assessing Organizational Readiness for Implementing ERP System Using Fuzzy Expert System Approach. *International Journal of Enterprise Information Systems*, *13*(1), 67–85. doi:10.4018/IJEIS.2017010105

Haldorai, A., Ramu, A., & Murugan, S. (2018). Social Aware Cognitive Radio Networks: Effectiveness of Social Networks as a Strategic Tool for Organizational Business Management. In H. Bansal, G. Shrivastava, G. Nguyen, & L. Stanciu (Eds.), *Social Network Analytics for Contemporary Business Organizations* (pp. 188–202). Hershey, PA: IGI Global. doi:10.4018/978-1-5225-5097-6.ch010

Hall, O. P. Jr. (2017). Social Media Driven Management Education. *International Journal of Knowledge-Based Organizations*, *7*(2), 43–59. doi:10.4018/IJKBO.2017040104

Hanifah, H., Halim, H. A., Ahmad, N. H., & Vafaei-Zadeh, A. (2017). Innovation Culture as a Mediator Between Specific Human Capital and Innovation Performance Among Bumiputera SMEs in Malaysia. In N. Ahmad, T. Ramayah, H. Halim, & S. Rahman (Eds.), *Handbook of Research on Small and Medium Enterprises in Developing Countries* (pp. 261–279). Hershey, PA: IGI Global. doi:10.4018/978-1-5225-2165-5.ch012

Hartlieb, S., & Silvius, G. (2017). Handling Uncertainty in Project Management and Business Development: Similarities and Differences. In Y. Raydugin (Ed.), *Handbook of Research on Leveraging Risk and Uncertainties for Effective Project Management* (pp. 337–362). Hershey, PA: IGI Global. doi:10.4018/978-1-5225-1790-0.ch016

Hass, K. B. (2017). Living on the Edge: Managing Project Complexity. In Y. Raydugin (Ed.), *Handbook of Research on Leveraging Risk and Uncertainties for Effective Project Management* (pp. 177–201). Hershey, PA: IGI Global. doi:10.4018/978-1-5225-1790-0.ch009

Hassan, A., & Privitera, D. S. (2016). Google AdSense as a Mobile Technology in Education. In J. Holland (Ed.), *Wearable Technology and Mobile Innovations for Next-Generation Education* (pp. 200–223). Hershey, PA: IGI Global. doi:10.4018/978-1-5225-0069-8.ch011

Hassan, A., & Rahimi, R. (2016). Consuming "Innovation" in Tourism: Augmented Reality as an Innovation Tool in Digital Tourism Marketing. In N. Pappas & I. Bregoli (Eds.), *Global Dynamics in Travel, Tourism, and Hospitality* (pp. 130–147). Hershey, PA: IGI Global. doi:10.4018/978-1-5225-0201-2.ch008

Hawking, P., & Carmine Sellitto, C. (2017). Developing an Effective Strategy for Organizational Business Intelligence. In M. Tavana (Ed.), *Enterprise Information Systems and the Digitalization of Business Functions* (pp. 222–237). Hershey, PA: IGI Global. doi:10.4018/978-1-5225-2382-6.ch010

Hawking, P., & Sellitto, C. (2017). A Fast-Moving Consumer Goods Company and Business Intelligence Strategy Development. *International Journal of Enterprise Information Systems, 13*(2), 22–33. doi:10.4018/IJEIS.2017040102

Hawking, P., & Sellitto, C. (2017). Business Intelligence Strategy: Two Case Studies. *International Journal of Business Intelligence Research, 8*(2), 17–30. doi:10.4018/IJBIR.2017070102

Haynes, J. D., Arockiasamy, S., Al Rashdi, M., & Al Rashdi, S. (2016). Business and E Business Strategies for Coopetition and Thematic Management as a Sustained Basis for Ethics and Social Responsibility in Emerging Markets. In M. Al-Shammari & H. Masri (Eds.), *Ethical and Social Perspectives on Global Business Interaction in Emerging Markets* (pp. 25–39). Hershey, PA: IGI Global. doi:10.4018/978-1-4666-9864-2.ch002

Hee, W. J., Jalleh, G., Lai, H., & Lin, C. (2017). E-Commerce and IT Projects: Evaluation and Management Issues in Australian and Taiwanese Hospitals. *International Journal of Public Health Management and Ethics, 2*(1), 69–90. doi:10.4018/IJPHME.2017010104

Hernandez, A. A. (2018). Exploring the Factors to Green IT Adoption of SMEs in the Philippines. *Journal of Cases on Information Technology, 20*(2), 49–66. doi:10.4018/JCIT.2018040104

Hernandez, A. A., & Ona, S. E. (2016). Green IT Adoption: Lessons from the Philippines Business Process Outsourcing Industry. *International Journal of Social Ecology and Sustainable Development, 7*(1), 1–34. doi:10.4018/IJSESD.2016010101

Hollman, A., Bickford, S., & Hollman, T. (2017). Cyber InSecurity: A Post-Mortem Attempt to Assess Cyber Problems from IT and Business Management Perspectives. *Journal of Cases on Information Technology, 19*(3), 42–70. doi:10.4018/JCIT.2017070104

Igbinakhase, I. (2017). Responsible and Sustainable Management Practices in Developing and Developed Business Environments. In Z. Fields (Ed.), *Collective Creativity for Responsible and Sustainable Business Practice* (pp. 180–207). Hershey, PA: IGI Global. doi:10.4018/978-1-5225-1823-5.ch010

Ilahi, L., Ghannouchi, S. A., & Martinho, R. (2016). A Business Process Management Approach to Home Healthcare Processes: On the Gap between Intention and Reality. In M. Cruz-Cunha, I. Miranda, R. Martinho, & R. Rijo (Eds.), *Encyclopedia of E-Health and Telemedicine* (pp. 439–457). Hershey, PA: IGI Global. doi:10.4018/978-1-4666-9978-6.ch035

Iwata, J. J., & Hoskins, R. G. (2017). Managing Indigenous Knowledge in Tanzania: A Business Perspective. In P. Jain & N. Mnjama (Eds.), *Managing Knowledge Resources and Records in Modern Organizations* (pp. 198–214). Hershey, PA: IGI Global. doi:10.4018/978-1-5225-1965-2.ch012

Jabeen, F., Ahmad, S. Z., & Alkaabi, S. (2016). The Internationalization Decision-Making of United Arab Emirates Family Businesses. In N. Zakaria, A. Abdul-Talib, & N. Osman (Eds.), *Handbook of Research on Impacts of International Business and Political Affairs on the Global Economy* (pp. 1–22). Hershey, PA: IGI Global. doi:10.4018/978-1-4666-9806-2.ch001

Jain, P. (2017). Ethical and Legal Issues in Knowledge Management Life-Cycle in Business. In P. Jain & N. Mnjama (Eds.), *Managing Knowledge Resources and Records in Modern Organizations* (pp. 82–101). Hershey, PA: IGI Global. doi:10.4018/978-1-5225-1965-2.ch006

Jamali, D., Abdallah, H., & Matar, F. (2016). Opportunities and Challenges for CSR Mainstreaming in Business Schools. *International Journal of Technology and Educational Marketing*, *6*(2), 1–29. doi:10.4018/IJTEM.2016070101

James, S., & Hauli, E. (2017). Holistic Management Education at Tanzanian Rural Development Planning Institute. In N. Baporikar (Ed.), *Management Education for Global Leadership* (pp. 112–136). Hershey, PA: IGI Global. doi:10.4018/978-1-5225-1013-0.ch006

Janošková, M., Csikósová, A., & Čulková, K. (2018). Measurement of Company Performance as Part of Its Strategic Management. In R. Leon (Ed.), *Managerial Strategies for Business Sustainability During Turbulent Times* (pp. 309–335). Hershey, PA: IGI Global. doi:10.4018/978-1-5225-2716-9.ch017

Jean-Vasile, A., & Alecu, A. (2017). Theoretical and Practical Approaches in Understanding the Influences of Cost-Productivity-Profit Trinomial in Contemporary Enterprises. In A. Jean Vasile & D. Nicolò (Eds.), *Sustainable Entrepreneurship and Investments in the Green Economy* (pp. 28–62). Hershey, PA: IGI Global. doi:10.4018/978-1-5225-2075-7.ch002

Jha, D. G. (2016). Preparing for Information Technology Driven Changes. In S. Tiwari & L. Nafees (Eds.), *Innovative Management Education Pedagogies for Preparing Next-Generation Leaders* (pp. 258–274). Hershey, PA: IGI Global. doi:10.4018/978-1-4666-9691-4.ch015

Joia, L. A., & Correia, J. C. (2018). CIO Competencies From the IT Professional Perspective: Insights From Brazil. *Journal of Global Information Management*, *26*(2), 74–103. doi:10.4018/JGIM.2018040104

Juma, A., & Mzera, N. (2017). Knowledge Management and Records Management and Competitive Advantage in Business. In P. Jain & N. Mnjama (Eds.), *Managing Knowledge Resources and Records in Modern Organizations* (pp. 15–28). Hershey, PA: IGI Global. doi:10.4018/978-1-5225-1965-2.ch002

K., I., & A, V. (2018). Monitoring and Auditing in the Cloud. In K. Munir (Ed.), *Cloud Computing Technologies for Green Enterprises* (pp. 318-350). Hershey, PA: IGI Global. doi:10.4018/978-1-5225-3038-1.ch013

Kabra, G., Ghosh, V., & Ramesh, A. (2018). Enterprise Integrated Business Process Management and Business Intelligence Framework for Business Process Sustainability. In A. Paul, D. Bhattacharyya, & S. Anand (Eds.), *Green Initiatives for Business Sustainability and Value Creation* (pp. 228–238). Hershey, PA: IGI Global. doi:10.4018/978-1-5225-2662-9.ch010

Kaoud, M. (2017). Investigation of Customer Knowledge Management: A Case Study Research. *International Journal of Service Science, Management, Engineering, and Technology*, *8*(2), 12–22. doi:10.4018/IJSSMET.2017040102

Kara, M. E., & Fırat, S. Ü. (2016). Sustainability, Risk, and Business Intelligence in Supply Chains. In M. Erdoğdu, T. Arun, & I. Ahmad (Eds.), *Handbook of Research on Green Economic Development Initiatives and Strategies* (pp. 501–538). Hershey, PA: IGI Global. doi:10.4018/978-1-5225-0440-5.ch022

Katuu, S. (2018). A Comparative Assessment of Enterprise Content Management Maturity Models. In N. Gwangwava & M. Mutingi (Eds.), *E-Manufacturing and E-Service Strategies in Contemporary Organizations* (pp. 93–118). Hershey, PA: IGI Global. doi:10.4018/978-1-5225-3628-4.ch005

Khan, M. A. (2016). MNEs Management Strategies in Developing Countries: Establishing the Context. In M. Khan (Ed.), *Multinational Enterprise Management Strategies in Developing Countries* (pp. 1–33). Hershey, PA: IGI Global. doi:10.4018/978-1-5225-0276-0.ch001

Khan, M. A. (2016). Operational Approaches in Organizational Structure: A Case for MNEs in Developing Countries. In M. Khan (Ed.), *Multinational Enterprise Management Strategies in Developing Countries* (pp. 129–151). Hershey, PA: IGI Global. doi:10.4018/978-1-5225-0276-0.ch007

Kinnunen, S., Ylä-Kujala, A., Marttonen-Arola, S., Kärri, T., & Baglee, D. (2018). Internet of Things in Asset Management: Insights from Industrial Professionals and Academia. *International Journal of Service Science, Management, Engineering, and Technology*, *9*(2), 104–119. doi:10.4018/IJSSMET.2018040105

Klein, A. Z., Sabino de Freitas, A., Machado, L., Freitas, J. C. Jr, Graziola, P. G. Jr, & Schlemmer, E. (2017). Virtual Worlds Applications for Management Education. In L. Tomei (Ed.), *Exploring the New Era of Technology-Infused Education* (pp. 279–299). Hershey, PA: IGI Global. doi:10.4018/978-1-5225-1709-2.ch017

Kożuch, B., & Jabłoński, A. (2017). Adopting the Concept of Business Models in Public Management. In M. Lewandowski & B. Kożuch (Eds.), *Public Sector Entrepreneurship and the Integration of Innovative Business Models* (pp. 10–46). Hershey, PA: IGI Global. doi:10.4018/978-1-5225-2215-7.ch002

Kumar, J., Adhikary, A., & Jha, A. (2017). Small Active Investors' Perceptions and Preferences Towards Tax Saving Mutual Fund Schemes in Eastern India: An Empirical Note. *International Journal of Asian Business and Information Management*, *8*(2), 35–45. doi:10.4018/IJABIM.2017040103

Lassoued, Y., Bouzguenda, L., & Mahmoud, T. (2016). Context-Aware Business Process Versions Management. *International Journal of e-Collaboration*, *12*(3), 7–33. doi:10.4018/IJeC.2016070102

Lavassani, K. M., & Movahedi, B. (2017). Applications Driven Information Systems: Beyond Networks toward Business Ecosystems. *International Journal of Innovation in the Digital Economy*, *8*(1), 61–75. doi:10.4018/IJIDE.2017010104

Lazzareschi, V. H., & Brito, M. S. (2017). Strategic Information Management: Proposal of Business Project Model. In G. Jamil, A. Soares, & C. Pessoa (Eds.), *Handbook of Research on Information Management for Effective Logistics and Supply Chains* (pp. 59–88). Hershey, PA: IGI Global. doi:10.4018/978-1-5225-0973-8.ch004

Lederer, M., Kurz, M., & Lazarov, P. (2017). Usage and Suitability of Methods for Strategic Business Process Initiatives: A Multi Case Study Research. *International Journal of Productivity Management and Assessment Technologies*, *5*(1), 40–51. doi:10.4018/IJPMAT.2017010103

Lee, I. (2017). A Social Enterprise Business Model and a Case Study of Pacific Community Ventures (PCV). In V. Potocan, M. Üngan, & Z. Nedelko (Eds.), *Handbook of Research on Managerial Solutions in Non-Profit Organizations* (pp. 182–204). Hershey, PA: IGI Global. doi:10.4018/978-1-5225-0731-4.ch009

Lee, L. J., & Leu, J. (2016). Exploring the Effectiveness of IT Application and Value Method in the Innovation Performance of Enterprise. *International Journal of Enterprise Information Systems*, *12*(2), 47–65. doi:10.4018/IJEIS.2016040104

Lee, Y. (2016). Alignment Effect of Entrepreneurial Orientation and Marketing Orientation on Firm Performance. *International Journal of Customer Relationship Marketing and Management, 7*(4), 58–69. doi:10.4018/IJCRMM.2016100104

Leon, L. A., Seal, K. C., Przasnyski, Z. H., & Wiedenman, I. (2017). Skills and Competencies Required for Jobs in Business Analytics: A Content Analysis of Job Advertisements Using Text Mining. *International Journal of Business Intelligence Research, 8*(1), 1–25. doi:10.4018/IJBIR.2017010101

Leu, J., Lee, L. J., & Krischke, A. (2016). Value Engineering-Based Method for Implementing the ISO14001 System in the Green Supply Chains. *International Journal of Strategic Decision Sciences, 7*(4), 1–20. doi:10.4018/IJSDS.2016100101

Levy, C. L., & Elias, N. I. (2017). SOHO Users' Perceptions of Reliability and Continuity of Cloud-Based Services. In M. Moore (Ed.), *Cybersecurity Breaches and Issues Surrounding Online Threat Protection* (pp. 248–287). Hershey, PA: IGI Global. doi:10.4018/978-1-5225-1941-6.ch011

Levy, M. (2018). Change Management Serving Knowledge Management and Organizational Development: Reflections and Review. In N. Baporikar (Ed.), *Global Practices in Knowledge Management for Societal and Organizational Development* (pp. 256–270). Hershey, PA: IGI Global. doi:10.4018/978-1-5225-3009-1.ch012

Lewandowski, M. (2017). Public Organizations and Business Model Innovation: The Role of Public Service Design. In M. Lewandowski & B. Kożuch (Eds.), *Public Sector Entrepreneurship and the Integration of Innovative Business Models* (pp. 47–72). Hershey, PA: IGI Global. doi:10.4018/978-1-5225-2215-7.ch003

Lhannaoui, H., Kabbaj, M. I., & Bakkoury, Z. (2017). A Survey of Risk-Aware Business Process Modelling. *International Journal of Risk and Contingency Management, 6*(3), 14–26. doi:10.4018/IJRCM.2017070102

Li, J., Sun, W., Jiang, W., Yang, H., & Zhang, L. (2017). How the Nature of Exogenous Shocks and Crises Impact Company Performance?: The Effects of Industry Characteristics. *International Journal of Risk and Contingency Management, 6*(4), 40–55. doi:10.4018/IJRCM.2017100103

Lu, C., & Liu, S. (2016). Cultural Tourism O2O Business Model Innovation-A Case Study of CTrip. *Journal of Electronic Commerce in Organizations, 14*(2), 16–31. doi:10.4018/JECO.2016040102

Machen, B., Hosseini, M. R., Wood, A., & Bakhshi, J. (2016). An Investigation into using SAP-PS as a Multidimensional Project Control System (MPCS). *International Journal of Enterprise Information Systems*, *12*(2), 66–81. doi:10.4018/IJEIS.2016040105

Malega, P. (2017). Small and Medium Enterprises in the Slovak Republic: Status and Competitiveness of SMEs in the Global Markets and Possibilities of Optimization. In M. Vemić (Ed.), *Optimal Management Strategies in Small and Medium Enterprises* (pp. 102–124). Hershey, PA: IGI Global. doi:10.4018/978-1-5225-1949-2.ch006

Malewska, K. M. (2017). Intuition in Decision-Making on the Example of a Non-Profit Organization. In V. Potocan, M. Üngan, & Z. Nedelko (Eds.), *Handbook of Research on Managerial Solutions in Non-Profit Organizations* (pp. 378–399). Hershey, PA: IGI Global. doi:10.4018/978-1-5225-0731-4.ch018

Maroofi, F. (2017). Entrepreneurial Orientation and Organizational Learning Ability Analysis for Innovation and Firm Performance. In N. Baporikar (Ed.), *Innovation and Shifting Perspectives in Management Education* (pp. 144–165). Hershey, PA: IGI Global. doi:10.4018/978-1-5225-1019-2.ch007

Martins, P. V., & Zacarias, M. (2017). A Web-based Tool for Business Process Improvement. *International Journal of Web Portals*, *9*(2), 68–84. doi:10.4018/IJWP.2017070104

Matthies, B., & Coners, A. (2017). Exploring the Conceptual Nature of e-Business Projects. *Journal of Electronic Commerce in Organizations*, *15*(3), 33–63. doi:10.4018/JECO.2017070103

McKee, J. (2018). Architecture as a Tool to Solve Business Planning Problems. In M. Khosrow-Pour, D.B.A. (Ed.), Encyclopedia of Information Science and Technology, Fourth Edition (pp. 573-586). Hershey, PA: IGI Global. doi:10.4018/978-1-5225-2255-3.ch050

McMurray, A. J., Cross, J., & Caponecchia, C. (2018). The Risk Management Profession in Australia: Business Continuity Plan Practices. In N. Bajgoric (Ed.), *Always-On Enterprise Information Systems for Modern Organizations* (pp. 112–129). Hershey, PA: IGI Global. doi:10.4018/978-1-5225-3704-5.ch006

Meddah, I. H., & Belkadi, K. (2018). Mining Patterns Using Business Process Management. In R. Hamou (Ed.), *Handbook of Research on Biomimicry in Information Retrieval and Knowledge Management* (pp. 78–89). Hershey, PA: IGI Global. doi:10.4018/978-1-5225-3004-6.ch005

Mendes, L. (2017). TQM and Knowledge Management: An Integrated Approach Towards Tacit Knowledge Management. In D. Jaziri-Bouagina & G. Jamil (Eds.), *Handbook of Research on Tacit Knowledge Management for Organizational Success* (pp. 236–263). Hershey, PA: IGI Global. doi:10.4018/978-1-5225-2394-9.ch009

Mnjama, N. M. (2017). Preservation of Recorded Information in Public and Private Sector Organizations. In P. Jain & N. Mnjama (Eds.), *Managing Knowledge Resources and Records in Modern Organizations* (pp. 149–167). Hershey, PA: IGI Global. doi:10.4018/978-1-5225-1965-2.ch009

Mokoqama, M., & Fields, Z. (2017). Principles of Responsible Management Education (PRME): Call for Responsible Management Education. In Z. Fields (Ed.), *Collective Creativity for Responsible and Sustainable Business Practice* (pp. 229–241). Hershey, PA: IGI Global. doi:10.4018/978-1-5225-1823-5.ch012

Muniapan, B. (2017). Philosophy and Management: The Relevance of Vedanta in Management. In P. Ordóñez de Pablos (Ed.), *Managerial Strategies and Solutions for Business Success in Asia* (pp. 124–139). Hershey, PA: IGI Global. doi:10.4018/978-1-5225-1886-0.ch007

Muniapan, B., Gregory, M. L., & Ling, L. A. (2016). Marketing Education in Sarawak: Looking at It from the Employers' Viewpoint. In B. Smith & A. Porath (Eds.), *Global Perspectives on Contemporary Marketing Education* (pp. 112–130). Hershey, PA: IGI Global. doi:10.4018/978-1-4666-9784-3.ch008

Murad, S. E., & Dowaji, S. (2017). Using Value-Based Approach for Managing Cloud-Based Services. In A. Turuk, B. Sahoo, & S. Addya (Eds.), *Resource Management and Efficiency in Cloud Computing Environments* (pp. 33–60). Hershey, PA: IGI Global. doi:10.4018/978-1-5225-1721-4.ch002

Mutahar, A. M., Daud, N. M., Thurasamy, R., Isaac, O., & Abdulsalam, R. (2018). The Mediating of Perceived Usefulness and Perceived Ease of Use: The Case of Mobile Banking in Yemen. *International Journal of Technology Diffusion*, *9*(2), 21–40. doi:10.4018/IJTD.2018040102

Naidoo, V. (2017). E-Learning and Management Education at African Universities. In N. Baporikar (Ed.), *Management Education for Global Leadership* (pp. 181–201). Hershey, PA: IGI Global. doi:10.4018/978-1-5225-1013-0.ch009

Naidoo, V., & Igbinakhase, I. (2018). Opportunities and Challenges of Knowledge Retention in SMEs. In N. Baporikar (Ed.), *Knowledge Integration Strategies for Entrepreneurship and Sustainability* (pp. 70–94). Hershey, PA: IGI Global. doi:10.4018/978-1-5225-5115-7.ch004

Nayak, S., & Prabhu, N. (2017). Paradigm Shift in Management Education: Need for a Cross Functional Perspective. In N. Baporikar (Ed.), *Management Education for Global Leadership* (pp. 241–255). Hershey, PA: IGI Global. doi:10.4018/978-1-5225-1013-0.ch012

Ndede-Amadi, A. A. (2016). Student Interest in the IS Specialization as Predictor of the Success Potential of New Information Systems Programmes within the Schools of Business in Kenyan Public Universities. *International Journal of Information Systems and Social Change*, *7*(2), 63–79. doi:10.4018/IJISSC.2016040104

Nedelko, Z., & Potocan, V. (2016). Management Practices for Processes Optimization: Case of Slovenia. In G. Alor-Hernández, C. Sánchez-Ramírez, & J. García-Alcaraz (Eds.), *Handbook of Research on Managerial Strategies for Achieving Optimal Performance in Industrial Processes* (pp. 545–561). Hershey, PA: IGI Global. doi:10.4018/978-1-5225-0130-5.ch025

Nedelko, Z., & Potocan, V. (2017). Management Solutions in Non-Profit Organizations: Case of Slovenia. In V. Potocan, M. Üngan, & Z. Nedelko (Eds.), *Handbook of Research on Managerial Solutions in Non-Profit Organizations* (pp. 1–22). Hershey, PA: IGI Global. doi:10.4018/978-1-5225-0731-4.ch001

Nedelko, Z., & Potocan, V. (2017). Priority of Management Tools Utilization among Managers: International Comparison. In V. Wang (Ed.), *Encyclopedia of Strategic Leadership and Management* (pp. 1083–1094). Hershey, PA: IGI Global. doi:10.4018/978-1-5225-1049-9.ch075

Nedelko, Z., Raudeliūnienė, J., & Črešnar, R. (2018). Knowledge Dynamics in Supply Chain Management. In N. Baporikar (Ed.), *Knowledge Integration Strategies for Entrepreneurship and Sustainability* (pp. 150–166). Hershey, PA: IGI Global. doi:10.4018/978-1-5225-5115-7.ch008

Nguyen, H. T., & Hipsher, S. A. (2018). Innovation and Creativity Used by Private Sector Firms in a Resources-Constrained Environment. In S. Hipsher (Ed.), *Examining the Private Sector's Role in Wealth Creation and Poverty Reduction* (pp. 219–238). Hershey, PA: IGI Global. doi:10.4018/978-1-5225-3117-3.ch010

Nycz, M., & Pólkowski, Z. (2016). Business Intelligence as a Modern IT Supporting Management of Local Government Units in Poland. *International Journal of Knowledge and Systems Science*, *7*(4), 1–18. doi:10.4018/IJKSS.2016100101

Obaji, N. O., Senin, A. A., & Olugu, M. U. (2016). Supportive Government Policy as a Mechanism for Business Incubation Performance in Nigeria. *International Journal of Information Systems and Social Change*, *7*(4), 52–66. doi:10.4018/IJISSC.2016100103

Obicci, P. A. (2017). Risk Sharing in a Partnership. In *Risk Management Strategies in Public-Private Partnerships* (pp. 115–152). Hershey, PA: IGI Global. doi:10.4018/978-1-5225-2503-5.ch004

Obidallah, W. J., & Raahemi, B. (2017). Managing Changes in Service Oriented Virtual Organizations: A Structural and Procedural Framework to Facilitate the Process of Change. *Journal of Electronic Commerce in Organizations*, *15*(1), 59–83. doi:10.4018/JECO.2017010104

Ojasalo, J., & Ojasalo, K. (2016). Service Logic Business Model Canvas for Lean Development of SMEs and Start-Ups. In N. Baporikar (Ed.), *Handbook of Research on Entrepreneurship in the Contemporary Knowledge-Based Global Economy* (pp. 217–243). Hershey, PA: IGI Global. doi:10.4018/978-1-4666-8798-1.ch010

Ojo, O. (2017). Impact of Innovation on the Entrepreneurial Success in Selected Business Enterprises in South-West Nigeria. *International Journal of Innovation in the Digital Economy*, *8*(2), 29–38. doi:10.4018/IJIDE.2017040103

Okdinawati, L., Simatupang, T. M., & Sunitiyoso, Y. (2017). Multi-Agent Reinforcement Learning for Value Co-Creation of Collaborative Transportation Management (CTM). *International Journal of Information Systems and Supply Chain Management*, *10*(3), 84–95. doi:10.4018/IJISSCM.2017070105

Ortner, E., Mevius, M., Wiedmann, P., & Kurz, F. (2016). Design of Interactional Decision Support Applications for E-Participation in Smart Cities. *International Journal of Electronic Government Research*, *12*(2), 18–38. doi:10.4018/IJEGR.2016040102

Pal, K. (2018). Building High Quality Big Data-Based Applications in Supply Chains. In A. Kumar & S. Saurav (Eds.), *Supply Chain Management Strategies and Risk Assessment in Retail Environments* (pp. 1–24). Hershey, PA: IGI Global. doi:10.4018/978-1-5225-3056-5.ch001

Palos-Sanchez, P. R., & Correia, M. B. (2018). Perspectives of the Adoption of Cloud Computing in the Tourism Sector. In J. Rodrigues, C. Ramos, P. Cardoso, & C. Henriques (Eds.), *Handbook of Research on Technological Developments for Cultural Heritage and eTourism Applications* (pp. 377–400). Hershey, PA: IGI Global. doi:10.4018/978-1-5225-2927-9.ch018

Parry, V. K., & Lind, M. L. (2016). Alignment of Business Strategy and Information Technology Considering Information Technology Governance, Project Portfolio Control, and Risk Management. *International Journal of Information Technology Project Management*, *7*(4), 21–37. doi:10.4018/IJITPM.2016100102

Pashkova, N., Trujillo-Barrera, A., Apostolakis, G., Van Dijk, G., Drakos, P. D., & Baourakis, G. (2016). Business Management Models of Microfinance Institutions (MFIs) in Africa: A Study into Their Enabling Environments. *International Journal of Food and Beverage Manufacturing and Business Models, 1*(2), 63–82. doi:10.4018/IJFBMBM.2016070105

Patiño, B. E. (2017). New Generation Management by Convergence and Individual Identity: A Systemic and Human-Oriented Approach. In N. Baporikar (Ed.), *Innovation and Shifting Perspectives in Management Education* (pp. 119–143). Hershey, PA: IGI Global. doi:10.4018/978-1-5225-1019-2.ch006

Pawliczek, A., & Rössler, M. (2017). Knowledge of Management Tools and Systems in SMEs: Knowledge Transfer in Management. In A. Bencsik (Ed.), *Knowledge Management Initiatives and Strategies in Small and Medium Enterprises* (pp. 180–203). Hershey, PA: IGI Global. doi:10.4018/978-1-5225-1642-2.ch009

Pejic-Bach, M., Omazic, M. A., Aleksic, A., & Zoroja, J. (2018). Knowledge-Based Decision Making: A Multi-Case Analysis. In R. Leon (Ed.), *Managerial Strategies for Business Sustainability During Turbulent Times* (pp. 160–184). Hershey, PA: IGI Global. doi:10.4018/978-1-5225-2716-9.ch009

Perano, M., Hysa, X., & Calabrese, M. (2018). Strategic Planning, Cultural Context, and Business Continuity Management: Business Cases in the City of Shkoder. In A. Presenza & L. Sheehan (Eds.), *Geopolitics and Strategic Management in the Global Economy* (pp. 57–77). Hershey, PA: IGI Global. doi:10.4018/978-1-5225-2673-5.ch004

Pereira, R., Mira da Silva, M., & Lapão, L. V. (2017). IT Governance Maturity Patterns in Portuguese Healthcare. In S. De Haes & W. Van Grembergen (Eds.), *Strategic IT Governance and Alignment in Business Settings* (pp. 24–52). Hershey, PA: IGI Global. doi:10.4018/978-1-5225-0861-8.ch002

Perez-Uribe, R., & Ocampo-Guzman, D. (2016). Conflict within Colombian Family Owned SMEs: An Explosive Blend between Feelings and Business. In J. Saiz-Álvarez (Ed.), *Handbook of Research on Social Entrepreneurship and Solidarity Economics* (pp. 329–354). Hershey, PA: IGI Global. doi:10.4018/978-1-5225-0097-1.ch017

Pérez-Uribe, R. I., Torres, D. A., Jurado, S. P., & Prada, D. M. (2018). Cloud Tools for the Development of Project Management in SMEs. In R. Perez-Uribe, C. Salcedo-Perez, & D. Ocampo-Guzman (Eds.), *Handbook of Research on Intrapreneurship and Organizational Sustainability in SMEs* (pp. 95–120). Hershey, PA: IGI Global. doi:10.4018/978-1-5225-3543-0.ch005

Petrisor, I., & Cozmiuc, D. (2017). Global Supply Chain Management Organization at Siemens in the Advent of Industry 4.0. In L. Saglietto & C. Cezanne (Eds.), *Global Intermediation and Logistics Service Providers* (pp. 123–142). Hershey, PA: IGI Global. doi:10.4018/978-1-5225-2133-4.ch007

Pierce, J. M., Velliaris, D. M., & Edwards, J. (2017). A Living Case Study: A Journey Not a Destination. In N. Silton (Ed.), *Exploring the Benefits of Creativity in Education, Media, and the Arts* (pp. 158–178). Hershey, PA: IGI Global. doi:10.4018/978-1-5225-0504-4.ch008

Radosavljevic, M., & Andjelkovic, A. (2017). Multi-Criteria Decision Making Approach for Choosing Business Process for the Improvement: Upgrading of the Six Sigma Methodology. In J. Stanković, P. Delias, S. Marinković, & S. Rochhia (Eds.), *Tools and Techniques for Economic Decision Analysis* (pp. 225–247). Hershey, PA: IGI Global. doi:10.4018/978-1-5225-0959-2.ch011

Radovic, V. M. (2017). Corporate Sustainability and Responsibility and Disaster Risk Reduction: A Serbian Overview. In M. Camilleri (Ed.), *CSR 2.0 and the New Era of Corporate Citizenship* (pp. 147–164). Hershey, PA: IGI Global. doi:10.4018/978-1-5225-1842-6.ch008

Raghunath, K. M., Devi, S. L., & Patro, C. S. (2018). Impact of Risk Assessment Models on Risk Factors: A Holistic Outlook. In K. Strang, M. Korstanje, & N. Vajjhala (Eds.), *Research, Practices, and Innovations in Global Risk and Contingency Management* (pp. 134–153). Hershey, PA: IGI Global. doi:10.4018/978-1-5225-4754-9.ch008

Raman, A., & Goyal, D. P. (2017). Extending IMPLEMENT Framework for Enterprise Information Systems Implementation to Information System Innovation. In M. Tavana (Ed.), *Enterprise Information Systems and the Digitalization of Business Functions* (pp. 137–177). Hershey, PA: IGI Global. doi:10.4018/978-1-5225-2382-6.ch007

Rao, Y., & Zhang, Y. (2017). The Construction and Development of Academic Library Digital Special Subject Databases. In L. Ruan, Q. Zhu, & Y. Ye (Eds.), *Academic Library Development and Administration in China* (pp. 163–183). Hershey, PA: IGI Global. doi:10.4018/978-1-5225-0550-1.ch010

Ravasan, A. Z., Mohammadi, M. M., & Hamidi, H. (2018). An Investigation Into the Critical Success Factors of Implementing Information Technology Service Management Frameworks. In K. Jakobs (Ed.), *Corporate and Global Standardization Initiatives in Contemporary Society* (pp. 200–218). Hershey, PA: IGI Global. doi:10.4018/978-1-5225-5320-5.ch009

Renna, P., Izzo, C., & Romaniello, T. (2016). The Business Process Management Systems to Support Continuous Improvements. In W. Nuninger & J. Châtelet (Eds.), *Handbook of Research on Quality Assurance and Value Management in Higher Education* (pp. 237–256). Hershey, PA: IGI Global. doi:10.4018/978-1-5225-0024-7.ch009

Rezaie, S., Mirabedini, S. J., & Abtahi, A. (2018). Designing a Model for Implementation of Business Intelligence in the Banking Industry. *International Journal of Enterprise Information Systems, 14*(1), 77–103. doi:10.4018/IJEIS.2018010105

Riccò, R. (2016). Diversity Management: Bringing Equality, Equity, and Inclusion in the Workplace. In J. Prescott (Ed.), *Handbook of Research on Race, Gender, and the Fight for Equality* (pp. 335–359). Hershey, PA: IGI Global. doi:10.4018/978-1-5225-0047-6.ch015

Romano, L., Grimaldi, R., & Colasuonno, F. S. (2017). Demand Management as a Success Factor in Project Portfolio Management. In L. Romano (Ed.), *Project Portfolio Management Strategies for Effective Organizational Operations* (pp. 202–219). Hershey, PA: IGI Global. doi:10.4018/978-1-5225-2151-8.ch008

Rostek, K. B. (2016). Risk Management: Role and Importance in Business Organization. In D. Jakóbczak (Ed.), *Analyzing Risk through Probabilistic Modeling in Operations Research* (pp. 149–178). Hershey, PA: IGI Global. doi:10.4018/978-1-4666-9458-3.ch007

Rouhani, S., & Savoji, S. R. (2016). A Success Assessment Model for BI Tools Implementation: An Empirical Study of Banking Industry. *International Journal of Business Intelligence Research, 7*(1), 25–44. doi:10.4018/IJBIR.2016010103

Ruan, Z. (2016). A Corpus-Based Functional Analysis of Complex Nominal Groups in Written Business Discourse: The Case of "Business". *International Journal of Computer-Assisted Language Learning and Teaching, 6*(2), 74–90. doi:10.4018/IJCALLT.2016040105

Ruhi, U. (2018). Towards an Interdisciplinary Socio-Technical Definition of Virtual Communities. In M. Khosrow-Pour, D.B.A. (Ed.), Encyclopedia of Information Science and Technology, Fourth Edition (pp. 4278-4295). Hershey, PA: IGI Global. doi:10.4018/978-1-5225-2255-3.ch371

Ryan, J., Doster, B., Daily, S., & Lewis, C. (2016). A Case Study Perspective for Balanced Perioperative Workflow Achievement through Data-Driven Process Improvement. *International Journal of Healthcare Information Systems and Informatics, 11*(3), 19–41. doi:10.4018/IJHISI.2016070102

Safari, M. R., & Jiang, Q. (2018). The Theory and Practice of IT Governance Maturity and Strategies Alignment: Evidence From Banking Industry. *Journal of Global Information Management*, *26*(2), 127–146. doi:10.4018/JGIM.2018040106

Sahoo, J., Pati, B., & Mohanty, B. (2017). Knowledge Management as an Academic Discipline: An Assessment. In B. Gunjal (Ed.), *Managing Knowledge and Scholarly Assets in Academic Libraries* (pp. 99–126). Hershey, PA: IGI Global. doi:10.4018/978-1-5225-1741-2.ch005

Saini, D. (2017). Relevance of Teaching Values and Ethics in Management Education. In N. Baporikar (Ed.), *Management Education for Global Leadership* (pp. 90–111). Hershey, PA: IGI Global. doi:10.4018/978-1-5225-1013-0.ch005

Sambhanthan, A. (2017). Assessing and Benchmarking Sustainability in Organisations: An Integrated Conceptual Model. *International Journal of Systems and Service-Oriented Engineering*, *7*(4), 22–43. doi:10.4018/IJSSOE.2017100102

Sambhanthan, A., & Potdar, V. (2017). A Study of the Parameters Impacting Sustainability in Information Technology Organizations. *International Journal of Knowledge-Based Organizations*, *7*(3), 27–39. doi:10.4018/IJKBO.2017070103

Sánchez-Fernández, M. D., & Manríquez, M. R. (2018). The Entrepreneurial Spirit Based on Social Values: The Digital Generation. In P. Isaias & L. Carvalho (Eds.), *User Innovation and the Entrepreneurship Phenomenon in the Digital Economy* (pp. 173–193). Hershey, PA: IGI Global. doi:10.4018/978-1-5225-2826-5.ch009

Sanchez-Ruiz, L., & Blanco, B. (2017). Process Management for SMEs: Barriers, Enablers, and Benefits. In M. Vemić (Ed.), *Optimal Management Strategies in Small and Medium Enterprises* (pp. 293–319). Hershey, PA: IGI Global. doi:10.4018/978-1-5225-1949-2.ch014

Sanz, L. F., Gómez-Pérez, J., & Castillo-Martinez, A. (2018). Analysis of the European ICT Competence Frameworks. In V. Ahuja & S. Rathore (Eds.), *Multidisciplinary Perspectives on Human Capital and Information Technology Professionals* (pp. 225–245). Hershey, PA: IGI Global. doi:10.4018/978-1-5225-5297-0.ch012

Sarvepalli, A., & Godin, J. (2017). Business Process Management in the Classroom. *Journal of Cases on Information Technology*, *19*(2), 17–28. doi:10.4018/JCIT.2017040102

Satpathy, B., & Muniapan, B. (2016). Ancient Wisdom for Transformational Leadership and Its Insights from the Bhagavad-Gita. In U. Aung & P. Ordoñez de Pablos (Eds.), *Managerial Strategies and Practice in the Asian Business Sector* (pp. 1–10). Hershey, PA: IGI Global. doi:10.4018/978-1-4666-9758-4.ch001

Saygili, E. E., Ozturkoglu, Y., & Kocakulah, M. C. (2017). End Users' Perceptions of Critical Success Factors in ERP Applications. *International Journal of Enterprise Information Systems, 13*(4), 58–75. doi:10.4018/IJEIS.2017100104

Saygili, E. E., & Saygili, A. T. (2017). Contemporary Issues in Enterprise Information Systems: A Critical Review of CSFs in ERP Implementations. In M. Tavana (Ed.), *Enterprise Information Systems and the Digitalization of Business Functions* (pp. 120–136). Hershey, PA: IGI Global. doi:10.4018/978-1-5225-2382-6.ch006

Seidenstricker, S., & Antonino, A. (2018). Business Model Innovation-Oriented Technology Management for Emergent Technologies. In M. Khosrow-Pour, D.B.A. (Ed.), Encyclopedia of Information Science and Technology, Fourth Edition (pp. 4560-4569). Hershey, PA: IGI Global. doi:10.4018/978-1-5225-2255-3.ch396

Senaratne, S., & Gunarathne, A. D. (2017). Excellence Perspective for Management Education from a Global Accountants' Hub in Asia. In N. Baporikar (Ed.), *Management Education for Global Leadership* (pp. 158–180). Hershey, PA: IGI Global. doi:10.4018/978-1-5225-1013-0.ch008

Sensuse, D. I., & Cahyaningsih, E. (2018). Knowledge Management Models: A Summative Review. *International Journal of Information Systems in the Service Sector, 10*(1), 71–100. doi:10.4018/IJISSS.2018010105

Sensuse, D. I., Wibowo, W. C., & Cahyaningsih, E. (2016). Indonesian Government Knowledge Management Model: A Theoretical Model. *Information Resources Management Journal, 29*(1), 91–108. doi:10.4018/irmj.2016010106

Seth, M., Goyal, D., & Kiran, R. (2017). Diminution of Impediments in Implementation of Supply Chain Management Information System for Enhancing its Effectiveness in Indian Automobile Industry. *Journal of Global Information Management, 25*(3), 1–20. doi:10.4018/JGIM.2017070101

Seyal, A. H., & Rahman, M. N. (2017). Investigating Impact of Inter-Organizational Factors in Measuring ERP Systems Success: Bruneian Perspectives. In M. Tavana (Ed.), *Enterprise Information Systems and the Digitalization of Business Functions* (pp. 178–204). Hershey, PA: IGI Global. doi:10.4018/978-1-5225-2382-6.ch008

Shaikh, A. A., & Karjaluoto, H. (2016). On Some Misconceptions Concerning Digital Banking and Alternative Delivery Channels. *International Journal of E-Business Research, 12*(3), 1–16. doi:10.4018/IJEBR.2016070101

Shams, S. M. (2016). Stakeholder Relationship Management in Online Business and Competitive Value Propositions: Evidence from the Sports Industry. *International Journal of Online Marketing, 6*(2), 1–17. doi:10.4018/IJOM.2016040101

Shamsuzzoha, A. (2016). Management of Risk and Resilience within Collaborative Business Network. In R. Addo-Tenkorang, J. Kantola, P. Helo, & A. Shamsuzzoha (Eds.), *Supply Chain Strategies and the Engineer-to-Order Approach* (pp. 143–159). Hershey, PA: IGI Global. doi:10.4018/978-1-5225-0021-6.ch008

Shaqrah, A. A. (2018). Analyzing Business Intelligence Systems Based on 7s Model of McKinsey. *International Journal of Business Intelligence Research, 9*(1), 53–63. doi:10.4018/IJBIR.2018010104

Sharma, A. J. (2017). Enhancing Sustainability through Experiential Learning in Management Education. In N. Baporikar (Ed.), *Management Education for Global Leadership* (pp. 256–274). Hershey, PA: IGI Global. doi:10.4018/978-1-5225-1013-0.ch013

Shetty, K. P. (2017). Responsible Global Leadership: Ethical Challenges in Management Education. In N. Baporikar (Ed.), *Innovation and Shifting Perspectives in Management Education* (pp. 194–223). Hershey, PA: IGI Global. doi:10.4018/978-1-5225-1019-2.ch009

Sinthupundaja, J., & Kohda, Y. (2017). Effects of Corporate Social Responsibility and Creating Shared Value on Sustainability. *International Journal of Sustainable Entrepreneurship and Corporate Social Responsibility, 2*(1), 27–38. doi:10.4018/IJSECSR.2017010103

Škarica, I., & Hrgović, A. V. (2018). Implementation of Total Quality Management Principles in Public Health Institutes in the Republic of Croatia. *International Journal of Productivity Management and Assessment Technologies, 6*(1), 1–16. doi:10.4018/IJPMAT.2018010101

Smuts, H., Kotzé, P., Van der Merwe, A., & Loock, M. (2017). Framework for Managing Shared Knowledge in an Information Systems Outsourcing Context. *International Journal of Knowledge Management, 13*(4), 1–30. doi:10.4018/IJKM.2017100101

Soares, E. R., & Zaidan, F. H. (2016). Information Architecture and Business Modeling in Modern Organizations of Information Technology: Professional Career Plan in Organizations IT. In G. Jamil, J. Poças Rascão, F. Ribeiro, & A. Malheiro da Silva (Eds.), *Handbook of Research on Information Architecture and Management in Modern Organizations* (pp. 439–457). Hershey, PA: IGI Global. doi:10.4018/978-1-4666-8637-3.ch020

Sousa, M. J., Cruz, R., Dias, I., & Caracol, C. (2017). Information Management Systems in the Supply Chain. In G. Jamil, A. Soares, & C. Pessoa (Eds.), *Handbook of Research on Information Management for Effective Logistics and Supply Chains* (pp. 469–485). Hershey, PA: IGI Global. doi:10.4018/978-1-5225-0973-8.ch025

Spremic, M., Turulja, L., & Bajgoric, N. (2018). Two Approaches in Assessing Business Continuity Management Attitudes in the Organizational Context. In N. Bajgoric (Ed.), *Always-On Enterprise Information Systems for Modern Organizations* (pp. 159–183). Hershey, PA: IGI Global. doi:10.4018/978-1-5225-3704-5.ch008

Steenkamp, A. L. (2018). Some Insights in Computer Science and Information Technology. In *Examining the Changing Role of Supervision in Doctoral Research Projects: Emerging Research and Opportunities* (pp. 113–133). Hershey, PA: IGI Global. doi:10.4018/978-1-5225-2610-0.ch005

Studdard, N., Dawson, M., Burton, S. L., Jackson, N., Leonard, B., Quisenberry, W., & Rahim, E. (2016). Nurturing Social Entrepreneurship and Building Social Entrepreneurial Self-Efficacy: Focusing on Primary and Secondary Schooling to Develop Future Social Entrepreneurs. In Z. Fields (Ed.), *Incorporating Business Models and Strategies into Social Entrepreneurship* (pp. 154–175). Hershey, PA: IGI Global. doi:10.4018/978-1-4666-8748-6.ch010

Sun, Z. (2016). A Framework for Developing Management Intelligent Systems. *International Journal of Systems and Service-Oriented Engineering*, *6*(1), 37–53. doi:10.4018/IJSSOE.2016010103

Swami, B., & Mphele, G. T. (2016). Problems Preventing Growth of Small Entrepreneurs: A Case Study of a Few Small Entrepreneurs in Botswana Sub-Urban Areas. In N. Baporikar (Ed.), *Handbook of Research on Entrepreneurship in the Contemporary Knowledge-Based Global Economy* (pp. 479–508). Hershey, PA: IGI Global. doi:10.4018/978-1-4666-8798-1.ch020

Tabach, A., & Croteau, A. (2017). Configurations of Information Technology Governance Practices and Business Unit Performance. *International Journal of IT/Business Alignment and Governance*, *8*(2), 1–27. doi:10.4018/IJITBAG.2017070101

Talaue, G. M., & Iqbal, T. (2017). Assessment of e-Business Mode of Selected Private Universities in the Philippines and Pakistan. *International Journal of Online Marketing*, *7*(4), 63–77. doi:10.4018/IJOM.2017100105

Tam, G. C. (2017). Project Manager Sustainability Competence. In *Managerial Strategies and Green Solutions for Project Sustainability* (pp. 178–207). Hershey, PA: IGI Global. doi:10.4018/978-1-5225-2371-0.ch008

Tambo, T. (2018). Fashion Retail Innovation: About Context, Antecedents, and Outcome in Technological Change Projects. In I. Management Association (Ed.), Fashion and Textiles: Breakthroughs in Research and Practice (pp. 233-260). Hershey, PA: IGI Global. doi:10.4018/978-1-5225-3432-7.ch010

Tambo, T., & Mikkelsen, O. E. (2016). Fashion Supply Chain Optimization: Linking Make-to-Order Purchasing and B2B E-Commerce. In S. Joshi & R. Joshi (Eds.), *Designing and Implementing Global Supply Chain Management* (pp. 1–21). Hershey, PA: IGI Global. doi:10.4018/978-1-4666-9720-1.ch001

Tandon, K. (2016). Innovative Andragogy: The Paradigm Shift to Heutagogy. In S. Tiwari & L. Nafees (Eds.), *Innovative Management Education Pedagogies for Preparing Next-Generation Leaders* (pp. 238–257). Hershey, PA: IGI Global. doi:10.4018/978-1-4666-9691-4.ch014

Tantau, A. D., & Frăţilă, L. C. (2018). Information and Management System for Renewable Energy Business. In *Entrepreneurship and Business Development in the Renewable Energy Sector* (pp. 200–244). Hershey, PA: IGI Global. doi:10.4018/978-1-5225-3625-3.ch006

Teixeira, N., Pardal, P. N., & Rafael, B. G. (2018). Internationalization, Financial Performance, and Organizational Challenges: A Success Case in Portugal. In L. Carvalho (Ed.), *Handbook of Research on Entrepreneurial Ecosystems and Social Dynamics in a Globalized World* (pp. 379–423). Hershey, PA: IGI Global. doi:10.4018/978-1-5225-3525-6.ch017

Trad, A., & Kalpić, D. (2016). The E-Business Transformation Framework for E-Commerce Architecture-Modeling Projects. In I. Lee (Ed.), *Encyclopedia of E-Commerce Development, Implementation, and Management* (pp. 733–753). Hershey, PA: IGI Global. doi:10.4018/978-1-4666-9787-4.ch052

Trad, A., & Kalpić, D. (2016). The E-Business Transformation Framework for E-Commerce Control and Monitoring Pattern. In I. Lee (Ed.), *Encyclopedia of E-Commerce Development, Implementation, and Management* (pp. 754–777). Hershey, PA: IGI Global. doi:10.4018/978-1-4666-9787-4.ch053

Trad, A., & Kalpić, D. (2018). The Business Transformation Framework, Agile Project and Change Management. In M. Khosrow-Pour, D.B.A. (Ed.), Encyclopedia of Information Science and Technology, Fourth Edition (pp. 620-635). Hershey, PA: IGI Global. doi:10.4018/978-1-5225-2255-3.ch054

Trad, A., & Kalpić, D. (2018). The Business Transformation and Enterprise Architecture Framework: The Financial Engineering E-Risk Management and E-Law Integration. In B. Sergi, F. Fidanoski, M. Ziolo, & V. Naumovski (Eds.), *Regaining Global Stability After the Financial Crisis* (pp. 46–65). Hershey, PA: IGI Global. doi:10.4018/978-1-5225-4026-7.ch003

Turulja, L., & Bajgoric, N. (2018). Business Continuity and Information Systems: A Systematic Literature Review. In N. Bajgoric (Ed.), *Always-On Enterprise Information Systems for Modern Organizations* (pp. 60–87). Hershey, PA: IGI Global. doi:10.4018/978-1-5225-3704-5.ch004

van Wessel, R. M., de Vries, H. J., & Ribbers, P. M. (2016). Business Benefits through Company IT Standardization. In K. Jakobs (Ed.), *Effective Standardization Management in Corporate Settings* (pp. 34–53). Hershey, PA: IGI Global. doi:10.4018/978-1-4666-9737-9.ch003

Vargas-Hernández, J. G. (2017). Professional Integrity in Business Management Education. In N. Baporikar (Ed.), *Management Education for Global Leadership* (pp. 70–89). Hershey, PA: IGI Global. doi:10.4018/978-1-5225-1013-0.ch004

Vasista, T. G., & AlAbdullatif, A. M. (2017). Role of Electronic Customer Relationship Management in Demand Chain Management: A Predictive Analytic Approach. *International Journal of Information Systems and Supply Chain Management, 10*(1), 53–67. doi:10.4018/IJISSCM.2017010104

Vergidis, K. (2016). Rediscovering Business Processes: Definitions, Patterns, and Modelling Approaches. In P. Papajorgji, F. Pinet, A. Guimarães, & J. Papathanasiou (Eds.), *Automated Enterprise Systems for Maximizing Business Performance* (pp. 97–122). Hershey, PA: IGI Global. doi:10.4018/978-1-4666-8841-4.ch007

Vieru, D., & Bourdeau, S. (2017). Survival in the Digital Era: A Digital Competence-Based Multi-Case Study in the Canadian SME Clothing Industry. *International Journal of Social and Organizational Dynamics in IT, 6*(1), 17–34. doi:10.4018/IJSODIT.2017010102

Vijayan, G., & Kamarulzaman, N. H. (2017). An Introduction to Sustainable Supply Chain Management and Business Implications. In M. Khan, M. Hussain, & M. Ajmal (Eds.), *Green Supply Chain Management for Sustainable Business Practice* (pp. 27–50). Hershey, PA: IGI Global. doi:10.4018/978-1-5225-0635-5.ch002

Vlachvei, A., & Notta, O. (2017). Firm Competitiveness: Theories, Evidence, and Measurement. In A. Vlachvei, O. Notta, K. Karantininis, & N. Tsounis (Eds.), *Factors Affecting Firm Competitiveness and Performance in the Modern Business World* (pp. 1–42). Hershey, PA: IGI Global. doi:10.4018/978-1-5225-0843-4.ch001 von Rosing, M., Fullington, N., & Walker, J. (2016). Using the Business Ontology and Enterprise Standards to Transform Three Leading Organizations. *International Journal of Conceptual Structures and Smart Applications*, *4*(1), 71–99. doi:10.4018/IJCSSA.2016010104

von Rosing, M., & von Scheel, H. (2016). Using the Business Ontology to Develop Enterprise Standards. *International Journal of Conceptual Structures and Smart Applications*, *4*(1), 48–70. doi:10.4018/IJCSSA.2016010103

Walczak, S. (2016). Artificial Neural Networks and other AI Applications for Business Management Decision Support. *International Journal of Sociotechnology and Knowledge Development*, *8*(4), 1–20. doi:10.4018/IJSKD.2016100101

Wamba, S. F., Akter, S., Kang, H., Bhattacharya, M., & Upal, M. (2016). The Primer of Social Media Analytics. *Journal of Organizational and End User Computing*, *28*(2), 1–12. doi:10.4018/JOEUC.2016040101

Wang, C., Schofield, M., Li, X., & Ou, X. (2017). Do Chinese Students in Public and Private Higher Education Institutes Perform at Different Level in One of the Leadership Skills: Critical Thinking?: An Exploratory Comparison. In V. Wang (Ed.), *Encyclopedia of Strategic Leadership and Management* (pp. 160–181). Hershey, PA: IGI Global. doi:10.4018/978-1-5225-1049-9.ch013

Wang, F., Raisinghani, M. S., Mora, M., & Wang, X. (2016). Strategic E-Business Management through a Balanced Scored Card Approach. In I. Lee (Ed.), *Encyclopedia of E-Commerce Development, Implementation, and Management* (pp. 361–386). Hershey, PA: IGI Global. doi:10.4018/978-1-4666-9787-4.ch027

Wang, J. (2017). Multi-Agent based Production Management Decision System Modelling for the Textile Enterprise. *Journal of Global Information Management*, *25*(4), 1–15. doi:10.4018/JGIM.2017100101

Wiedemann, A., & Gewald, H. (2017). Examining Cross-Domain Alignment: The Correlation of Business Strategy, IT Management, and IT Business Value. *International Journal of IT/Business Alignment and Governance*, *8*(1), 17–31. doi:10.4018/IJITBAG.2017010102

Wolf, R., & Thiel, M. (2018). Advancing Global Business Ethics in China: Reducing Poverty Through Human and Social Welfare. In S. Hipsher (Ed.), *Examining the Private Sector's Role in Wealth Creation and Poverty Reduction* (pp. 67–84). Hershey, PA: IGI Global. doi:10.4018/978-1-5225-3117-3.ch004

Wu, J., Ding, F., Xu, M., Mo, Z., & Jin, A. (2016). Investigating the Determinants of Decision-Making on Adoption of Public Cloud Computing in E-government. *Journal of Global Information Management*, *24*(3), 71–89. doi:10.4018/JGIM.2016070104

Xu, L., & de Vrieze, P. (2016). Building Situational Applications for Virtual Enterprises. In I. Lee (Ed.), *Encyclopedia of E-Commerce Development, Implementation, and Management* (pp. 715–724). Hershey, PA: IGI Global. doi:10.4018/978-1-4666-9787-4.ch050

Yablonsky, S. (2018). Innovation Platforms: Data and Analytics Platforms. In *Multi-Sided Platforms (MSPs) and Sharing Strategies in the Digital Economy: Emerging Research and Opportunities* (pp. 72–95). Hershey, PA: IGI Global. doi:10.4018/978-1-5225-5457-8.ch003

Yusoff, A., Ahmad, N. H., & Halim, H. A. (2017). Agropreneurship among Gen Y in Malaysia: The Role of Academic Institutions. In N. Ahmad, T. Ramayah, H. Halim, & S. Rahman (Eds.), *Handbook of Research on Small and Medium Enterprises in Developing Countries* (pp. 23–47). Hershey, PA: IGI Global. doi:10.4018/978-1-5225-2165-5.ch002

Zanin, F., Comuzzi, E., & Costantini, A. (2018). The Effect of Business Strategy and Stock Market Listing on the Use of Risk Assessment Tools. In *Management Control Systems in Complex Settings: Emerging Research and Opportunities* (pp. 145–168). Hershey, PA: IGI Global. doi:10.4018/978-1-5225-3987-2.ch007

Zgheib, P. W. (2017). Corporate Innovation and Intrapreneurship in the Middle East. In P. Zgheib (Ed.), *Entrepreneurship and Business Innovation in the Middle East* (pp. 37–56). Hershey, PA: IGI Global. doi:10.4018/978-1-5225-2066-5.ch003

About the Contributors

Md Mashiur Rahman, an author and banker, is currently working in Bank Asia Ltd., Credit Risk Management Division of Corporate Office, Dhaka, Bangladesh. He has 15 years of glorious banking experience and worked in different divisions of the bank with profound satisfaction. He has written a number of books, articles in international journals, chapters of book and columns in daily newspapers. He is also working as Book Editor of IGI Global: International Academic Publisher, USA and Taylor & Francis Group, USA. Mr. Rahman was born in Hosnabad under Barishal District, Bangladesh. Heintroduced two models namely "Wealth and Welfare Business Model: sustainable business model" and "Mahdia Banking Model: sustainable banking model" which address the problem of existing capitalistic business and banking models and provides solutions with some correction of existing models. The models were presented in different national and international conferences and also are under consideration for publication by the USA publishers. He has completed Secondary Study from Hosnabad High School, Higher Secondary from Dhaka Imperial College and Bachelor&Master's in Marketing from Dhaka University, Bangladesh. He is keen to study and likes to work for humanity. He believes that working to solve human problems can make us rich and happy. He lost his father when he was in class eight and lost his mother after completion of post-graduation. He has a daughter and a son. His spouse is an entrepreneur.

Richa Goel is Assistant Professor-Economics and International Business at Amity International Business School, Amity University Noida. She is a Ph.D. in Management and has a journey of almost 18 years in academic and consistently striving to create a challenging and engaging learning environment where students become life-long scholars and learners. Imparting lectures using different teaching strategies, she is an avid teacher, researcher, and mentor. She has to her credit a number of publications in reputed national and international journals accompanied with participation in conferences. She is serving as a member of review committee for conferences journals and acting as Lead Editor of Annual International Referred Journal and Research Coordinator with Amity International Business School. Her area of interest includes Economics, Business Law, Human Resource Management and Diversity Management.

Anthony P. Gomes, originally from Dhaka, Bangladesh, moved to USA in 1993. After doing his Master's in business management from Dhaka University, Bangladesh, he ventured into private sector management positions including one of the leading NGO in Bangladesh, World Vision. After moving to USA, Mr. Gomes changed his career path and began his journey in the IT field and now working with TeamPeople, Washington D.C. Mr. Gomes has almost 40 years of experience in community development, he is a social activist playing a key role in many social organizations in Washington metro area and beyond in North American. He is also a creative writer and editor with almost 40 years of experiences. He has written a lot of valuable articles in local and regional publications in Bangladesh as well as in USA and most of his contributions were focusing on the social welfare, equality and community development for the betterment of the society. He has worked as the Chief Editor for many publications in last four decades including some of the special publications of the leading nationwide events in Bangladeshi community in USA. He brings a rich experience of professional, social and literary talents and contributing member of the community in USA. He has been involved with numerous socio-cultural organizations and still contributing towards the social welfare with his intellectual resources. He has been involved with a lot of organizations from the beginning of his involvement with social works and he dreams of a better, more equitable just society and contribute towards building a better future for the next generation!

Md Almas Uzzaman is a Bangladeshi born Australian Citizen, living in Sydney involved in analyzing, buying and selling of shares, stocks and securities in New York Stock Exchange (NYSE), AMEX, ASX, LSE, XETRA, HKSE, DSE. He helps investors in analyzing shares and stocks in capital markets. He advises and guides in doing business, international business, and social research when researchers ask help in conducting research. He closely observes and analyzes of individual persons and groups to take better decisions for income, employment and business management. He enjoys take classes for training and education. Mr. Almas loves to create sustainable and welfare business for less fortunate people, helping them to become small trader/entrepreneur, helping less educated, less fortunate people/ students to become valuable and demanding human capital. He conducts brain storming sessions in finding to generate income, employment and stress free happy life management. He was additional Director General of Bangladesh Customs, Excise and Value Added Tax; Assistant Secretary of Ministry of Foreign Affairs, Peoples Republic of Bangladesh and Lecturer of the Department of Marketing, University of Dhaka.

* * *

P. C. Bahuguna is Associate Professor in the area of Organizational Behaviour and Human Resource Management at School of Business, University of Petroleum and Energy Studies, Dehradun, U.K., India. His major teaching interests focus on general areas of human resource management, strategic human resource management, organizational behaviour and economics. He has presented/contributed research papers in national and international journals of repute. His research interests focus on talent management and strategic human resource management. He also has industry experience as administrator, consultant and a trainer in companies that include Consultancy Services, Hospitality and Printing industry. While working in the industry he was responsible for Recruitment & Selection, Training & Development, Performance Management, and budgeting etc. Besides organizing and conducting in-house training programs, he acts as a resource person for conducting sessions on people skills and performance management for organizations from oil and gas and power sector. His academic assets include a Bachelor Degree in Science, Master in Arts (Economics), Master of Business Administration and Doctorate in Management.

S. K. Baral did his M. Com, LL. B, MBA, and Ph.D. (Awarded in the year 1999) from Utkal University, Bhubaneswar, Orissa. He has authored 18 books with most current, comprehensive and state-of-art analysis to fulfil the need of Commerce & Management students, professionals and executives working in related fields. He has been conferred with 20 National and International Awards. He has been associated as the Life Member of 17 prestigious Indian Organizations and as an active academician, he has been closely associated with several Indian and foreign Universities. He is the Chief Editor of the 'Splint International Journal of Professionals', a Quarterly Peer Reviewed International Journal, ISSN 2349 – 6045, published by Indianjournals.com, indexed and abstracted @ ProQuest, USA, J-Gate, Indian Citation Index and International Scientific Indexing. He has contributed 131 Research Articles in different referred National and International Journals to his credit and working as Professor, Department of Commerce, Faculty of Commerce & Management at Indira Gandhi National Tribal University (A Central University of Govt. of India), Amarkantak, Madhya Pradesh, India.

Kazi Lamia Haque is a student at the School of Business and Economics at North South University. She is currently pursuing a Bachelor's degree majoring in Accounting and Finance. Besides her current educational background, she is currently exploring her research interests in various fields. Her research interests include Sustainability, Sustainable Business Models, Financial Inclusion, and Alternative Accounting Standards.

Betül Inam currently works as an assistant professor at the Department of Accounting and Taxation of Bilecik Seyh Edebali University. Her research topics are as follow: public expenditures, income inequality, public finance, and taxation.

Quazi Tafsirul Islam is a Lecturer of Strategy and Human Resources at the School of Business and Economics in North South University. He has obtained his Masters in Management & HR from the University of Dundee, Scotland, the UK, with a Distinction and was awarded the 'MSc Management Award' as a class valedictorian for 2017. Before this, he studied at North South University, Bangladesh, pursuing a bachelor's degree majoring in Finance, Accounting & Human Resources Management which he also completed with a distinction. Before joining Academia, he worked for a few years in leading global and local banks in Bangladesh in different capacities and roles. His research interest includes Sustainability, Organizational Behavior, Technology Adoption, and Case Study.

Mikail Kar is working as an academic at Bursa Uludag University, Department of Economics. He completed his undergraduate degree at Istanbul Marmara University, his master's degree at the State University of New York, and his PhD degree at Bursa Uludag University. He mainly works on economic theory, market analysis, methodological issues, economic policy, industrial economics. He has many book chapters and articles published in distinguished international publishing houses and journals in these fields of study. He is still continuing his academic studies at Bursa Uludag University and giving lectures in the field of economic theory.

Chitra Krishnan is Assistant Professor – Human Resource Management & Behavioral Science at Amity International Business School, Amity University Noida. She has done several International assignments and also worked with the Ministry of Manpower, Oman. Before her academic career, she has worked in the industry in various positions of responsibility. In her academic career of 14 years, she has been actively involved in rigorous academic pursuits in the field of higher professional education to enhance skill sets that promote the holistic development of learners. She has to her credit a number of books edited chapters, case studies, and research papers published in reputed national and international journals, and has participated at many professional conferences as well. She has been empaneled as a member of the review committee for conferences and journals of repute and also serving as Editor of the Annual International Referred Journal. Her area of interest includes Human Resource Management, Organisation Behavior, Talent Management, Diversity Management, Employee Satisfaction, and Knowledge Management.

Sheakh Reyad Muhammad Noor has graduated from Marketing Department, Dhaka University, Dhaka. After completion of graduation he was joined in renowned machinery indenting company where he worked for 8 years. Now he has been doing import business and name of his enterprise is Chandradeep. Corporate Office of the business is located at Purana Paltan, Dhaka. He is also an independent researcher and column writer. Mr. Noor is very much eager about human welfare. His spouse is a teacher in Botany of a colleges. They have two kids and they are very much happy in family life.

Dilek Murat currently works as an associate professor at the Department of Econometrics of Bursa Uludag University. Her research topics are as follow: statistical experimental design, multivariate statistical analysis methods and multi criteria decision making methods.

Tilottama Singh is a certified HR analyst and trained academic, researcher, and trainer with 9 years of experience in the field of Human Resources and Work Dynamics. She is currently employed as an Assistant Professor in Amity University, Noida, UP. Her areas of expertise are: Human Resources & Strategy and her teaching concentration include Human resource, strategy, and law. She is also involved in the course and syllabus designing and developing on various Management topics, including analytics, wellbeing, and management curriculum. She also serves as the member of AIMA and acts to lead and liaise between the student community and the industry delegates, with a keen interest in training.

Md. Shamim Talukder is currently an Assistant Professor in the Department of Management, North South University, Bangladesh. He received Ph.D. degree major in Management Science and Engineering from the School of Management, Huazhong University of Science and Technology, Wuhan, China, and MBA in Management Information Systems from the University of Dhaka, Bangladesh. His teaching and research interests include Human-Computer Interaction, Mobile Computing, IoT in Healthcare, Wearable Technology for social care, the impact of social media uses and e-government/open data. His research has been published in journals such as Technological Forecasting and Social Change, Industrial Management and Data Systems, Technology in Society, Journal of Systems and Information Technology, and Foresight. He serves as a reviewer for many peer-review journals including Information Technology and People, Enterprise Information System, the Bottom Line, and the Journal of Systems and Information Technology.

Index

G

H

I

L

M

N

P

R

S

T

U

W

www.ingramcontent.com/pod-product-compliance
Lightning Source LLC
LaVergne TN
LVHW081328300926
849161LV00008B/1910